THE UNITED NATIONS AND PEACEKEEPING

The United Nations and Peacekeeping

Results, Limitations and Prospects:
The Lessons of 40 Years of Experience

Edited by

Indar Jit Rikhye

President, International Peace Academy
New York

and

Kjell Skjelsbaek

Acting Director
Norwegian Institute of International Affairs, Oslo

St. Martin's Press   New York

First published in the United States of America in 1991

Printed in Great Britain

ISBN 0-312-05364-9

Library of Congress Cataloging-in-Publication Data
The United Nations and peacekeeping : results, limitations, and
    prospects : the lessons of 40 years of experience / edited by Indar
Jit Rikhye and Kjell Skjelsbaek.
        p. cm.
    Papers presented at a workshop held in Oslo, Norway, December
12–14, 1988, co-sponsored by the Norwegian Institute of
International Affairs and the International Peace Academy.
    Includes index.
    ISBN 0-312-05364-9
    1. United Nations—Armed Forces—Congresses. I. Rikhye, Indar
Jit, 1920– . II. Skjelsbaek, Kjell. III. Norsk utenrikspolitisk
institutt. IV. International Peace Academy.
JX1981.P7U413 1991
341.7′3—dc20   90-43358
                                                       CIP

Contents

Editors' Preface

In response to the increased interest in peacekeeping and the 40th anniversary of the first UN peacekeeping operation, the Norwegian Institute of International Affairs (NUPI) and the International Peace Academy (IPA) agreed to co-sponsor a workshop entitled 'The UN and Peacekeeping: Results, Limitations and Prospects: The Lessons of 40 Years of Experience' in Oslo, Norway, 12–14 December 1988.

The idea behind the workshop was to bring together a select group of peacekeeping practitioners, diplomats, and academicians with particular interest in this area in order to evaluate briefly the historical experiences of peacekeeping and to analyse critically its present potentials and problems.

We were pleased to bring together an outstanding group of professionals with first-hand experience in areas of peacekeeping. We were especially fortunate that the Chairman was Sir Brian Urquhart, the former UN Under-Secretary-General for Special Political Affairs, who has been associated with peacekeeping from its inception. Norway's strong endorsement of peacekeeping and the support for this workshop became obvious with the participation of two of its cabinet members, Dr Johan Jørgen Holst, Minister of Defence and Mr Thorvald Stoltenberg, Minister of Foreign Affairs. The list of other participants is included in this publication.

This publication includes the papers presented at the Oslo workshop and the reflections of the Chairman. The workshop participants agreed on the agenda for further research, which is presently being undertaken by NUPI, the Centre for International and Strategic Studies, York University, Canada, and the IPA.

We wish to express our sincere appreciation to the Ford Foundation, especially to Dr Enid Schoettle, to the MacArthur Foundation, to the Canadian Institute for International Security, and to the Samuel Freeman Charitable Trusts, for their support of this workshop and publication.

Indar Jit Rikhye, Major-General (ret.), President,
International Peace Academy

Kjell Skjelsbaek, Acting Director, Norwegian Institute of
International Affairs

List of Abbreviations

AMAL	Afwaj Al-Muqamah Al-Lubnaniyya
AO	Area of Operation
CAO	Chief Administrative Officers
CBMs	Confidence Building Measures
CDE	Conference on Disarmament in Europe
CIA	Central Intelligence Agency
CIIPS	Canadian Institute for International Peace and Security
CMF	Commonwealth Monitoring Force
CSCE	Conference on Security and Cooperation in Europe
DOMREP	Mission of the Representative of the Secretary-General in the Dominican Republic
EOSG	Executive Office of the Secretary-General
FIJIBATT	Fijian Battalion
FINBATT	Finnish Battalion
FOD	Field Operations Division
FRENCHBATT	French Battalion
FRG	Federal Republic of Germany
GHANBATT	Ghanaian Battalion
GSS	General Security Service
ICCS	International Commission for Control and Supervision
ICRC	International Committee of the Red Cross
ICSC	International Commission for Supervision and Control
IDF	Israel Defence Force
ILO	International Labour Organisation
INF	Intermediate Nuclear Force
IPA	International Peace Academy
IRISHBATT	Irish Battalion
MFO	Multinational Force and Observers in the Sinai
MNF I & II	Multinational Force in Beirut I and II
MNR	Mozambique National Resistance
NEPBATT	Nepalese Battalion
NGO	Non-Governmental Organisation
NORBATT	Norwegian Battalion

NUPI	Norwegian Institute of International Affairs
OAU	Organisation of African Unity
OFOESA	Office of Field Operations and External Support Activities
ONUC	United Nations Operation in the Congo
OSPA	Office for Special Political Affairs
OUSGSPA	Office of the Under-Secretary-General for Special Political Affairs
PLO	Palestine Liberation Organisation
POLISARIO	Frente Popular para Liberacion de Saguia el Hamra y Rio de Oro
SARC	South Asian Association for Regional Cooperation
SENBATT	Senegalese Battalion
SLA	South Lebanese Army
SSOD	Special Session on Disarmament
SWAPO	South West Africa People's Organisation
TRNC	Turkish Republic of Northern Cyprus
UN	United Nations
UNAVEM	United Nations Angola Verification Mission
UNDOF	United Nations Disengagement Observer Force
UNDOMREP	United Nations Observer Group in The Dominican Republic
UNEF I & II	United Nations Emergency Force I and II
UNFICYP	United Nations Peacekeeping Force in Cyprus
UNGOMAP	United Nations Good Offices Mission in Afghanistan and Pakistan
UNIFIL	United Nations Interim Force in Lebanon
UNIIMOG	United Nations Iran–Iraq Military Observer Group
UNITA	Uniao Nacional para a Independencia Total de Angola
UNITAR	United Nations Institute for Training and Research
UNMOGIP	United Nations Military Observer Group in India and Pakistan
UNMOs	United Nations Military Observers
UNOGIL	United Nations Observation Group in Lebanon
UNTAG	United Nations Transition Assistance Group in Namibia

UNTEA/UNSF	United Nations Temporary Executive Authority/United Nations Security Force in West New Guinea
UNTSO	United Nations Truce Supervision Organisation
UNYOM	United Nations Yemen Observation Mission
US	United States of America
USG	Under-Secretary-General
USSR	Union of Soviet Socialist Republics
ZANU	Zimbabwe African National Union
ZANU PF	Zimbabwe African National Union (Patriotic Front)

List of Tables

Notes on the Contributors

Günther G. Greindl is currently serving as Brigadier-General in the Austrian Ministry of Defence. Until recently he was Commander of UNFICYP and was also former Commander of UNDOF.

Marianne Heiberg is Research Associate at the Norwegian Institute of International Affairs, Oslo. She was formerly Research Fellow at the International Peace Research Institute, Oslo.

Johan Jørgen Holst is currently Minister of Defence of Norway. He was formerly Director of the Norwegian Institute of International Affairs, Oslo and State Secretary in the Ministries of Defence and Foreign Affairs.

Alan M. James is currently Professor and Head of Department, Department of International Relations at the University of Keele, UK. He was formerly Senior Lecturer and Reader, Department of International Relations, London School of Economics.

James O. C. Jonah is currently Assistant Secretary-General for Research and the Collection of Information, United Nations, New York. He was formerly Assistant Secretary-General for Field Operational and External Support Activities, Director of the Office of the Under-Secretaries-General for Special Political Affairs, and Political Adviser to the Commander of UNEF II.

Augustus Richard Norton is currently permanent Associate Professor of Comparative Politics, Department of Social Sciences, United States Military Academy, West Point. He has served with the UN Truce Supervision Organisation in South Lebanon and has had a range of assignments with the US Army Airborne Division.

Susan R. Mills is currently UN Deputy Controller/Director, Financial Management and Control Division, Office of Programme and Planning, Budget and Finance. She was formerly Chief of the Financial Management and Control Systems Unit of the Office of Financial Services, and Management Officer in the Administrative Management Service of the Department of Administration and Management.

Indar Jit Rikhye is currently President of the International Peace Academy. He is a retired Major-General of the Indian Army. He was formerly Military Adviser to the United Nations Secretary-General; Chief of Staff and later Commander, UNEF I; and Acting Special Representative of the Secretary-General in the Congo.

Kjell Skjelsbaek is currently Acting Director of the Norwegian Institute of International Affairs and leader of the Institute's research programme on peacekeeping. He was formerly Professor of International Relations, Department of Political Science, University of Oslo; and Special Fellow at the UN Institute for Training and Research (UNITAR).

Brian Urquhart is Scholar-in-Residence at the Ford Foundation. He was formerly Under-Secretary-General for Special Political Affairs at the United Nations. He took part in the organisation and direction of UNEF I and II and served as Assistant to the Secretary-General's Special Representative in the Congo and as UN Representative in Katanga, Congo. He joined the UN at its foundation.

Thomas G. Weiss is currently Executive Director of the International Peace Academy. He was formerly Economic Affairs Officer with UNCTAD in Geneva. He has been a staff member at the World Policy Institute, UNITAR and the International Labour Organisation (ILO) as well as a lecturer at Colgate, Princeton and New York Universities.

Henry Wiseman is currently a professor at the University of Guelph, Ontario. His activities and research have focused on peacekeeping and defence policy. He was formerly Director of Peacekeeping Programmes at the International Peace Academy.

List of Participants

Dr John Barrett
Deputy Director
Canadian Centre for Arms Control and Disarmament

Professor Roddick B. Byers
Professor of Political Science
and Senior Research Fellow
Centre for International and Strategic Studies,
York University, Canada

Professor David Dewitt
Director
Centre for International and Strategic Studies,
York University, Canada

Mr Aage Eknes
Director of Conflict Management and Peacekeeping Programs,
International Peace Academy

Mr Urs Freiburghaus
Head of the Service of International Law
and Information
General Staff (Military Department)
Ministry of Defence, Switzerland

Colonel Martin L. Ganderson
Chief of Staff
US Military Delegation to the United Nations
United States Mission to the United Nations

Captain 1 Rank Aleksandr S. Gorokhov
Counsellor
Permanent Mission of the Union of Soviet Socialist
Republics to the United Nations

Mr Marrack I. Goulding
Under-Secretary-General for Special Political Affairs
United Nations

Major-General Günther G. Greindl
Force Commander, UNFICYP

Mr Hideki Harashima
Minister and Head of Chancery
Permanent Mission of Japan to the United Nations

Dr Marianne Heiberg
Researcher
Norwegian Institute of International Affairs

Dr Johan Jørgen Holst
Minister of Defence, Norway

Colonel Ole Huusa
Headquarters Defence Command, Norway

Dr Alan M. James
Department of International Relations
University of Keele, United Kingdom

Dr James O. C. Jonah
Assistant Secretary-General
Office for Research and the Collection of Information
United Nations

Ms Susan R. Mills
Deputy Controller
Office of Programme Planning, Budget and Finance
United Nations

Lt. Col. W. Alexander Morrison, CD
Minister-Counsellor
Permanent Mission of Canada to the United Nations

Colonel Martin Hjelmervik Ness
Counsellor (Military Adviser)
Permanent Mission of Norway to the United Nations

Professor Augustus Richard Norton
Permanent Associate Professor of Comparative Politics
United States Military Academy, West Point

Major-General (ret.) Indar Jit Rikhye
President
International Peace Academy

Dr Enid B. Schoettle
Director, International Affairs Programs
The Ford Foundation

Dr Kjell Skjelsbaek
Director
Norwegian Institute of International Affairs

Mr Bjorn Skogmo
Deputy Director General
Ministry of Foreign Affairs, Norway

Mr Thorvald Stoltenberg
Minister of Foreign Affairs, Norway

Lt. Colonel Ilkka H. Tiihonen
Commanding Officer of UN Training Centre
Finland

Sir Brian E. Urquhart
Scholar in Residence, International Affairs Programs
The Ford Foundation

Mr Karel E. Vosskuhler
Program Officer, International Affairs Programs
The Ford Foundation

Major-General Bengt Wallroth
Chief, International Department
Ministry of Defense, Sweden

Mr Wang Suobao
Deputy Navy Representative
Permanent Mission of the People's Republic of China
to the United Nations, New York

Dr Thomas G. Weiss
Executive Director
International Peace Academy

Dr Henry Wiseman
Professor of Political Studies,
University of Guelph, Canada.

Introduction
Indar Jit Rikhye

This evaluation of the historical experience of peacekeeping was conducted in order to analyse critically its present potentials and problems. It was based on the presentation of papers by select practitioners and scholars to generate a discussion between participants on major topics relating to peacekeeping. Peacekeepers, mainly military personnel, lack comprehension of the international political context of such operations. Discussion of this topic will facilitate consideration of the expectations, limitations and results of these operations.

An appraisal of the conduct of peacekeeping operations requires consideration of both the management and the financing of these operations. A related topic deserving attention is the attitude of the parties involved in peacekeeping, that is, parties to the conflict, including the host(s) and contributing states. It was assumed that the participants at the workshop would be ready to build on the past to project the future.

The volume begins with 'Reflections by the Chairman', by Brian Urquhart, and is followed in Chapter 2 by 'Rethinking Peacekeeping', a paper prepared by Professor Augustus Richard Norton and Dr Thomas G. Weiss, originally intended as a summary of the workshop's discussion. Written after the workshop, it reflects the debates that went on there, along with some of Norton's and Weiss's own views. It is a general paper on peacekeeping, which makes interesting reading on its own, as a background paper, though echoing many of the main points brought out in the chairman's analysis.

In his paper, 'Peacekeeping in the International Political Context: Historical Analysis and Future Directions', Henry Wiseman compares the present political and operational effectiveness of peacekeeping to show what should be avoided and what should be retained and developed for future appreciation.

In dealing with the much-debated relative importance of the General Assembly and the Security Council in authorising, as well as managing, peacekeeping operations, Wiseman concludes: 'It is now

1

well understood, without any apparent opposition by members of the UN, that peacekeeping should be mandated and maintained under the jurisdiction of the authority of the Security Council. Contentious disagreements about the residual authority of the General Assembly in matters of peacekeeping are, for the most part, overcome'. It is the voting pattern in the General Assembly which has brought about this change in advocacy and practice, yet without formal understanding.

Wiseman examines the main factors thematically, that is: the multiplicity of functions; the types of conflicts engendering peace-keeping responses; principles of consent and host country percep-tions; the principles and perceptions of neutrality; peacekeeping and the provision of security; peacekeeping and peacemaking and pre-crisis planning.

In describing the functions, he states, 'As the legitimacy of peacekeeping has increased and the mandates have become more elaborate, so have the number, diversity, difficulty and complexity of functions.... The functions can be roughly grouped ... into three categories – military, governmental/political and civil'. In suggesting this grouping, he cautions that the boundaries are not distinct. How true it is; and in fact any attempt to group them will be futile.

In discussing types of conflicts that lead to peacekeeping, Wiseman aptly says, 'Cease-fire lines are more or less readily defined upon cessation of hostilities between national armies in set piece territorial wars. They are not so readily defined in guerrilla-type civil wars conducted by non-state as well as state actors'. He says that of the eighteen conflicts almost half were civil conflicts. This is despite the unwillingness of most troop-contributing states to accept openly a role in internal strife. Indirect or open foreign military intervention has become a common feature of local and regional wars. However, Wiseman states, 'The international political climate has changed dramatically since that time. Gone are the cries that peacekeeping is a neo-colonialist imposition, a cry sounded so vehemently during and in the aftermath of the Congo operation'.

Wiseman emphasises the importance of the principle of consent. He argues that, with consent, peacekeeping operations have proved more successful. Host states have generally complied with agree-ments, although some states, for example Israel, have been offen-ders. Personally I think all host countries have been offenders, some more than others. Therefore peacekeeping missions have to keep a constant vigil for their compliance. Non-state actors usually have not co-operated, except when it has suited them. Whether they were The

Palestine Liberation Organisation (PLO), Afwaj Al-Muqamah Al-Lubnaniyya (AMAL), or the Party of God in Lebanon, or a Grivas-led group in Cyprus, they all did whatever they could in defiance of UN mandates.

Should peacekeeping operations be neutral or impartial? Wiseman cites Kjell Skjelsbaek who has argued that a peacekeeping force should be *strictly impartial*. He quotes an article written by Ernst B. Haas, 'Collective Management of International Conflict, 1945–84'[1] in dealing with the question of neutrality, but the examples he gives, that is, the concerted action of the Security Council to persuade Israel to stop fighting and to airlift the UN Emergency Force (UNEF) II in the Suez Canal area in the aftermath of the October 1973 war, and to airlift the UN Interim Force in Lebanon (UNIFIL) in South Lebanon in 1978, were part of the pre-negotiations to establish peacekeeping and have very little to do with the conduct of peacekeeping operations. Such operations are seldom neutral, but most must be impartial.

Wiseman concludes his historical analysis by suggesting that many of the challenges to peacekeeping operations, that is, diplomatic management of non-state parties, verification of arms control measures, delivery of humanitarian assistance, and so forth, were likely to be better debated in an academic setting rather than the Special Committee for Peacekeeping established by the UN General Assembly in 1964.

Kjell Skjelsbaek's paper 'UN Peacekeeping: Expectations, Limitations and Results: Forty Years of Mixed Experience' opens with an expression of legitimate concern that the award of the Nobel Peace Prize to UN Peacekeeping should not be allowed to cloud the fact that these operations have been politically controversial throughout the lifespan of their 40 years. He states that 'At the moment there is a world-wide trend toward greater appreciation. This trend could quickly be reversed, however.'

Skjelsbaek establishes two criteria by which peacekeeping can be judged, that is, that it cannot stop warfare by itself, and that peacekeeping is but one step on the road toward a lasting settlement. He refers to George L. Sherry's coined term *controlled impasse* which describes the essential task of peacekeeping. In a situation where neither party is convinced that it can absolve its principal objectives, and when efforts to achieve them by violent means appear too risky, an impasse may seem preferable. Skjelsbaek argues that the essential element in all peacekeeping operations is to sustain a controlled

4 *Introduction*

impasse. If this approach is accepted, his conclusion is that most UN peacekeeping operations have been successful.

He describes various aspects of the strength or capabilities of peacekeeping under two headings, military capability and political assets of UN peacekeeping. In the first instance, he deals with the size of the force, which is determined by the task, and the expected co-operation of the parties. He also describes the problems related to equipment: troop-contributing countries must provide what is needed for the early phases of the operations, since it takes a few months for the UN to build its supply levels. He also addresses the training and competence of peacekeeping troops, correctly assessing that the quality of the contingents varies significantly.

There is no more accurate observation than Skjelsbaek's statement: 'Peacekeeping is primarily a political and diplomatic activity.' He notes that UN peacekeeping represents the concerns of the international community, and argues that UN peacekeeping carries an international stamp of legitimacy. Unlike non-UN peacekeeping operations, the UN Blue Berets symbolise the power of the Security Council and the UN membership. Therefore 'An attack on a UN force deployed to uphold international values is different from an attack on other multinational forces without this moral clout.'

Skjelsbaek's well-structured paper concludes, 'there are trade-offs between the different military capabilities and political assets of peacekeeping operations. The weaker the political support for an operation, the more important it is to be strong on the ground. The more delinquent the members of the Security Council are in supporting its resolutions, the more critical the composition of the force and co-operation among troop-contributors'.

'Peacekeeping and Peacemaking: The Need for Patience' by Major-General Günther G. Greindl is a retrospective view of UN peacekeeping. Quoting a Japanese diplomat, Greindl says, 'Peacekeeping operations are not intended merely to be a guardian of the status quo, but rather, should facilitate efforts towards comprehensive settlement of the regional conflict in which they are involved'. Anxiety exists that peacekeeping might perpetuate the status quo, and diminish the channels of problem-solving.

Peacekeeping operations appear, on the surface, to be alike, but this is not the case in reality. The most important difference between peacekeeping operations is that the political context for each is unique. Greindl divides such operations into three categories: (1) operations launched as part of a politically-negotiated settlement, for example West Irian and Namibia; (2) forces deployed after a cease-fire agreement, for example the operations after the Arab–Israeli wars; and (3) forces interposed, without a prior written agreement, but with the consent of the conflicting parties to help end the conflict.

Drawing on his experience in the UN Peacekeeping Force in Cyprus (UNFICYP), Greindl suggests ways to minimise the negative effects of peacekeeping, since the public has the impression that as long as a peacekeeping mission is ongoing, the problem is not resolved. A good public relations system could minimise this problem. An additional problem is that local governments and the media have developed the habit of using the UN, and peacekeeping operations in particular, as a target to release frustrations arising from their own failure to achieve a political settlement. Greindl suggests that consideration should be given 'to developing a procedure to allow a reduction in the strength of a force during periods of relative calm'. Also the gradual introduction of military observers into a peacekeeping force offers another method of reducing troops. This should be accompanied by de-confrontation plans – in order to strengthen the cease-fire further – and improved monitoring and surveillance with the use of electronic equipment.

Greindl states that 'It is sometimes suggested ... that a viable option would be the withdrawal of all peacekeeping forces from the area in order to force the parties to settle their differences'. However, he feels that this option could be dangerous, particularly in the case of Cyprus.

In his paper, 'The Management of UN Peacekeeping', James O. C. Jonah deals mainly with the structural changes announced by the UN Secretary-General in November 1988. Ever since the UN peacekeeping operations in the Congo, the daily management of peacekeeping operations has been controversial, along with issues relating to authorisation and financing. The Soviet Union, from the inception of peacekeeping, has held the view that peacekeeping should be the sole responsibility of the Security Council, and that the Military Staff Committee would render any assistance required. Accordingly the role of the Secretary-General should be that of the Chief Executive Officer of the Organisation. This was contrary to the view of the Western powers and a large majority of the member states, who have held that the Military Staff Committee could only act if operations were authorised under Chapter VII of the Charter, that is, enforcement of peace, and that only the Secretary-General could effectively provide day-to-day management.

Jonah rightly states that their divergent views concerning how these operations should be managed remained unresolved 'until new life was given to peacekeeping in October, 1973', when UNEF II was established. The Secretary-General at that time, Kurt Waldheim, put forth suggestions reconciling the divergent views. 'He recognised that the Security Council retained overall authority over peacekeeping operations', and proposed, with the consensus of the Security Council, that 'the operations would come under the command of the UN, vested in the Secretary-General, but subject to the authority of the Security Council'.

Jonah discusses in detail how the Secretary-General makes arrangements for the management of peacekeeping operations within the Secretariat. UNEF I, the first peacekeeping force, was established by the General Assembly. First Dag Hammarskjöld, and later U Thant, played a special role in its management and eventual withdrawal. Since then the Security Council has authorised peacekeeping operations and has called for the Secretary-General to manage them. He is usually assisted by a small staff, including an Under-Secretary-General for Special Political Affairs. Administration of the operations is managed by Field Operations Division (FOD), a branch of the Office of General Services of the Secretariat. The administration of peacekeeping operations has proved most difficult.

When he was appointed Secretary-General, Javier Pérez de Cuéllar created an Assistant Secretary-General for Field Operations, reporting directly to him. This position was axed during the UN administrative reform in 1988 and the situation reverted to what it had been before. Apparently the Secretary-General expects to bring Field Service back to the executive office by placing it within the office of the Under-Secretary-General for Special Political Affairs in charge of peacekeeping. Such an arrangement would bring better co-ordination between the political and administrative functions of the Secretariat and would favourably influence relations in the field.

Jonah has pointed out that, 'throughout FOD, there is a very limited number of personnel with the necessary civilian background, in both field and Headquarters, required to develop policy or contingency plans for missions support'. He suggests that these weaknesses, and the need to reduce staff, make it necessary to obtain military staff from potential troop-contributors and UN staff from other secretariat branches. Such a course was possible in planning the UN Transition Assistance Group in Namibia (UNTAG), but usually there is little time in the authorisation of an operation and its implementation. Therefore, at best, what Jonah suggests is reliance on an *ad hoc* system in the most sensitive chain of the UN command of peacekeeping operations.

Jonah provides a clear description of the appointment of the military adviser by Dag Hammarskjöld and the evolution of that office since the early 1960s. Without commenting in any way on personalities, the military adviser's appointment remains controversial. In fact the ambiguity of his responsibilities relating to field service operations since the revival of this position recently is a serious drawback in the preparation of peacekeeping operations.

Jonah deals ably with the command and control problems in the field. Any lack of co-ordination between the political and administrative aspects at headquarters is reflected in the field. At one time the chief administrative officer responsible to FOD acted independently, making co-ordination difficult. This problem has been overcome by reorganising the head of the mission as the most senior UN official, that is, the chief of staff of observer group, and the commander of a force as the overall head. However, better co-ordination between the military and civilian is desirable and steps should be taken to improve it.

Jonah's paper is an important contribution to this volume, and he is to be commended for facing sensitive, yet important, controversial issues which must be resolved.

'The Financing of UN Peacekeeping Operations: The Need for a Sound Financial Basis' by Susan R. Mills, Deputy Controller of the United Nations, makes a clear and full presentation of the financial aspects of peacekeeping. Mills, with her thorough knowledge of UN administration and years of experience in financial management, opens her paper by stating that 'Not since the early 1960s, when peacekeeping operations precipitated a financial crisis for the UN, has the world community shown more than cursory interest in its financial stability'.

She provides a summary of financing methods. Six of fifteen peacekeeping operations initiated by the UN were financed from the regular budget and were, therefore, 'profoundly affected by the financial "health" of the UN in respect of the regular budget'. Two of the other nine, in Yemen and West Irian, were financed by the parties most directly concerned. The operation in Cyprus is financed by voluntary contributions and the remainder through special assessments.

After discussing Articles 17 and 19 of the UN Charter, that is, the legal regime covering assessments, she reviews the first peacekeeping operation, and the military observer groups (in the Middle East, in consequence of the Arab–Israeli conflict beginning in 1948, and between India and Pakistan following the conflict over Jammu and Kashmir). The assessments were not large and were paid regularly by member states. However, when the first peacekeeping force was established after the Suez War in 1956, some member states refused to pay their share 'on the basis of what they characterised as positions of principle, the primary reason given being that only the Security Council could authorise a peacekeeping operation'. Mills states further that 'These withholdings of assessed contributions also led to the beginning of a practice that has, unfortunately, continued to the present time – namely, delays in payment by the UN, because of a lack of resources, of amounts which the Organisation owes to troop-contributing countries.'

The peacekeeping operation in the Congo precipitated the 'first genuine *cash* crisis' in 1960. This operation was authorised by the Security Council, yet some countries refused to pay because they disagreed with the conduct of the operations. By the end of 1961, faced with a major financial crisis, the General Assembly authorised the issue of bonds up to $200 million. Ultimately $169 million of such bonds were sold and by 1988 were repaid by payments from the regular budget. The objecting states never paid this part of their dues. This eventually led to the Article 19 crisis, when the United States attempted to apply it to the Soviet Union, which was overdue for more than two years of assessed contributions. Realising that an application of Article 19 against the Soviet Union would lead to a serious crisis in the UN, it was decided by a gentleman's agreement that the General Assembly would transact no business that would require putting a question to vote. The Assembly, by a consensus decision, decided that the UN's financial difficulties should be solved through voluntary contributions.

A special account was established by the General Assembly in which the member states were encouraged to make voluntary contributions. Although many members gave generously, the Organisation has barely managed to meet its day-to-day cash commitments.

This led to a renewed search for ways to meet costs. In 1973 the General Assembly decided that: (a) 63.15 per cent of the total appropriation should be apportioned among the five Permanent Members of the Security Council (Group A); (b) 34.78 per cent should be paid by the 23 economically developed member states (Group B), excluding Group A; (c) 2.02 per cent should be paid by 82 member states characterised as economically less developed (Group C); and (d) 0.05 per cent should be apportioned among 25 specifically-named, least economically developed member states (Group D). Since 1973 the relative shares of cost have shifted, but these basic arrangements remain: Group A – 57.88 per cent; Group B – 39.51 per cent; Group C – 2.56 per cent; and Group D – no change.

The Forty-Third Session of the General Assembly was resumed in February 1989. It dealt especially with peacekeeping matters, including the problems of past operations, the imminent launching of UNTAG, the possibilities of new operations in Western Sahara and Cambodia, and lastly the overall financial situation of the UN.

Mills describes four of the main issues being discussed that deserve particular attention: (1) voluntary contributions in kind and the proposal by some members that these be accepted in lieu of assessed contributions – there are questions regarding the type of contribution and if it can be used; (2) voluntary contributions in cash – again it is proposed by some members that they be used to reduce the cost of the operations to the member concerned; (3) a peacekeeping reserve fund to meet costs until they are authorised and regular payments received; and (4) indirect costs and how they should be met.

The paper concludes by stating, 'Until and unless agreement is reached and all parties unreservedly abide by such an agreement, UN peacekeeping will continue to be placed in jeopardy'.

Johan Jørgen Holst's paper, 'Support and Limitations: Peacekeeping from the Point of View of Troop-Contributors', starts with the consideration of UN peacekeeping in the international context from a Norwegian perspective. He writes that, 'The means of communications have altered perceptions of distance, the media creates the conditions for instant awareness and involvement'.

Holst describes Norway's engagement in UN peacekeeping as based on a number of factors: (1) owing to her exposed position in an area which is dominated by the strategic interests of the major powers, Norway is particularly concerned about the possibility that distant conflicts could impact on the environment in Northern Europe; (2) smaller states are more easily accepted as disinterested parties; and (3) it constitutes an exercise in reality-testing for small and medium powers, which tend to view distant conflicts from rather abstract points of view.

In concluding, Holst says that there were some direct benefits to troop-contributing states. Great demands are made on the UN force, and personnel must be able to use weapons in self-defence. The peacekeeping mission involves significant challenges to the skills of each soldier, to leadership, and to discipline.

Alan M. James's paper, 'Peacekeeping and the Parties', deals with the host country or countries, as well as contributing states. At the outset, James states that 'peacekeeping rests on the consent of the state or states on whose territory the peacekeepers operate. If any such operation is to maximise its contribution to the maintenance of peace, it must also have the co-operation of all relevant disputants, whether or not they happen to be host states'. He continues, 'it is the parties [to the conflict] who play the crucial role, not only in respect of the success of a peacekeeping mission but also in its creation'.

The other important role belongs to the contributing states who provide the personnel and financing. These third party states provide the physical instrument and the means to establish a peacekeeping presence. However, the disputants and, more particularly, the host(s) possess a veto over the employment or otherwise of peace-keeping to help resolve conflicts. James has emphasised that not all quarrels have reached the stage where the parties are ready to embark on any of these (calming, containing or composing of a quarrel) directions. Sometimes the parties may choose to do without the help of a third party 'for there is no basis for the assumption that an impartial or non-forceful third party is essential'.

James describes three broad grounds on which parties may have reservations involving a peacekeeping body in their conflict: (1) a peacekeeping presence may have undesirable international repercussions, not just for the host(s) states, but for any non-host parties; (2) international consequences having an adverse effect on only the host(s); and (3) the domestic repercussions of having peacekeepers on one's soil.

In the first case, when an operation is within the borders of the host country, the non-host country, who might have a strong perceived need to intervene within the host country, would only be able to do so with some risk of international repercussions. The host country's co-operation is essential, but when not fully available, as is often the case, it will not entirely jeopardize the operation. The degree of co-operation, or lack of it, will influence the impression of the host country on not only the contributing states, but on other members of the international community.

In the second instance, reservations of a host country about agreeing to a peacekeeping operation relate to the obvious need for a third party to cover a state's weakness. Furthermore the presence of international watchdogs suggests 'A different kind of inferiority – moral rather than physical'. Besides this, a peacekeeping operation does infringe somewhat on a country's sovereignty.

Lastly, a peacekeeping operation would have an inevitable effect on domestic policies. It would involve relations with the populace and would affect national policies.

James suggests remedies to overcome these problems. While he writes little of the advantages of peacekeeping, he recommends that the problems must be seen in perspective. He argues that 'Neither conceptually nor practically is a state diminished by involving peace-keepers in its affairs'. He then stresses the importance of setting up a contract, as clearly as possible, to describe the way in which the peacekeepers are to operate. This mandate should be clearly under-stood by the states concerned. Finally, he advises that it must also be made abundantly evident that 'there must be complete and unques-tioned respect for the principle that a peacekeeping body operates on the basis of impartiality and non-forcefulness (except in self-defence – and that must be strictly defined)'.

Dr Marianne Heiberg, in her paper, 'Peacekeepers and Local Popu-lations: Some Comments on UNIFIL', employs her experience and skills as an anthropologist to focus on the relationship between UNIFIL and the culturally-complex local populations with which it deals. The paper includes a study of the UN contingents and their inter-relationships. At the outset she states that a relationship to local civilians built on communication and confidence is a necessary factor for success.

In the first part of her paper, she discusses general political and economic characteristics of the relation between UNIFIL and local Lebanese, focusing on their implications for a UNIFIL withdrawal.

She says that 'the presence over time of a peacekeeping force probably inevitably and usually unintentionally helps restructure the society in which it operates'.

In discussing the security zone along the Israeli border inside Lebanon, Heiberg says that 'Like all forces of occupation, the IDF [Israel Defence Force] has enhanced its effectiveness through an extensive network of local informers. Local collaboration is obtained through a series of positive and negative sanctions'. She states that the security zone is regarded by the Israelis as highly successful and essential. The larger numbers of local populace, who are not collaborators, look upon UNIFIL for protection. Thus collaborators, that is, members of the Christian militia and their families receiving special benefits, informers and a few traders, are hostile to the UN troops, whereas the others, who are the majority, trust the UN. However, UNIFIL is an alien element in the area. Only a small minority of UN personnel receive satisfactory political or cultural training about the area prior to their arrival. Inevitably the UN has been 'sucked into the economic and political fabric of the wider society in which it operates and of which it has become an integral part'. Besides, in complying with its mandate, the UN force has insisted upon upholding Lebanese legality.

In a comprehensive survey of the implications of UNIFIL withdrawal Heiberg has concluded: (a) that it would provoke an intense and complex civil war; and (b) that Israel would be compelled to reinforce the security zone escalating economic and human cost.

In the second part of her paper, Heiberg has discussed the force itself. Unlike a national military command, UNIFIL is made up of a number of national components. However, what is unique is that the units are each a *battalion*, a *kingdom*. Her own nation's contingent, the Norwegian battalion, located in the south, is the most isolated since there are no UN units on its flanks. It is the geography and the security zone which have created conditions previously unknown to UN peacekeeping. The relationship between the unit commanders and the force commanders is based on past UN experience and is not significantly different from other multinational forces.

Heiberg describes the different nationalities, with their cultures, policies and religion, that are within UNIFIL. Indeed there are few differences between soldiers who come voluntarily and those who are professionals. Certainly volunteers provide a variety of professional skills which can be used to advantage, whereas the professionals are primarily soldiers and only have a trade when recruited for that purpose. She has elaborated on the motivation of the soldiers, which includes a prevalence of greed and crime. Since soldiers are human, a body of soldiers constitutes a society, and as such, exhibit all human strengths and weaknesses. Thus the question to ask is whether or not there is greater crime and corruption in UNIFIL. Heiberg informs us that there is. If this is the case, then the UN command must set it right.

In a descriptive analysis of cultural differences and their impact on operations and inter-relationships between contingents and the populace, she discusses the Ghanaians briefly, and the Nepalese at some length. These soldiers are from the Third World, where their salaries are low and there is a lack of consumer goods. In one example, she describes the differences between the motives of Norwegians and Ghanaians as they pub-crawl together. Surely the Ghanaians may enjoy a beer and the Norwegians may feel safer with them from local molesters at bars; however, the 'buddy system' exists amongst all soldiers, regardless of colour, creed or nationality. This fact should not be ignored.

I must confess to being saddened to read her description of the Nepalese. They belong to a proud warrior race with a long tradition of competent service and chivalry. I have had the privilege of commanding Gurkha troops from Nepal, the same people who serve the kingdom of Nepal. I have travelled to Nepalese villages and visited their homes. I was surprised to read Heiberg's description and can only conclude that there has been intolerable lowering of standards which requires determined action by the UN and Nepalese authorities. I am a Hindu and by birth a Brahmin; I accept that inequities exist in the caste system. If the Kashatriyas, the warrior Nepalese class, will not attend to their latrines, where are the personnel who would normally attend to such tasks? My religion demands cleanliness and purity, which *are* more difficult to maintain in conditions of poverty and underdevelopment; however, it is possible to do so. Surely the UN has a responsibility to the Nepalese soldiers and must pay heed to the views of a respected scholar to eradicate unacceptable conditions that may still exist in UNIFIL.

At my request, Nancy Wright, a consultant, has reviewed my paper on the 'Future of Peacekeeping' which follows.

In a comprehensive evaluation of past achievements and future hopes of United Nations peacekeeping, General Indar Jit Rikhye stresses the need both to resolve ongoing problems and to explore new opportunities. He notes that the revival of UN peacekeeping, marked by the awarding of the 1988 Nobel Peace Prize to the UN peacekeeping forces, coincides with a new-found groundswell of interest in the UN as a vital instrument in the realisation and maintenance of global peace and security.

He then outlines a number of continuing problems. For example the Security Council resolutions by which peacekeeping missions are authorised are themselves at best a compromise. One of the greatest difficulties is in translating the diplomatic language of the resolutions into the precise instructions needed to carry out military operations. Although a Special Committee for Peacekeeping (the Committee of 34) was appointed in 1965 to recommend guidelines for peacekeeping to the General Assembly, this Committee has yet to agree on four essential issues: (1) establishing a sub-organ of the Security Council to manage the operations; (2) the appointment of the commander; (3) the composition of the forces, including support units; and (4) provisions of termination of the forces.

Yet another dilemma is that, owing to political differences and sensitivities, the UN has increasingly turned to the Secretary-General for leadership in peacekeeping. While this approach has proved valuable from a diplomatic standpoint, the decentralisation has complicated the co-ordination of peacekeeping operations.

In an effort to remedy this problem, the Secretary-General has consolidated management of peacekeeping operations through the office of the Under-Secretary-General for Special Political Affairs for Peacekeeping. At the same time the Secretary-General has limited this official's involvement in the political phase of the negotiations preceding the operations. As a result only one Under-Secretary-General for Special Political Affairs is responsible for peacekeeping, and is responsible for only the operational aspects.

At present, Rikhye explains, the two most important matters still needing attention are: (1) administrative and logistical support for peacekeeping and (2) the availability of military expertise to the Secretary-General. In order to formalise co-ordination between operations managed by an Under-Secretary-General for Special Political Affairs and the logistic support by Field Service under the Under-Secretary-General for Administration, UN Secretary-General Pérez de Cuéllar brought field operations to his own office and placed an Assistant Secretary-General in charge. With the two most important aspects of peacekeeping handled within the Executive Office of the Secretary-General, better co-ordination was achieved. However, under the recent administration reform and consequent reduction in senior Secretariat positions, field operations were reverted to Administration early in 1988. While this change may prove necessary in view of the present financial austerity, it is important to recognise the fundamental importance of maintaining a proper system of co-ordination for peacekeeping.

Although many efforts have been made to provide some military expertise to the Secretary-General and his staff, the results have not been very satisfactory, according to Rikhye. The political differences among the Permanent Members of the Security Council on key issues relating to the management of peacekeeping operations are central to the use of a military advisory staff for the Secretary-General. Therefore disagreements among the Permanent Members of the Security Council impede the management process.

Rikhye stresses that, despite the continued presence of the problems just described, UN peacekeeping has a dynamic legacy. An evaluation of past and present peacekeeping efforts, plus the current proliferation of international conflict, provides sufficient ground to underscore the importance of sustaining and strengthening the peacekeeping forces.

The renewed interest in peacekeeping should serve as an impetus for new roles for peacekeeping forces, Rikhye explains. Possible functions include: use during incipiency; border security; confidence-building measures; verification; use during civil wars and assistance in maintaining law and order; combating terrorism; humanitarian aid and security; drug interdiction; and naval peacekeeping.

In conclusion, Rikhye states:

> The possibility of establishing a more rigorous framework for the prevention and settlement of international disputes rests upon the common will of the UN member states and respect for national sovereignty and integrity as well as upon respect for international authority and compliance with its decisions. Since the eventual success of peacekeeping depends on the ability to promote peace-making, a greater effort by the UN is required in this respect. As peacekeeping is the start of the process of peacemaking, its success is essential for what will follow. Therefore the members of the Security Council must show greater will to support their resolutions, for there will be little progress if there are no teeth for implementing the Council's decisions.

Furthermore Rikhye underscores the important preventive function of peacekeeping, namely in conflict avoidance. Confidence-building measures and verification are likewise crucial to conflict prevention. Those involved in peacekeeping thus need to understand better the technology available to them in the realms of verification and confidence-building.

He stresses that the role of the Secretary-General in peacekeeping continues to be fundamental. Member states often may be able to call on the Good Offices of the Secretary-General when the political environment makes dependency on another part of the UN difficult or impossible.

In order for peacekeeping forces to be assured of the resources they need and deserve, Rikhye advocates enlarging the number of troop-contributing countries. He cites the present stand-by arrangements made by Canada and the Scandinavian countries, among others, as a useful example of what can be done in this regard.

Rikhye reaffirms the degree to which the future of peacekeeping depends largely on the extent to which national and international leaders are committed to finding solutions to current problems and to exploring new roles for peacekeeping forces. In particular he upholds the awarding of the 1988 Nobel Peace Prize to the UN Peacekeeping Forces as a promising sign of renewed faith in the United Nations and in global solutions to international problems.

REFERENCE

1. *The United Nations and the Maintenance of International Peace and Security* (Published for UNITAR by Martinus Nijhoff Publishers, 1987) p. 33.

1 Reflections by the Chairman

Brian E. Urquhart

It was a pleasure to chair an important meeting in Norway on peacekeeping that opened just after the award of the Nobel Peace Prize. I must congratulate the two sponsors not only for the initiative to hold such a workshop but also for their prescience.

Thorvald Stoltenberg, our host country's Foreign Minister and member of the IPA's Advisory Board, stated in his opening remarks that peacekeeping has become for many countries part of 'Realpolitik' and not merely an idealistic approach to international peace and security. The support of the great powers, political and financial, is a *sine qua non*, hence the importance of the drastic change in attitude by the Soviet Union and re-evaluation by the United States with a new administration taking office.

At the moment there is a better political climate to discuss peacekeeping as part of a viable system of international peace and security than at any time in the past 30 years. The declining validity of the use of force in what is obviously an interdependent and multipolar world, at least in terms of conventional warfare, makes it propitious to discuss how to make peacekeeping less improvisational than in the past.

The new role of the Security Council, functioning for the first time as a collegial body as anticipated in the Charter rather than a battleground for the great powers, opens up a number of possibilities for regional conflict management. While the millennium has not arrived, the fading of the Cold War provides new co-operative avenues for third parties as the recent progress in Angola–Namibia has demonstrated.

After having been in the doldrums for a decade since the establishment of UNIFIL, 1988 marked an important departure for peacekeeping: the change in the international political climate, particularly the change in attitude by the USSR and a greater willingness by both superpowers to utilise the UN; observers in Afghanistan as part of UN-brokered indirect talks; a new observer force to follow up the Iran–Iraq cease-fire; the Nobel Peace Prize. Meanwhile planning moves ahead for the UN Transition Assistance Group (UNTAG) and the Western Sahara while thought is being given to the possible use of outside forces as part of a settlement in Kampuchea. However, unrealistic expectations should not be raised that a new era has arrived, one in which peacekeeping will be utilised in all regional conflicts and will proceed smoothly and without hitches. The UN Good Offices Mission in Afghanistan and Pakistan (UNGOMAP) in Afghanistan was initiated outside of the Security Council and may yet come to haunt the Organisation.

The force observing the cease-fire between Iran–Iraq, the UN Iran–Iraq Military Observer Group (UNIIMOG), was fielded in the traditional manner and has broadened the base of troop-contributors by involving 26 countries, but there is still no official agreement between the parties. The UNTAG plans have been dusted off; but much has changed since their formulation in 1978, including the circumstances of the operation and an additional task to verify the withdrawal of Cuban troops.

Care should be taken in attempting to generalise excessively about peacekeeping and to improve upon what has been part of the recipe for success, namely improvisation. While modifications of past practice are clearly possible and desirable, one of the strengths of previous operations has been the creative and spontaneous adaptation of general principles to a specific situation. For example, attempting to determine in advance whether the great powers should be involved is not really useful, as it may or may not depend upon the context.

Impartiality is essential for successful peacekeeping operations. The parties to a conflict can represent practical problems of interpretation in operational decisions. Holding personal views is not an impediment to professional conduct in the field, provided that there are clear standards and solid leadership. Effective secretariat officials and peacekeepers can also be quite impartial in public but make known privately their views and thereby exercise a quiet diplomacy that can facilitate negotiations.

There is a much discussed link between peacekeeping and progress on political negotiations, or the process of peacemaking. It is useful to make a distinction between less and more controversial peacekeeping operations. In conflicts where peacekeepers are part of an agreement and will depart after a fixed period of time (for instance, Namibia and Western Sahara) or where they are a part of an agreed cease-fire and the parties are able to pay for the service (for instance, MFO) there are relatively few criticisms or frustrations among the troop-contributors. However, where peacekeeping forces are inter-posed to stop hostilities (for instance, the UN Peacekeeping Force in Cyprus (UNFICYP) or the UN Interim Force in Lebanon (UNIFIL) or in an inter-state war, like UNIIMOG) it is quite unlikely that negotiations will proceed quickly. Hence the international com-munity must patiently and squarely face the unfortunate reality of a long, controversial, and costly peacekeeping presence. In this context the possibility of increased humanitarian assistance to build bridges between factions should be explored to the fullest.

The Secretary-General has recently reorganised the management of peacekeeping. The new arrangements have strengthened the Secretary-General's role as the focal point for peacemaking and centralised the conduct of all ongoing peacekeeping operations and the planning of future ones in the Office of Special Political Affairs. On the other hand there is now a somewhat artificial division between peacemaking and peacekeeping; and problems still exist in the linkages to the Field Operations Division and related to the effective-ness of the Office of the Military Adviser. These are particularly serious in light of the likely expanded use of peacekeeping. There may be a role for the Military Staff Committee in an advisory capacity to the Secretary-General, but until there is an enforcement action, it cannot function as specified in the Charter in relation to the Security Council.

Questions are increasingly being asked concerning the willingness of the international community to finance an annual peacekeeping budget that could approach $1.5–$2 billion. The apt comparison is not with the present UN budget but rather with the cost of sophisti-cated weapons systems or indeed with the cost of conflict. The cost of two advanced strategic bombers would pay for one year's operations in Namibia. Nonetheless alternative means for financing – perhaps from beneficiaries in the private sector – should be considered, particularly in light of the overall UN financial crisis.

In fact the overall financial crisis of the United Nations circum-scribes the debate about the financial problems and future prospects for peacekeeping. There is an intimate link between the overall financial health of the Organisation and the effectiveness of peace-keeping operations. The regular budget provides not only the support staff in the secretariat for managing peacekeeping and peacemaking and the finances for certain operations, but also the working capital to help launch quickly the heavy start-up costs for new operations. As a result of the very high level of unpaid contributions for the regular budget and particularly for special assessments, peacekeeping continues largely through the forbearance and generosity of troop-contributors. The suggestion from the Sixth Committee of the General Assembly to establish a Working Capital Fund for peace-keeping should of course be supported; but there will be no adequate solution until member states universally respect their obligations to pay their assessments for the Organisation's peacekeeping operations. The fact that UNIIMOG is in deficit after only four months is disquieting. The imminent operation in Namibia, at approximately ten times the cost, risks becoming a political and financial crisis of major proportion. Efforts to reduce UNTAG for financial reasons are likely to have serious political consequences.

There is an obvious inability of developing countries that contribute troops to pay for deficits in operations; the ability and willingness of many industrialised troop-contributors to continue subsiding operations may also be limited.

Joint action by troop-contributing countries, both developing and developed, to influence financially delinquent countries in New York is one potentially useful means to exert pressure. It may also be useful for troop-contributors as a group to discuss common political and technical issues.

The consent of the parties to a conflict is the basis on which rests the essentially non-violent but firm device known as international peacekeeping. A certain war-weariness seems recently to have helped overcome the reluctance of conflicting parties to solicit the help of peacekeeping missions. The problems of consent need to be stressed in light of UNGOMAP's experience and the growing number of conflicts where the lack of consent of one or more insurgents would directly threaten peacekeepers. Questions related to the use of force also merit further study, especially in this context.

The relationship between Blue Berets and local populations is an important, yet relatively unexplored, variable influencing the effectiveness of peacekeeping operations. The multinational character of UN forces is the basis for their legitimacy, authority, and acceptability. At the same time, the cultural diversity of peacekeepers – including their varying rates of pay and spending patterns – combines with differences in military operational styles to affect their impact on local society. Such factors can be either supportive or destructive of a force's effectiveness as well as of the economic and social conditions of the country in which it operates. These matters, admirably described in the workshop paper on the subject, should become the object of internal discussion among the staffs and contingents of peacekeeping forces.

There is a need for more effective public relations and public education efforts in relation to peacekeeping. Serious misconceptions exist about what this unusual tool of conflict management can and cannot do, not only among the public at large but also among the media and decision-makers in governments and parliaments. Academics could well play a useful role here.

Participants disagreed as to whether the Ad Hoc Committee on Peacekeeping (now the Committee of 34) or more academic and non-governmental forums like the one organised by the Norwegian Institute of International Affairs (NIIA) and the International Peace Academy (IPA) were preferable vehicles for discussion of the future of peacekeeping. The answer is probably that both should look into the needs for reform in such areas as training, logistics, finance, management, and technology as well as more forward looking uses for peacekeeping – for example, at sea, in drug interdiction, against terrorism, in the delivery of humanitarian aid, in preventive diplomacy, and in civil wars.

More analysis by both academics and practitioners of past peacekeeping successes and failures – both UN and non-UN operations – as well as imaginative studies of its future applications – are clearly necessary. Insights from related areas (for example, verification of Confidence Building Measures (CBMs) in the arms control field) may also be applicable.

2 Rethinking Peacekeeping

Augustus Richard Norton and
Thomas G. Weiss

INTRODUCTION

In December 1988 the International Peace Academy (IPA) of New York and the Norwegian Institute of International Affairs (NUPI) sponsored an off-the-record workshop outside Oslo in which some thirty-five practitioners and analysts of peacekeeping discussed the rapidly changing context of international peace and security at the end of the 1980s. The timing for these discussions was propitious. They began the day after the award of the Nobel Peace Prize to forty years of United Nations peacekeeping, in which context the UN had been publicised suddenly as a viable instrument for international conflict management.

The point of departure for the three-day retrospective look at the problems and the prospects for peacekeeping was the extreme fluctuation in international support for this unusual vehicle to help mitigate disputes in the Third World. Envisioned as an instrument for preserving peace in the post-war world, the image of the United Nations was badly tarnished by its inability to stand above the fray of international politics. Rent by East–West and North–South polarities, denied support by the superpowers and encumbered by bureaucracy, the UN's inability to prevent or resolve peacefully international conflicts almost became a mockery of its idealistic origins. It was pointed out that while analysts tended to compliment the economic and social programs of the specialised agencies, they usually dismissed the prospects for UN action on the political and security fronts. A new nadir in multilateralism was reached with the financial crisis of 1986–87.

Then, in the new international climate of 1988, the UN began playing an energetic role in ending an impressive list of enduring conflicts. It showed a new vitality in performing what may be its most important role, the peaceful resolution of international conflict. The list of recent diplomatic successes and potential undertakings was impressive. The Gulf War spluttered to a close, Soviet troops withdrew from Afghanistan, the fighting in the Western Sahara slowed and considerable headway was made in the decolonisation process to end strife in Namibia. There was also promising progress toward a negotiated settlement in Kampuchea. Progress even seemed possible in the stubborn Cyprus dispute.

There was a general conviction that the availability of the peace-keeping option had helped to make much of this progress possible, underlined dramatically by the Nobel Prize. After a decade in the doldrums, peacekeeping was taken off the shelf for every region in the Third World. In 1988 unarmed UN observers were dispatched to Afghanistan and the Iraqi–Iranian border. Peacekeeping forces were planned for the Western Sahara, and a long-awaited United Nations peacekeeping force was under active preparation for Namibia. Yet another peacekeeping force was being discussed for Cambodia, while the needs for verification were also being planned for Central America.

After several decades in which the scope for UN action in the Third World had been narrowly circumscribed, the IPA and NUPI understood the importance of the present historical moment. They asked the distinguished international contingent of scholars and practitioners to analyse peacekeeping as part of a viable, alternative system of international peace and security. It was not necessary to reinvent the peacekeeping wheel. Both the possibilities as well as the limitations of this unusual tool of international conflict management were discussed. Six main themes emerged from the exchange of views in Oslo.

Superpower Relations

The resolution of conflict by third parties is arduous and frustrating work, but it is a hopeless task unless the participants in war choose peace. The first and most obvious element in successful conflict management is the need for diplomatic support from the major players in conflicts. Moreover, initiatives by the Secretary-General lacking a firm base of diplomatic support, especially from the super powers, are likely to come to naught.

Thus there was a general agreement that a key factor had been the recent dramatic improvement of relations between Moscow and Washington. The Security Council has been reinvigorated and functions as a collegial body as anticipated in the Charter rather than as a battleground for great and not-so-great powers to score cheap rhetorical victories.

For its part the Soviet Union has come to the conclusion that UN conflict management serves its own national interests. Moscow has traditionally been extremely sceptical about UN peacekeeping. It refused to support financially most operations; and it was seldom invited to participate. Over the past two years though, Soviet diplomats and scholars have stressed the UN as a co-operative institution with which to reduce international tension and to resolve specific crises. Concrete actions have buttressed the new Soviet lexicon, including the beginning of repaying arrears on Soviet peacekeeping assessments, the acceptance of UN participation in monitoring the withdrawal of Soviet troops from Afghanistan, and behind-the-scenes actions with Cuba and Vietnam to foster negotiated settlements in Angola and Kampuchea. Less than a week before the workshop, General Secretary Gorbachev enthusiastically addressed the General Assembly, an action that symbolised the seachange in Soviet attitudes.

Ironically the USSR's new interest in multilateral instruments for security and conflict resolution coincided with the Reagan era decline in US support for these very same mechanisms and an increased reliance by Washington on unilateral actions. However, the shift in Soviet attitudes has apparently begun to evoke positive reponses from the United States, including behind-the-scenes co-operation over specific conflicts. President Reagan's final speech to the General Assembly in September 1988 noted that 'the United Nations has the opportunity to live and breathe and work as never before', a remarkable about-face from an administration which had brought about financial crisis in cutting budgetary allocations and in unleashing political forces that were commonly labelled as 'UN-bashing'. President Reagan's comments were viewed optimistically by many who hoped that the Bush Administration would return to the traditional US willingness at least to give multilateralism a chance.

Despite general enthusiasm about a resurgent United Nations, participants cautioned against attempts to revive the idea of collective security – international peace enforcement of Chapter VII of the Charter. However, this does not mean that concerted international action is futile. With the Soviet Union showing enthusiasm for peacekeeping, China showing interest for the first time, the western Permanent Members of the Security Council – especially the US – indicating a renewed dedication to peacekeeping, there will be new opportunities to quell conflict.

Limitations of Peacekeeping and the Need for Peacemaking

Participants were not too distracted by flights of doves to recognise that the dispatch of UN peacekeeping forces or observers does not signal the end of a conflict, but rather the beginning of an opportunity to resolve it. Peacekeeping is a means of facilitating peacemaking, but it is not a solution in and of itself, except insofar as it meets the commendable humanitarian goals of saving lives and easing human suffering.

International peacekeeping is intended as an interim step to buy time for conflict resolution and diplomacy. The breathing space purchased by a peacekeeping force is often absolutely necessary to allow passions to quiet and enmities to dissipate. It is a way of disentangling a volatile situation from the international system. The deployment of a lightly-armed peacekeeping force is a kind of international declaration of danger. In its essence it is the symbolic, seemingly even the theatrical, deployment of impeccably neutral military units which are interposed between belligerents and use force only as an absolutely last resort in self-defence. Peacekeeping forces are lightly armed and often derive much of their influence from the moral weight of the international community. The very fact that the force is put in place – as a moral but not normally a physical barrier to external intervention – emphasises the danger inherent in the situation and, at least, the momentary intention of the international community to pull out all of the diplomatic stops to limit the conflict. The moral weight which peacekeeping forces symbolise may not always hold much sway, but these forces can make a stunning difference.

Once established however, peacekeeping operations often take on lives of their own. Participants, particularly those from the traditional troop-contributing countries, regretted that the illusionary calm of stabilised disorder often dissipates the momentum for concerted diplomacy. The temporary stopgap of peacekeeping thus ends up being confused with a solution. Internal conflicts fester, often abetted by external powers which are undeterred by the presence of an international force.

Not surprisingly some of the most useful and successful UN peacekeeping ventures have been in tandem with bilateral peace-making or disengagement efforts, for example the UN Disengagement Observer Force (UNDOF). Several participants agreed that peacekeeping is often a sort of diplomatic sleight of hand, allowing states to extricate themselves from adventures that they find burdensome or no longer sensible. For instance, in 1958, Secretary-General Dag Hammarskjöld deftly helped to justify the exit of US marines from Lebanon and British troops from Jordan by increasing the number of United Nations military observers, a move not too dissimilar, in the view of one participant, from the face-saving 'fig leaf' of UN observers in Afghanistan.

In this regard participants made a distinction between less and more difficult peacekeeping operations. When they are deployed in support of a settlement – as with the Multinational Force and Observers (MFO) in the Sinai or when they are to depart by a specific date – as planned in Namibia and the Western Sahara, peacekeepers generally face little criticism, if predictable frustrations. However, when peacekeepers are interposed to stop hostilities in which the belligerents have little interest in negotiating a solution (as in Cyprus, Lebanon or, perhaps, on the Iran–Iraq border) their task is much more formidable, and their contributions often considerably more thankless. In such situations the international community must patiently and squarely face the unfortunate reality of a long, controversial, and costly peacekeeping presence. Financial decisions about peacekeeping resemble those about refugees and disasters: they are normally based on the fiction of short-term inputs. There was a general agreement that troop-contributors and funders should dispel such illusions for many operations.

The Use of Force and Civil Wars

Participants were concerned about the levels of force increasingly required of peacekeepers, particularly in civil wars. Paradoxically peacekeepers eschew violence, but their operations often occur in extremely violent situations. Peacekeepers can separate warring armies, observe cease-fires, report violations, even provide humanitarian services, but they may use force only as an absolutely last resort and in self-defence. Soldiers as peacekeepers must walk a very fine line. Not only must they operate with impeccable neutrality, and exemplify military professionalism, but they must demonstrate restraint and self-control. International peacekeepers serve as a form of moral suasion to justify non-violence. If peacekeepers regress to combatants, they are likely to be quickly outgunned and they will soon find themselves unwelcome.

The 'preferred' and certainly the least problematic role for an international peacekeeping force is to deploy between belligerents who have agreed to stabilise an armed peace. The United Nations Disengagement Observer Force (UNDOF), based on the Golan Heights and separating the Israeli and Syrian armies, is a good illustration. However, not all peacekeeping forces are deployed in circumstances where the tasks are so neatly drawn.

Peacekeeping forces also have been deployed within states, rather than between them. Violent internal conflict, often between different ethnic, tribal or religious groups, poses one of the most daunting challenges that peacekeepers have had or are likely to face.

The most chaotic circumstances for a UN operation were in the Congo (1960–64) where the forces became embroiled in a civil war and were widely criticised by many parties but with particularly lasting effect in the Soviet bloc and many African countries for not imposing a political solution. The Congo has become a negative lesson about the limits of peacekeeping, but peacekeeping operations in internal wars continue. For instance, the United Nations Interim Force in Lebanon (UNIFIL), which had been created in 1978 to oversee the withdrawal of Israeli forces from Lebanon and the reestablishment of Lebanese governmental authority in southern Lebanon, was a focal point for discussion. UNIFIL quickly found itself in the midst of a truly incredible array of gunmen and militiamen, who, in the aggregate, represent nearly every active conflict in the Middle East. UNIFIL has failed to fulfil its mandate, but it has lent a modicum of stability to south Lebanon. Participants agreed with most analysts: no one would enjoy contemplating the consequences of its withdrawal.

While the use of force has recently been minimal, it was felt that Cyprus also remains a potential powder keg. Since 1974 the United Nations Force in Cyprus (UNFICYP) has served as a buffer separating the Turkish-occupied northern from the southern part of the island, where the internationally-recognised government resides. From 1964 to 1974 UNFICYP was deployed throughout the island, where it functioned with considerable success as a constabulary force attempting to quell inter-communal bloodshed. The force is alternately condemned for freezing the partition of the island, and praised for forestalling additional episodes of aggression between NATO members Greece and Turkey.

Participants agreed that an example of the type of operation to avoid was the Multinational Force in Beirut (MNF). By design a non-UN force deployed after the Israeli invasion of 1982, it brought together contingents from the United States, France, Italy and Britain in an effort to bring stability to Lebanon. Initially the MNF was to be only a short-duration force (it had a 30-day mandate) tasked to oversee the withdrawal of Palestinian combatants from Lebanon, a mission that it fulfilled competently and promptly. Shortly after being withdrawn, it was hastily reinserted following the slaughter in the Sabra and Chatila refugee camps in September 1982. Within a year of its return, it came to be viewed by opponents of the government of President Amin Gemayel as the 'international militia'. The MNF sacrificed the moral authority that usually underlies successful peacekeeping, and instead became a participant in the complex Lebanese conflict. Spurning military advice, civilian policy-makers were blind to the limitations of the MNF and acted as though it were an expeditiary force. After the notorious attacks on the French and US contingent in the Autumn of 1983, the MNF was disbanded in early 1984, leaving behind a Lebanon engulfed by conflict.

The MNF example illustrates that it is tempting to ask too much of peacekeepers, to expect them to do what diplomats have not been able to do. Participants emphasised that the hard-won lessons of past operations underline the wisdom of strictly constrained rules of engagement for peacekeepers to avoid the liabilities inherent in the over-zealous use of force.

Of course the non-use of force can be a disabling credo, if it is interpreted to preclude resolve and resourcefulness. Participants pointed out that UN doctrine had already evolved from 'individual' to 'institutional' self-defence and that artillery in Lebanon, as it had been earlier in the Congo, goes far beyond light weapons. In locales where savage violence reigns – such as Mozambique, Ethiopia, the Sudan, Kampuchea and Afghanistan – some participants argued that less restrictive guidelines would be required if peacekeeping forces were to be deployed. However, the practical aversion of troop-contributing countries to sending their soldiers into combat and to sustaining heavy casualties even in the name of peacekeeping probably makes the creation of such forces close to impossible. However, it was noted that there is an apparent willingness of regional partners whose own security is threatened to run higher risks in 'peacekeeping' efforts – India in Sri Lanka or the Frontline States in Mozambique.

The Management of Peacekeeping

The Secretary-General has recently reorganised the management of peacekeeping in order to ensure a more adequate linkage to peace-making. The new arrangements have sought to strengthen the Secretary-General's role as the focal point for negotiations and centralised the conduct of ongoing peacekeeping operations and the planning of future ones in the Office of Special Political Affairs. In the view of some participants, however, there is now a somewhat artificial division between peacekeeping and peacemaking, which should be seen as a continuum and part of the world body's gamut of conflict management tools. Unsolved and serious problems also remain concerning the adequacy of the support provided for field operations and of the effectiveness of military counsel available to the Secretary-General. Experienced and knowledgeable personnel, both civilian and military, are inadequate in the secretariat to cover even ongoing operations; if expansion occurs, there would simply not be adequate support.

Many participants did not conceal their view that a major weakness has been the uneven leadership of peacekeeping forces. Peace-keeping is no place for tired or marginally competent generals with little command or combat experience. The Secretary-General should have a list of resourceful and talented generals who can pass muster and who will be released promptly by their governments when the UN needs them. As a minimum the Secretary-General should insist on multiple nominations. This is an area where the firm support of the Security Council would be essential.

A final, and largely unresolved, question related to the purely military aspects of peacekeeping operations. While peacekeeping is predominantly political, many participants believed that some acutely military problems – command and control, logistics, intelligence, and civilian/military relations – required much more analysis and critical attention than in the past. In particular there was consensus about the need to clarify mandates. What was characterised as their 'woolly' nature had led to a situation in which there were too many and too controversial operational decisions in the field.

The Soviet suggestion to revive the Military Staff Committee met with little enthusiasm from either representatives of troop-contributors or sources of financing. Though sometimes bent – as in Cyprus where the British have played a major role in the operation since its inception – there has been a working rule against the use of Permanent Member's forces in such operations. Participants judged this to be a sensible rule; but following it does not preclude great power assistance, including logistical support, training and perhaps intelligence sharing as well as possible support to the humanitarian side of peacekeeping operations.

Finance

The long-standing problems related to the lack of adequate financing for peacekeeping operations were a central preoccupation of participants. In spite of the renaissance in peacekeeping, the financial quibbling surrounding the launching of the Namibia operation indicated that myopia still characterises the judgements of the major powers. The five Permanent Members ignored the concerns of African and non-aligned states about the drastically reduced complement of personnel for the UN Transition Assistance Group (UNTAG) in Namibia. In determining to cut the costs of UNTAG, the five indicated clearly that the financial tail is still wagging the political dog. Questions are increasingly asked about the ability of the international community to finance an annual peace-keeping budget that could be from $1 to 2 billion dollars. Participants underlined that the apt question pertained to the cost of alternatives, not only in financial terms but in terms of threats to regional stability throughout the Third World. For purposes of a relative cost comparison, it was pointed out that the estimated cost of one Stealth Bomber would be more than a year's operations in Namibia.

Participants believed that a different type of financial calculation was desirable. On the part of the traditional troop-contributing countries, for example, support for peacekeeping has reflected hard-headed calculations about national defence policy. For instance, the Nordic countries (Finland, Norway, Sweden, Denmark) and neutrals like Austria and Ireland, as well as the NATO member Canada, view peacekeeping as a realisation of multilateralism; and some also view such service as realistic training for their soldiers. Moreover providing troops to a UN force is a form of burden-sharing in the view of NATO allies like Norway, and deserves to be so recognised.

Future Challenges

Peacekeeping forces, by the very nature of the circumstances that spawn them, are usually created in moments of utter haste, when other options have withered or have been vetoed by one or more of the Permanent Members of the Security Council. Participants emphasised that care must be taken not to impede the flexibility of the Secretary-General, the day-to-day commander-in-chief, because one of the secrets of success has been creative improvisation. Lessons certainly need to be gleaned from experience; but one of the strengths of the past has been creative and spontaneous adaptations of general principles – neutral interposition, the non-use of force except in self-defence, consent of the parties, and non-interference in internal affairs – to the specific needs of each new crisis and continuous, *ad hoc* adjustments to changing circumstances within each crisis.

At the instant of creation there is no opportunity dispassionately to conduct research or establish lengthy training programmes. The lessons of previous undertakings must be on hand, if not already assimilated. This argues strongly for the predesignation of a national contingent, which are trained and ready for deployment on short notice. By no means does this preclude the creative exploration of other missions for UN forces, including perhaps a role in interdicting drug trafficking, or on the high seas, or confronting humanitarian emergencies in places like the southern Sudan. Participants urged that these and other possibilities be analysed in light of the most propitious climate in some forty years for the expanded use of the multilateral machinery for the management of international conflict.

They urged the International Peace Academy and the Norwegian Institute of International Affairs to continue their exploration of the lessons from ongoing operations. They stressed the importance of a workshop on 'the future challenges of peacekeeping', which would be co-sponsored in mid 1990 by the IPA, NUPI and the Centre for Strategic and International Studies of York University.

NOTE

Brief portions of this essay were the basis for 'Turning Again to U.N. Peacekeepers', *New Leader*, vol. LXXII (1989) no. 6, pp. 12–14. Reprinted with permission.

3 Peacekeeping in the International Political Context: Historical Analysis and Future Directions
Henry Wiseman

INTRODUCTION

A reading of the current political climate depicts a renewal of faith in the UN and in the competence and utility of peacekeeping. Indeed peacekeeping has entered a promising stage of revival. There are new opportunities and challenges which could dramatically reaffirm the strength of the UN in the maintenance of international peace and security; but the future is not automatically assured. There are a great many hurdles to overcome.

Why then look back to compare past with present? Has not the past been analytically mined close to the point of exhaustion? Should not our enquiry be directed exclusively to the horizon of new opportunities?

The historical literature is certainly rich with ideas and proposals for extending the techniques of peacekeeping into many new areas, such as arms control verification, monitoring the delivery of humanitarian aid, new methodologies for the anticipation and containment of conflict before the crisis stage, and so forth. While I share the belief that some of these ideas may be desirable, even possible in the future, I intend to be true – or at least largely so – to my mandate to compare the past and present political and operational effectiveness of peacekeeping, to show what should be avoided and what should be retained and developed for future applications.

I will focus on the UN experience, but not exclusively. To restrict the analysis to the UN would be to ignore the valuable lessons, good and bad, of peacekeeping by regional organisations and *ad hoc* arrangements. That is not the only reason. Should the UN make more frequent future use of peacekeeping, then we must certainly assume that new operations may be applied to situations where heretofore it could not venture because of the nature of the conflict, regional concerns and direct involvement of the Permanent Members of the Security Council; reasons why regional or *ad hoc* arrangements rather than those of the UN were applied. For example, had the US and the USSR been more 'accommodating' in 1975 as they now seem to be, then the second UN Emergency Force (UNEF II) might have been extended and not replaced by the *ad hoc* Multinational and Observer Force in the Sinai (MFO). Similarly the UN Interim Force in Lebanon (UNIFIL) could have been used, as the Soviets proposed, to supervise the withdrawal of the Palestinians from Beirut in 1982 and the subsequent disaster to the *ad hoc* multinational force (MNF) could possibly have been avoided. Again, the *ad hoc* arrangements in 1954 in Vietnam proved to be totally ineffective. A UN operation was then, for obvious reasons, out of the question. Yet 34 years later the UN has been invited into a comparable situation in Afghanistan.

Raising the 'what if's' of history is not my purpose, which is to extract the lessons from historical and current endeavours wherever they are to be found. The examination will deal therefore with the following factors without, at the outset, differentiating between what are commonly known as 'peace observer' and 'peacekeeping' operations. These factors will be examined thematically rather than in a chronological order of operations.

- the multiplicity of peacekeeping and peace observation functions
- types of crises evoking peacekeeping responses and characteristics of parties in conflict
- principles of consent and the operational implications – the use of force
- host party perceptions and the principle and practice of neutrality and impartiality
- provision of security
- peacekeeping, peacemaking and pre-crisis planning

Even before embarking on this examination, some of the preliminary findings are already self-evident. These are: (1) the increasing complexity of the conflict situations, (2) the extensive involvement of non-governmental parties, (3) the frequent political support and military assistance of one or more of the Permanent Members to one or another of the parties in conflict, and (4) the growing multiplicity of military, civilian and governmental functions undertaken by peace-keeping operations. Though seemingly apparent, the implications of these matters and their relationship to the complexity of corresponding developments in the international system are fundamental. To ignore them would restrict the study of peacekeeping to a legal and structural analysis.

It is now well understood, without any apparent opposition by members of the UN, that peacekeeping should be mandated and maintained under the jurisdiction of the authority of the Security Council. Contentious disagreement about the residual authority of the General Assembly in matters of peacekeeping are, for the most part, overcome. The primacy of the Security Council in the maintenance of international peace and security is not challenged; and so the Council is now engaged through the instrumentalities of peacekeeping in a very wide range of civilian and what are normally considered governmental activities as listed above.

When the UN was established, peace and security were defined essentially in terms of specific dispute settlement techniques, negotiation, mediation, arbitration, judicial procedures, under Chapter VI of the Charter and by military means, under Chapter VII. Pacific instrumentalities are drawn from nineteenth-century ideas on how to manage Europe and the balance of power. The experiences of World War I and World War II and the many wars since then show, however, that the world continues to rely chiefly on military means. Indeed much of the world still operates within the confines of the military paradigm. Consequently the founders of the UN jurisdictionally empowered the Security Council to command large-scale military forces and established the Military Staff Committee as its only sub-organ. The subsequent innovative development of peacekeeping, without charter provisions, was a response to historical necessity; but it brought in its wake an entirely new set of functions. It should therefore be clear to all that the traditional conception of peace and security in purely or predominantly military terms is no longer sufficient for the management of the international system.

MULTIPLICITY OF FUNCTIONS

As the legitimacy of peacekeeping has increased and the mandates have become more elaborate, so have the number, diversity, difficulty and complexity of functions. They range from the 'relatively' simple task of the observation of cease-fires all the way to the assumption of 'governmental' authority over a given territory. The functions can be roughly grouped (the boundaries are not distinct) into three categories – military, governmental/political, and civil – each with its own range of procedures and problems. The following list is not exhaustive, but includes some examples where they have been either implemented or proposed:

Military Functions: observation and monitoring of cease-fires; supervision of the withdrawal of forces; maintenance of buffered zones (UNEF I, UNEF II, UN Observation Group in Lebanon (UNOGIL)); regulation of the disposition and movement of military forces (West Irian, Rhodesia, Namibia, and Western Sahara); prevention of infiltration (Lebanon 1958, 1980), and prevention of civil war (Congo).

Governmental/Political Functions: maintenance of territorial integrity, provision of law and order; ensuring political independence (Congo); assisting in the establishment of a viable government (Congo); security of the population (Western Sahara); management of communal strife, a socio-political function (Cyprus); coping/negotiating with non-governmental entities (Congo, Cyprus, Lebanon, Afghanistan, and Western Sahara); assumption of temporary governmental authority and administration (West Irian, Rhodesia/Zimbabwe, Namibia, Western Sahara, Gaza); administration of an election of a constituent assembly to write a constitution (Namibia); conduct of elections and referendum (Kashmir, Rhodesia, Namibia, Western Sahara) (elections were also provided for in the 1954 *ad hoc* arrangements for the unification of North and South Vietnam); and assisting in the formation of local administration (UNIFIL).

Civil Functions: provision of humanitarian assistance (Gaza, Congo, Cyprus); monitoring and regulation of the flow of refugees (Zimbabwe, Namibia, Cyprus, and Lebanon); and management of local disputes.

These functions, whether military, civilian or governmental, are each becoming more frequent, more elaborate, and more interrelated. This trend will surely continue, and as will be argued later, will require the formation of clearer guidelines, more training, more resources and more complex machinery

TYPES OF CONFLICTS ENGENDERING PEACEKEEPING RESPONSES

Cease-fire lines are more or less readily defined upon cessation of hostilities between national armies in set piece territorial wars. They are not so readily defined in guerrilla-type civil wars conducted by non-state as well as state actors. Of the fifteen UN peacekeeping operations mounted since 1948, all, with the exception of the Mission of the Representative of the Secretary-General in the Dominican Republic (DOMREP) and the UN Peacekeeping Force in Cyprus (UNFICYP), were interstate wars. Depending on the criteria for pacification, it might also be argued that because of the large-scale US military intervention, the Dominican Republic was also an interstate conflict. Similarly, because of the Greek Enosis Movement and the Turkish invasion of Cyprus, UNFICYP too could be classified as an interstate conflict.

Nevertheless one of the most outstanding features is that, of the 15 conflicts which produced a peacekeeping response, six were also civil conflicts involving non-state domestic actors. When the Balkan and Indonesian conflicts of the immediate post-war period and the current situations in Namibia and Western Sahara are included, the ratio becomes nine out of nineteen. Furthermore, of seven non-UN peacekeeping operations – Vietnam 1954, International Commission for Supervision and Control (ICSC), Vietnam 1973, International Commission for Control and Supervision (ICCS), Sinai 1975, Multi-national Force and Observers (MFO), Sinai 1979 (the reformation of the MFO), Rhodesia/Zimbabwe 1979, Commonwealth Monitoring Force (CMF) and Beirut 1982, Multinational Forces in Beirut (MNF I and MNF II) – all but one were interstate conflicts. Yet again, four of these were also civil wars involving non-state actors. All this very clearly demonstrates that the modality of peacekeeping, from whatever mandate source, is frequently applied to conflicts which are at one and the same time a confusing and incendiary mix of state and non-state actors.

This is not at all surprising. Most classifications of conflicts and war over decolonisation, national self-determination, interstate and domestic struggles for power, in the last 40 years display these same characteristics; and most have been embroiled in the global disease of the Cold War. According to one comparative study, 79 per cent of wars between 1900 and 1941 were between states. By contrast, from 1945 to 1969, 85 per cent were internal civil wars.[1] The evidence shows quite clearly that civil wars have increased in regularity as well as severity from 1945 well into the 1970s, diminishing somewhat as the process of decolonisation drew to a close.[2]

Most researchers also show that indirect or open foreign military interventions have become a common feature of local and regional wars in recent decades. One study reports that the proportion of wars which have become internationalised rose from 18 per cent in the 1919–39 period to 27 per cent in the 1946–65 period and rising to 36 per cent in the period 1966–77.[3] This is also the pattern of those conflict situations subjected to UN and other forms of peacekeeping operations (for example Israel and its neighbours in 1948, the Suez crisis of 1956 with Great Britain and France, the US in Vietnam from 1968 to 1973, the Soviet Union in Afghanistan in 1979 and US counter-support to Pakistan). There are no hard and fast categories, but heavy-handed support and supply of arms by the USSR, the US and others to one or another party in conflict is a common feature of the international system. Most significantly, superpower and other military support have continued after as well as before cease-fires have been declared and peacekeeping operations have been put in place. It is relevant to note that from 1965 to 1984, of the five Permanent Members, the Soviet Union and the United States ranked alternatively first and second among the highest exporters of arms, followed by France and the United Kingdom. China ranked seventh after Italy and the Federal Republic of Germany.[4] Furthermore, 'according to Central Intelligence Agency (CIA) estimates, 69 680 military personnel from developing countries were trained in the Soviet Union between 1955 and 1985; and according to the Department of Defense, the United States trained 457 675 personnel from the Third World during the same period.[5]

Indigenous conflicts that could possibly have been regionally contained have become pawns of the Cold War. The United States and Soviet partisanship toward opposing sides have typified throughout those conflicts which have been subjected to UN and non-UN peacekeeping operations. Largely for these reasons, from 1945 to 1964, there was not one of the six cases where both the US and USSR voted in favour of a peacekeeping operation in the Council or the General Assembly.[6] In all seven non-UN cases, from Vietnam

(ICSC) in 1954 to the British managed Commonwealth Monitoring Force (CMF) in Rhodesia in 1979, each situation was aggravated or undermined by US/Soviet rivalry. Oddly enough, the MFO was established to monitor the Sinai because the Soviet Union opposed the continuation of UNEF II to supervise the peace treaty between Israel and Egypt; whereas in 1982, the situation was reversed when the USSR called for the deployment of UNIFIL to supervise the withdrawal of the Forces of the Palestine Liberation Organisation (PLO) from Beirut which Israel and the US opposed; hence the *ad hoc* MNF operation.

The international political climate has changed dramatically since that time. Gone are the cries that peacekeeping is a neo-colonialist imposition, a cry sounded so vehemently during and in the aftermath of the Congo Operation. Gone are the days when peacekeeping was such a divisive issue that it almost wrecked the UN itself. Gone are the days when socialist states were unwilling or unwelcome contributors to peacekeeping operations. Now over 60 states comprising more than 40 per cent of UN Members from all parts of the world have become 'peacekeepers'. The phrase 'equitable geographic composition' has been given full expression. The present prospects are for more representative composition and the more frequent and efficacious use of peacekeeping, with possibilities of application in complex and violent situations heretofore too controversial and intractable for the intervention of UN peacekeeping. These include: Kampuchea, Mozambique, Central America or even the Gaza Strip. Each of these and others that might readily come to mind are, however, cases of civil conflict involving domestic and other non-state actors encumbered by foreign intervention and strategic and ideological rivalry. These are the endemic characteristics of conflict in this chaotic age.

THE PRINCIPLE OF CONSENT AND HOST COUNTRY PERCEPTIONS

Consent is one of the primary and fundamental requirements of peacekeeping. It is a principle that has been operative in every UN and non-UN operation. As long as peacekeeping, however amplified, stays short of enforcement action, the principle of consent will prevail. Although this principle has been much applauded, the political and operative consequences have not been fully examined.

Is consent granted willingly or under pressure? What are the reasons for acceptance? Are these reasons based on short-term relief or on long-term policy objectives? The answers to all these and related questions will in each case directly affect the actions of the parties and therefore the performance of a peacekeeping mandate.

Of related and equivalent importance is whether the Security Council is forced to take precipitous action in calling for a peace-keeping mandate when hostilities reach their most critical stage, or whether time and the nature of the conflict permits reasoned consultation with the parties. The two most recent cases – Afghanistan and Iran/Iraq – are both the result of considerable negotiation and definition of the mandate and functions, even though the first was established after lengthy negotiations and the latter over a much shorter period of time. The other two operations under active consideration – Namibia and Western Sahara – will be, if and when implemented, the result of very extensive negotiations. Prior to these events, however, only three of the thirteen UN operations were based upon amply negotiated agreements, namely West Irian, UN Yemen Observation Mission (UNYOM) and UN Disengagement Observer Force (UNDOF). In none of these situations have hostilities resumed. In all the others where the UN intervened at the height of crises, hostilities were resumed in seven out of twelve cases; in six of the seven, non-state parties were involved in the hostilities (United Nations Military Observer Group in India and Pakistan (UNMOGIP), United Nations Truce Supervision Organization (UNTSO), UNEF I, UNOGIL, United Nations Operation in the Congo (ONUC), and UNFICYP). The exceptions were DOMREP and UNEF II; the latter being unique in several ways. It was established at the most critical moment of the 1973 Arab–Israeli war under intense pressure from the US and the USSR, which were at the same time arming the war machines of their respective allies. Yet the ensuing process of a UN-mandated cease-fire and UNEF II in its several configurations among other matters resulted in un-precedented face-to-face negotiations and eventually a peace treaty between Israel and Egypt.

We might surmise, or more confidently assume, that when negotia-tions leading to a cessation of hostilities supervised by a peacekeeping operation are comprehensive in consultation and substance, then the likelihood of the renewal of hostilities will be considerably reduced. Still there is a further coincidence of factors that must be noted. Among the three cases cited above, West Irian, UNYOM and

UNDOF, which were founded upon comprehensive agreements and where hostilities had not been renewed, all can be basically classified as interstate conflicts with little or no involvement of non-state parties. On the other hand, among the seven cases where there were no extended and comprehensive negotiations, nor any prior agreement, there were five in which non-state parties were deeply involved. This leads to their classification as intrastate conflicts (legal or political jargon for domestic violence or civil war).

Assuming therefore that the non-renewal of violence or hostilities is a mark of successful peacekeeping, even when no overall peace settlement is achieved, then we may safely argue that peacekeeping is at best a hazardous process when hurriedly imposed at the most acute stage of hostilities. By contrast the more advance preparation and comprehensive agreement of peacekeeping modalities, the less the likelihood of further eruption of hostilities.

The most difficult problems arise out of the involvement of non-state parties. An in-depth analysis will show that these entities do not fully partake in nor seriously observe the behavioural implications of the principle of consent. The Palestinian Fedayeen never granted their 'consent' in 1948 or 1956 and subsequently violated it as their interest dictated; Moise Tshombe in the province of Katanga was not a consenting party to the establishment of ONUC and adhered to the mandate only after being forcibly subdued; the Greek Nationalist Movement in Cyprus was not consulted about the UNFICYP mandate and violated it at will. The PLO, the Hazbolah and the Christian militia, acting as a surrogate for Israel, were not direct parties to the establishment of UNIFIL and for them the principle of consent had none or little operational significance. In Afghanistan, the Geneva Accords, so skillfully negotiated by Diego Cordovez between the Governments of Afghanistan and Pakistan and 'guaranteed' by the Soviet Union and the United States,[7] continued to be violated by Afghan factions which refused to sign the Accords: in effect, no consent.

Of course these non-state parties are not the sole violators of UN mandates. Israel has been a grave and consistent offender and so has Egypt, particularly in 1967. However, the reasons for the failure of non-state parties to participate fully in the granting and adherence to the conditions of consent is that revolutionary, counter-revolutionary or movements of national self-determination, by their very nature, operate outside conventional state-centred political norms because their goals are absolutely vital to their existence. They are therefore generally unyielding in the pursuit of these goals, less subject to the strictures of international law and more immune to pressures or sanctions exerted by states or international organisations. Major exceptions to this pattern were the non-state parties of Robert Mugabe of the Zimbabwe African National Union – Patriotic Front (ZANU PF) and Joshua Nkomo of the Zimbabwe African National Union (ZANU). Though sometimes engaged in bloody struggles for black majority rule, they agreed to participate in the Lancaster House negotiations in 1979 which resulted in the cease-fire and elections in Rhodesia, now called Zimbabwe. In that case, all the parties – state and non-state – were subjected to and responded to strong international pressures. Similar outcomes with the UN Transition Assistance Group (UNTAG) for Namibia and the negotiations for the withdrawal of Cuban troops from Angola are undoubtedly the result of considerable external pressures.

All these matters deserve a lot more examination before clear lessons or conclusions may be drawn. However, all the evidence suggests that where non-state parties are major rather than marginal actors, it is better to bring them into the negotiating process at the early stages in the international management of conflict. History shows that they almost always end up there any way (for example, the Viet Cong in Vietnam, ZANU PF and ZANU in Rhodesia, the South West Africa People's Organization (SWAPO) in Namibia and Jonas Savimbe of the Union for the Total Independence of Angola (UNITA) in Angola; but, like all similar cases, the fundamental issues at stake are primarily political. These must be fully appreciated before the principles and modalities of peacekeeping and peace-making can be successfuly applied.

THE PRINCIPLE AND PERCEPTIONS OF NEUTRALITY

The effectiveness of a peacekeeping operation is therefore profoundly influenced by the perceptions and expectations of the parties. Where these differ from the intent of the mandate, problems are sure to arise. When considering 'threats to international peace and security', the Security Council has the right and, I would argue, the obligation to intervene; but when the intervention is in the form of a peacekeeping operation, the reason why host countries grant consent is very important. History provides a rich variety of reasons: because a cease-fire was preferred to the alternative of further military losses

(Egypt 1973); because of a hiatus in the fighting which enabled military forces to regroup and prepare for later attack (Israeli/Palestine 1948); because peacekeeping provided a face-saving device for British and French withdrawal in 1967; because Lebanon in 1982 expected UNIFIL to provide political and military security and the territorial integrity of the state; and because, for the Greek community in Cyprus, UNFICYP maintained the status quo which preserved their position of dominance.

It is therefore very clear that the motives and objectives of parties consenting or acknowledging a peacekeeping or peace observer operation are many and varied. Some may be identical or ancillary to the stated objectives of the UN peacekeeping mandates and of their elaboration into specific functions determined by the Secretary-General – others, not at all. International peace and security is best served when the parties in conflict – the Security Council as a body and the Permanent Members in particular – actively agree on the objectives and functions of a mandate. There is enough evidence in the record to confirm this proposition.

One of the most fundamental features of peacekeeping is the issue and ramifications of neutrality; or, more explicitly, operational objectivity and impartiality. The matter is very complex. As an interpository force, especially in cease-fire situations, neutrality is imperative unless otherwise designated by the mandate or by the Secretary-General. Yet this quality is sometimes misunderstood with serious consequences by the parties in conflict. 'Neutrality' was challenged with unwelcome results in the Congo, abused for years by South Africa to deny UN neutrality in regard to UNTAG because the General Assembly had recognised SWAPO as the legitimate representative of the people of Namibia, and denied by many of the factions in Lebanon which accused UNIFIL of being partial to either Israeli or Arab factions. The same occurred in Rhodesia during the 1980 cease-fire and elections when Robert Mugabe and Joshua Nkomo accused the British governor, Lord Soames, of being partial to the political ambitions of the white-supported Government of Bishop Abel T. Muzorewa. Although in principle UN peacekeeping forces should be perceived and acknowledged by all parties as being fully impartial, in practice this is close to impossible.

The more complex the situation – ones which are well beyond the demarcation of cease-fire lines – the more likely there are to be perceptions and accusations of partisanship. This is particularly so where the threshold between inter and intra-state conflict is blurred or non-existent. A most extreme case was that of the overly ambitious peacekeeping mandate of the Organization of African Unity (OAU) in Chad in 1979, which was intended to demilitarise the capital of N'Djamena, enforce the cease-fire, control the Chadian airforce and ensure the free movement of the population; but each of the military factions of Goukouni Oueddie in control of N'Djamena and of Hissene Habre, who tried to dislodge him, expected the Nigerian battalion acting on behalf of the OAU to come to its aid. When the Nigerians emphatically held to their position of neutrality, they were harassed and attacked by both sides and eventually forced to withdraw. This was a gross misinterpretation of the peacekeeping mandate which was designed to separate the forces in preparation for a negotiated settlement and not intended to impose the will of one party upon another. Charges of partiality were more common in the earlier period of UN peacekeeping associated with the process of decolonisation encumbered by Cold War rivalry.

However, the necessity for 'impartiality' in word and deed continues to be imperative. Yet this will be all the more difficult to ensure in multifaceted civil conflicts which are overburdened with the partisanship of one or more of the Permanent Members. Impartiality is not only a principled requirement of UN peacekeeping operations, it must also be perceived as such by the parties in conflict and actively expressed in word and deed by the Permanent Members. Under these conditions impartiality could take on new meaning and greater significance in the sought-after shift from unilateral and bilateral to multilateral management of conflict.

The lesson, it is hoped, will be taken seriously by the Permanent Members; but it is not their responsibility alone. The ideological nature of many contemporary conflicts, insistence on narrow doctrinal conformity and the uncompromising pursuit of singular objectives leaves little room for the appreciation, let alone the practice, of objectivity, impartiality and neutrality. (I recall participating in the conduct of a peacekeeping simulation based on a wholly imaginary conflict situation located on a non-existent island in the Pacific Ocean. Yet the moment some 'peacekeepers' – military personnel from Latin America – identified one of the fictitious parties in conflict with a real life adversary, all objectivity was lost. That fictitious party became the enemy that had to be obliterated.)

Once in place, a UN peacekeeping force should, as argued by Kjell Skjelbaek, be 'strictly impartial'.[8] It should at least adhere as closely to a quality of impartiality as the political situation will allow. Neutrality may not be required for success in cases where, as Hass argues, the Permanent Members act in concert. The 1973 war and UNEF II was such an occasion where both superpowers leaned heavily on Israel, and did so again in the aftermath of the Israeli invasion of Lebanon in 1982. Once in the field, however, all parties would have to be treated with the same impartiality or a UN force would quickly lose credibility and viability. That would surely be the case in the ongoing operations in Cyprus, the Golan Heights, Iran Iraq, Afghanistan, as well as in the proposed operations in Western Sahara and Namibia.

The International Peace Academy and some defence colleges teach the principles and practices of peacekeeping to future peacekeeping personnel; but what instruction is offered to the potential subjects of peacekeeping operations? This is not a trivial matter. The meaning of international peace and security in the UN Charter presupposes that the Security Council can and should invoke a common good. Short of enforcement, which presumes guilt, peacekeeping is designed to be impartial. It might be very helpful if the politically and culturally diverse membership of the General Assembly could comprehend and adopt an operational definition of the terms impartiality, objectivity and neutrality. Definition in law or lexicon are inadequate. If the attempt to agree on a functional definition failed, it would regrettably demonstrate how shallow and inadequate was the appreciation of the concept. If the attempt succeeded, how well it would reify existing beliefs and be used directly to infuse peacekeeping with greater independence, credibility and effectiveness.

Hass could be right that neutrality may not be relevant where a UN mandate adopted by consensus of the Permanent Members would name the 'guilty party' or would call for an imposed solution, but not otherwise. There are too many occasions where the term peace-keeping has been usurped by unilateral military actions, such as the US naval offshore bombardment in Beirut. The distinction between peacekeeping and peace enforcement must be maintained, even though the threshold between them has become somewhat blurred. The use of violence against peacekeepers in the Congo and in Lebanon which forced them to respond in kind, are cases in point. Mandates which require the maintenance of law and order always, I am sure, raise the sensitive question: what measures may be under-taken to do so? For the very first time, the mandate for UNIIMOG

Resolution 598 (1987) declared the Security Council to be 'acting under Articles 39 and 40 of the Charter'. By inference, if not in fact, peacekeeping in this case was shifted from the void between Chapters VI and VII of the Charter, where it now resides, into Chapter VII, 'Actions with Respect to Threats to the Peace Breaches of the Peace and Acts of Aggression'.

This is a most interesting and important development. As has been argued elsewhere, peacekeepers have all too often come under military assault and been pushed to reply beyond the parameters of the non-use of force. The threshold between non-use and use of force must be maintained. Yet there are occasions when commanders in the field or the Secretary-General are called upon to use their discretion to stretch the meaning of a mandate. The high levels of violence and UN casualties in Lebanon are sufficient example.

These kinds of occasions are sure to arise in the future. Only the most naïve would expect a peacekeeping operation in Kampuchea, Southern Africa or Central America to be totally free of violence. Surely, when food becomes a key weapon in a civil war situation, as in the Sudan, then the Blue Berets themselves would be put at risk if they attempted to guarantee delivery on humanitarian grounds. At the risk of redundancy, there are many recurrent occasions where non-governmental parties or their agents are unrestrained by the international moral sanction of the Blue Berets. Beyond these occasions, there have been direct acts of war where UN forces were overrun and bypassed as in the Middle East War of 1967 and more recent occasions of Israeli action in Lebanon.

It is conceivable, even probable, that a more politically coherent and determined Security Council could find means to curtail incidences of 'mid level violence' through political pressure or by upgrading the quality of the peacekeeping mandate. Again an example can be found in the Congo where the Security Council authorised the Secretary-General to take such 'vigorous action including the use of the requisite measure of force, if necessary, for the immediate apprehension, detention . . . and/or deportation of all foreign military and paramilitary personnel'.[9] The very possibility that the Security Council might undertake such measures could serve as a deterrent to limit or prevent the erosion of the credibility and effectiveness of peacekeepers in the field. As to the curtailment or prevention of acts of war – that is a matter well beyond consideration in a study of peacekeeping.

PEACEKEEPING AND THE PROVISION OF SECURITY

Relief from violence, war and the threat of death are the gifts of peace, however transitory, that a cease-fire bestows on belligerents and non-combatants alike. Blue Berets on the scene where former battles took place are the affirmation that a cease-fire will hold. The peace-keepers are both the symbol and the instrument of security. Beyond that, the peacekeepers are expected, as they have been frequently charged, to do one or another of the following: 'secure and supervise the cessation of hostilities';[10] 'use its best efforts to prevent a recurrence of fighting';[11] 'use the Papuan (West Irianese) police as a UN security force to maintain law and order at his discretion (the Secretary-General); use Indonesian armed forces',[12] 'the Force will use its best efforts to prevent the recurrence of fighting and to ensure that its area of operation will not be utilized for hostile activities of any kind'[13]; and other UN mandates which contain the words 'maintain' or 'supervise' a cease-fire or otherwise prevent the recurrence of hostilities.

These are critical clauses defining the function and responsibilities of UN forces and are acknowledged as such by the respective parties; but what happens thereafter? How do the parties in conflict, especially the combatants and non-combatants in the field interpret these clauses which many have never read or understood, into personal, local or national perceptions of their own 'security' requirements? This may range all the way from personal safety and communal protection to the sovereign security of national territory. Such expectations may well be beyond the intent and capability of a UN force. UN commanders and field officers would probably have much to say on this subject. Yet this gap between UN mandated functions and the expectation of the parties is a very serious matter, not-withstanding the heroic efforts of UN personnel to provide and maintain individual and communal security. They are sometimes caught in the Catch-22 dilemma of trying to provide protection and security for groups or parties which believe themselves free to infiltrate and attack UN forces while, at the same time, insisting that the UN forces provide them with security from the 'other side'. An even more serious situation may develop where a host country, such as Israel, views the peacekeepers at best as a fig leaf for their military security, at worst as an obstacle.

I don't know the answer to this problem, if there is one. All that can be suggested at this point in time is that the UN should clearly develop and publicise appropriate guidelines with an accompanying explanation, not solely in legal language or as written in operational manuals, but in the language of the layman. Beyond that, more effective measures might be considered by the Security Council. Some possibilities are the raising of the level of economic or political sanctions against the offending parties, or by militarily reinforcing the UN contingent and lowering the threshold for the authorised use of force. Otherwise there is the constant danger, as experience shows, of the erosion of freedom of movement and the mitigation of political impact on the parties in conflict and on the general situation. Perpetuation rather than resolution of the situation is a general result. The prospects for conflict resolution fade away.

PEACEKEEPING AND PEACEMAKING AND PRE-CRISIS PLANNING

The UN deservedly enjoys a great deal of credit for its peacekeeping record. The same cannot be said for peacemaking in relation to the same events. Of the 13 operations beginning with UNMOGIP 1948, only two conflicts can be said to have been truly resolved – West Irian and the peace treaty between Egypt and Israel emanating from UNEF II. Six of the others continue to this very day, UNMOGIP, UNTSO, UNFICYP, UNDOF and UNIFIL. One, UNEF I, was withdrawn in the heat of war. Another, ONUC, is more difficult to assess – partial success, might be the appropriate characterisation. As for DOMREP, the conflict can best be described, at the risk of contradiction, as having been resolved through repression. Of the current and proposed operations, the conflict in Afghanistan continues while the situation in Iran–Iraq, considering the bloodiness of the war, is reasonably stable. Prospects for UNTAG and Western Sahara look very good. When put in place, the integral electoral components in each should ensure the resolution of these violent and longstanding conflicts. The parallel process and outcome of the non-UN peacekeeping operation in Rhodesia (now Zimbabwe) is a highly relevant model.

This takes us back to the actual moment in time when the Security Council is seized of conflicts which threaten international peace and security. The record is absolutely clear. The Security Council has not been, to date, very successful in managing crises before they explode. The reasons are equally clear: one or another of the Permanent Members is heavily engaged in upholding the cause of one of the

parties in conflict; a superpower categorically opposes any multilateral intervention that it cannot control within its own declared area
of strategic dominance; and/or a general reluctance to overtly violate
Article 2 (7) of the Charter, the non-interference 'in matters which
are essentially within the domestic jurisdiction of any state'. Incidences of all three are numerous. France opposed the UN operation
in the Congo because of possible similar action in Algeria. The Soviet
Union opposed any UN action in Hungary following its own military
intervention in 1956. The United States would not allow any UN role
in Vietnam, nor it seems, in the current situation in Central America.
Exceptions are the Middle East in 1956 and Afghanistan in 1988.

These barriers, however, seem to be breaking down. Article 2 (7)
is cited almost exclusively in a defensive mode, ignored in the
offensive mode. The Soviet Union has accepted a UN Peace Observation Mission in Afghanistan and has in general reversed its
traditional antipathy to UN peacekeeping. The United States has in
general dropped its attack on the UN. China has adopted a more
positive approach and the non-aligned have become very supportive.
The desire to strengthen peacekeeping has been echoed through the
halls of the UN and in the various capitals of the world – Norway,
Canada and Austria are foremost among them. The fact that 26 states
have elected to participate in UNIIMOG and in UNGOMAP – many,
including Argentina, Hungary, Indonesia and Turkey, which have
never before contributed to any similar UN operation – is solid
evidence of the growing willingness to use the UN in the management
of conflict; but there is still resistance in many quarters. It would not
do to exaggerate the situation. Yet, should the Permanent Members
shift from unilateral to multilateral endeavours in the maintenance of
international peace and security there is firm ground for optimism
that the Security Council may be strengthened. The Council could
then possibly adopt pre-crisis conflict management measures.

It is here that the Secretary-General is extensively engaged in
preventive diplomacy and related peacemaking functions through
the use of his good offices. His successes in quiet diplomacy in
Afghanistan, Iran–Iraq, Western Sahara and his current efforts in
Cyprus are weighty testimony to his impartiality, patience and
persistence which enable him to use his office to such good effect. A
more conciliatory and committed Council could use the Office of the
Secretary General to explore the use of peacekeeping-related
measures in the early stages of crises where it would be politically
undesirable or premature for the Council itself to venture.

This is in agreeable contrast to the Soviet attacks on Dag Hammarskjöld when he tried to use the independence of his office in just such a manner. The mutual confidence currently enjoyed by the Security Council and the Secretary-General augurs well for the whole process of peacemaking in pre-crisis situations. As Pérez de Cuéllar has himself noted, 'situations that threaten peace are usually highly complicated and require a flexible and finely tuned response'.[14]

The Soviet Union has recently proposed the 'promotion of UN capability to take effective preventive measures for averting international crises and conflicts,'[15] and has called for 'a more active use of the mechanisms for formal and informal consultations among Security Council Members with the participation of the Secretary General,'[16] adding that 'the Soviet Union wants to see the positive experience and practice of UN peacekeeping operations consolidated and further developed and put on a more solid legal and financial basis' (to which it added), 'these operations could be more extensively used for the implementation of Security Council decisions as well as for the prevention of emerging armed conflicts'.[17] If former President Reagan's praise for the UN in his address of September 1988 should be carried forward by President George Bush, then there are grounds for optimism for a more favourable US policy toward the UN.

WHAT NOW?

Peacekeeping has gone through a remarkable period of development in function, scope and application. When all the data is gathered together, several factors move to the forefront. The first is the clear trend that conflict in general has become more multidimensional and multilateral, involving many state and non-state parties. All are entwined in a complex web of conflicting objectives; and paradoxically there is a parallel, though a less certain trend, toward the successful combination of peacekeeping and peacemaking, as in West Irian, Zimbabwe and as hopefully will occur in Namibia, Angola and Western Sahara. Only some of the more significant features have been dealt with in this paper. Overall the possibility exists for even greater expansion and utilisation in the future. Much of the past 'ad hocary' has become institutionalised, the principles more or less accepted and the capability quite solidly based in the UN and among many member states. The choice now is either to let history take its course, or to attempt to strengthen the foundations and plan for the future. From 1964 to the present all efforts to set firm guidelines, especially those focused in the Special Committee on Peacekeeping Operations (the Committee of 33), have failed. Indeed there are those, particularly in the office of the Under-Secretary-General for Political Affairs, who believed all along that it would be a mistake to try and negotiate the modes of organisation and rules of engagement, that the end result would make the process more cumbersome and restrictive, rather than adaptive and flexible. There is much validity in this argument.

I believe, however, that the present situation is one in which the adaptive and flexible characteristics could be explored to great advantage without binding UN peacekeeping in narrow and rigid formalism. Yet I am not at all sure that this could be done in the Committee of 33. The Committee has too long a history of disagreement over what strictures should be applied to the Secretary-General, what role, if any, should be assigned to the Military Staff Committee, what procedures and guidelines, and under what auspices, should the 'international' training of peacekeepers be conducted, and other historically contentious issues. At no time, to my knowledge, has the formal agenda of the Committee included such items as fact-finding procedures in the early stages of conflict, 'diplomatic management' of non-state parties, establishment of international criteria for the administration of free and fair elections, peacekeeping delivery of humanitarian aid, verification of arms control measures, organisational structures designed for naval forces and guidelines for co-operative peacekeeping measures with regional organisations.

However, the characteristics of conflict in the international system and the nature and functions of peacekeeping tell us that these are matters that may well come into play in the future. Still it is difficult to imagine how these 'ideas' could be considered in a formal diplomatic setting. There are many states, however, that might be willing to consider these matters in an 'academic' setting where the injection of new ideas and the opening of horizons could be done through a series of academic papers which diplomatic and military participants could discuss at will without fear of authorship or commitment.

Obviously the International Peace Academy, the Norwegian Institute of International Affairs and the Canadian Institute of International Peace and Security are the kind of non-governmental institutions that could initiate this process 'diplomatically'. They could explore these ideas in many capitals, east, west, north and south. Then, with governmental support, they could plan the best means for creative deliberations on the future of peacekeeping. Subsequently, and preferably only after the intellectual and political process of exploration and filtration, should some of the recommendations be fed into the formal deliberative processes of the UN. The most opportune time for such a venture is now.

REFERENCES

1. I. Kende, 'Twenty-five years of local wars', *Journal of Peace Research* (1971) no. 8, pp. 7–12.
2. W. Eckhardt and E. A. Azar, 'Major World Conflicts and Interventions, 1945 to 1975', *International Relations*, 5 (1978) pp. 78–83.
3. M. Small and J. D. Singer, 'Conflict in the International System, 1916–1977: Historical Trends and Policy Futures', in C. W. Kegley, Jr and P. J. McGowan (eds), *Challenges to America: United States Foreign Policy in the 1980s*, (Beverly Hills: Sage, 1979) pp. 89–115.
4. *World Armaments and Disarmament SIPRI Yearbook 1985* (Stockholm: International Peace Research Institute, 1985) pp. 372–73.
5. R. L. Sivard, *World Military Expenditures* (Washington: World Priorities, 1988) p. 13.
6. Henry Wiseman, 'The United Nations and International Peacekeeping', in *The United Nations and the Maintenance of International Peace and Security* (Dordrecht: Martinus Nijhoff, 1987) p. 300.
7. 'Letter Dated 14 April, 1988, From The Secretary-General Addressed To The President Of The Security Council', UN Doc. S/19834, 26 April 1988.
8. 'Peaceful Settlement of Disputes by the United Nations and Other Intergovernmental Bodies', *Cooperation and Conflict*, vol. XXI (1986), no. 3, p. 147.
9. UN Doc. Security Council res. 169 (1961).
10. GA Res. 998 (ES-1), 1956.
11. Egypt/Israel, *Report of the Secretary-General*, Res. 340, 1973, UN Doc. S/11052.
12. Ratification of Agreement and Resolution between the Republic of Indonesia and the Kingdom of the Netherlands concerning West New Guinea, UNTS, vol. 437, p. 274.
13. Report of the Secretary-General on the implementation of Security Council Resolution 425 (1978), UN Doc. S/12611 re UNIFIL.
14. Quoted in Statement of Rafeeuddin Ahmed in an address on *The United Nations Role in Peace-Making* (Tokyo: 6 September 1988).
15. Ibid.
16. Ibid.
17. Ibid.

4 UN Peacekeeping: Expectations, Limitations and Results: Forty Years of Mixed Experience

Kjell Skjelsbaek

INTRODUCTION

Multinational peacekeeping is a novelty in the history of international affairs. In 1985 the United Nations published a survey of its operations up to that time.[1] The first operation recorded in this book is UN Truce Supervision Organization (UNTSO) which started its mission in June 1948. Thus the UN has had 40 years of experience with peacekeeping. The lessons which can be drawn from these 40 years are important for the development of the concept of peacekeeping and for the planning and execution of future operations. Lessons can also be drawn from a limited number of non-UN operations.

In the anniversary year, the UN was awarded the Nobel Peace Prize for its peacekeeping operations. The decision of the Nobel Committee was generally applauded. It should not be forgotten, however, that the applause would have been much more muted if the prize had been given four or five years ago. For a number of reasons the concept of peacekeeping has been politically controversial throughout the span of 40 years. At the moment there is a world-wide trend toward greater appreciation.

This trend could quickly be reversed however. Peacekeeping is a difficult business, fraught with dangers. Existing or future forces and military observer corps may run into problems on the ground, become victims of political squabbles in the region they operate and bones of contention in the rivalry between major powers. The UN operation in the Congo (ONUC, 1960–64) contained all these elements. Its repercussions were felt for years in the UN. The UN secretariat, potential troop-contributors and the major powers learned important lessons. With the possible exception of the UN Interim Force in Lebanon (UNIFIL) subsequent operations have

52

fared much better. Nevertheless there is no guarantee against a similarly dismal experience in the future. Although each one of these actors may pursue policies which are subjectively rational, their combination may produce a negative outcome for all concerned.

Because the vacillation between blame and praise of international peacekeeping is likely to continue, it is important both politically and academically to develop a set of criteria by which peacekeeping operations can be judged. The term 'peace' is not a propitious point of departure. In combination with the ambitious aims of the Charter of the United Nations it may create unrealistic expectations about the impact of peacekeeping operations. It is often not recognised that peacekeeping is not, and never was intended to be, an alternative to a system of collective security; but in the absence of such a system, as outlined in Chapter VII of the Charter, peacekeeping operations may be a useful instrument for the containment or management of conflict. In the following pages I shall identify some functions which UN peacekeeping forces and corps cannot perform, and some tasks which they properly may be expected to fulfil.

First, they cannot by themselves stop warfare. If one or more of the parties to a conflict are determined to use arms, neither the Security Council nor peacekeeping forces and corps can prevent them. The fate of the UN Emergency Force (UNEFI) in the Sinai in 1967, of the UN Peacekeeping Force in Cyprus (UNFICYP) during the civil war and interventions in Cyprus in 1974, and of UNIFIL during the Israeli invasion of Lebanon in 1982, illustrates this point. The mission of UNEF I was terminated just before the Israeli attack. UNFICYP and UNIFIL could do little more than protect non-combatants.

There is, however, a significant exception to this rule. Peace-keeping forces, usually infantry battalions with light arms, are capable of deterring and combating smaller military units, for example militias, which are not backed by larger forces, for instance, a regular national army.

Second, peacekeeping is but one step on the road toward a lasting settlement, a resolution of a given conflict. Conflict is often defined as the existence of incompatible political objectives. Incompatibility is the core of the conflict, but it is always associated with two other dimensions, conflict behaviour and conflict attitudes. Peacekeeping relates to these two dimensions as follows.

When the parties to a conflict accept a peacekeeping element in their relationship, they explicitly or implicitly renounce a particularly nasty kind of conflict behaviour – use of arms. The peacekeeping

force is charged with the task of helping the parties to avoid violence. Other forms of conflict behaviour, propaganda, economic sanctions, competition for allies and political support, appeals to world opinion and so on, are not proscribed. A peacekeeping element does not prevent the parties from continuing to wage their conflict by all available means except violence.

In most conflicts the parties have inadequate information about each other. The information they possess is often unreliable and distorted and tends to reinforce negative emotions toward the other side. One of the tasks of peacekeeping forces and observer corps is to reduce suspicion in the military field by providing reliable information based on thorough and impartial observation. The peacekeepers are unable, however, to influence the parties' general perceptions of and feelings toward one another. In most cases they have only limited contact with the local population, and they are not supposed to discuss political issues. They cannot serve as general channels of communication. The force commander and his staff meet regularly with the military leadership of the parties, and occasionally also with the political leadership; but their agendas are limited to problems related to the mandate of the force.

A genuine settlement of a conflict implies that the parties change their objectives so that they are no longer acutely incompatible, that they terminate their attempts to coerce or punish each other, that their mutual perceptions become more realistic and that the feeling of hostility subsides. This usually takes a very long time. 'Permanent settlements usually flow from a change in historical circumstances, which in the long run tend to make irrelevant even the most intractable conflict situations.'[2] In this perspective peacekeeping is little more than a stopgap measure, but it can be a helpful and indeed a necessary condition for starting a process toward conflict resolution.

CONTROLLED IMPASSE

George Sherry has coined the term 'controlled impasse' to describe the essential task of peacekeeping. In a situation where neither party is convinced that it can achieve its principal objectives, and where efforts to achieve them by violent means appear too risky, an impasse may seem preferable. Sometimes the parties realise this themselves, sometimes they are cajoled or pressured by friends and allies to live with a situation which they regard as highly unsatisfactory, but at least better than some of the likely alternatives. An ignominious truce may be better than continued war. Third parties, for instance, the Secretary-General of the United Nations, may also succeed in persuading the parties that the conflict is insoluble, and that they will have to learn to live with it, and to control the resulting impasse politically and militarily.[3] The task of the peacekeeping force then is to assist the parties to accept a situation none of them really likes.

I submit that this is the common element in all peacekeeping mandates. This is the appropriate criterion for assessing the success or failure of peacekeeping.

Some mandates are explicitly more ambitious. UNFICYP, for example, should not only use its best efforts to prevent the recurrence of fighting. It should also, as necessary, contribute to the maintenance and restoration of law and order and a return to normal conditions. The possibility of fulfilling the latter part of the mandate depends largely on factors beyond the control of UNFICYP. The tasks of UNIFIL are to confirm the withdrawal of Israeli forces from southern Lebanon, to restore international peace and security, and to assist the Government of Lebanon in ensuring the return of its effective authority in the area. The latter part of the mandate goes beyond controlling the situation, but has come to naught also in this case.

Controlled impasse means in practice a steady military situation without serious episodes that could easily escalate to large-scale fighting. Military observer corps may prevent deliberate initiation of incidents by being able to report objectively the course of events and identifying the culprits. When incidents take place, whether intentionally or not, they may intercede, appeal to the parties, assist in the separation of forces, and so on. Peacekeeping forces can of course do the same thing; but they are better suited for interpositioning. They are also better equipped for actually stopping infiltration into a demilitarised zone.

We now turn to some of the factors which are important for the achievement of this goal, which make the task more or less difficult and determine the degree of success or failure.

THE SIZE OF THE PROBLEM

UN peacekeeping missions have been carried out under very different conditions. Some missions have been, from an operational point of view, quite simple. Others have faced much more difficult challenges. The following are some of the factors which distinguish the different situations.

Terrain

Some peacekeeping operations have taken place in relatively flat and open deserts with excellent visibility and few hiding places. Under such conditions observing military activity is comparatively easy. Both the Sinai and Golan belong to this category.

Large parts of Cyprus and southern Lebanon are hilly and offer good hiding places. It is more difficult for a peacekeeping force to maintain adequate control in such a terrain. The problems are compounded when vegetation is dense. Terrain and vegetation suitable for guerrilla warfare may create almost unsurmountable difficulties for a peacekeeping mission. Other things being equal, peacekeeping in the landscapes of Central America or in Kampuchea may be considerably more demanding than peacekeeping in the deserts of Namibia or Western Sahara. Personnel requirements would be much larger in the former than in the latter examples.

Population

Peacekeeping is probably easier in sparsely populated areas than in areas of high population density. Guerrilla forces and militias can hide among civilians and store weapons in houses, barns, and so on. The protection of non-combatants, usually not part of the mandate but nevertheless an important concern of many peacekeeping forces, also requires additional personnel. The UN has some, but not very much, experience with peacekeeping in large cities. In Nicosia UNFICYP controls a narrow demilitarised zone where shooting incidents are not infrequent. The UN has still not tried to police a large city seething with struggle among different militias. The Multinational Force in Beirut (MNF) (1982–84) ran into serious difficulties and foundered. Several factors contributed to its failure, one of them being its inability to trace and apprehend troublemakers. A UN force in Beirut would probably have a better political platform than the unfortunate MNF. Nevertheless policing this city under present circumstances will probably be too costly in terms of personnel requirements and casualties.

The Pattern of Conflict

In several peacekeeping operations, the force or observer corps has been positioned between two regular disciplined armies. On other occasions they have found themselves in the midst of civil strife between militias of several political factions in shifting alliances. The Congo operation is the most extreme example, but the present situation in southern Lebanon is also highly complex and volatile. During UNFICYP's first years of operation, this force also confronted competing armed groups, especially within the Greek Cypriot community.

The Size of the Area

Other things being equal, the size of the area entrusted to a peacekeeping force, or the length of an armistice line to be patrolled and observed, are significant factors. Larger areas require more resources. If the UN posts/personnel are too widely dispersed, doubts about their ability to observe adequately the military situation and to prevent infiltration might arise. The Israelis have repeatedly accused UNIFIL of being unable to stop infiltration through its area of operations.

The Presence or Absence of an Agreement between the Parties

Most UN peacekeeping operations have been linked to an agreement between the parties, usually an armistice agreement. However, there have also been cases without any explicit agreement, or an agreement which excludes some of the relevant parties.

The establishment of UN Iran–Iraq Military Observer Group (UNIIMOG) is interesting in this respect. When both Iran and Iraq had announced that they would respect the call of the Security Council for a cease-fire, it was possible to deploy the observer corps after close consultation with the two governments. However, there is not as yet a formal cease-fire agreement.

The establishment of UNEF II is another case in point. This force was deployed in October 1973 when both Egypt and Israel accepted the Security Council's demand for cease-fires contained in resolutions 338–40 (1973). UNEF subsequently moved in steps eastward to help implement two disengagement agreements between Egypt and Israel negotiated with the help of the United States.

The United Nations Yemen Observation Mission (UNYOM) was established by the Security Council in 1963 following an agreement between Egypt, Saudi Arabia and Yemen to end the civil war there in which Egyptian and Saudi forces were also involved. After 15 months UNYOM had to be withdrawn because neither the Egyptians nor the Saudis complied with the agreement. The cost of the operation was to be borne by these two governments, and they did not wish to continue it.

UNIFIL is the most important deviant case. This force was established on the initiative of the United States and the Government of Lebanon. The Security Council voted on the US draft resolution less than a day after the formal presentation of the US proposal. Key members of the UN secretariat had serious doubts about the wisdom of placing a peacekeeping force in Lebanon. The US, however, wanted to present the Israelis with a *fait accompli* before Prime Minister Begin had a chance to mobilise parts of US public opinion against a UN force he did not want. The main adversary of Israel in southern Lebanon, the Palestine Liberation Organisation (PLO), was also not consulted. This organisation criticised bitterly the Security Council Resolution. Ironically the Government of Lebanon was the only Arab party which openly and explicitly supported the establishment of UNIFIL; but the Government of Lebanon had no effective military presence in the southern part of the country.

The absence of an agreement between the parties, or at least some tacit understanding, complicated the mission of UNIFIL from the very beginning. Both the PLO and Israel prevented UNIFIL from deploying in areas which these adversaries wanted to reserve for themselves. The presence of 'nests' of PLO soldiers in UNIFIL's area of operations was for many years a difficult issue in the relationship between the UN and the PLO. It further compromised UNIFIL in the eyes of the Government of Israel. The relationship to the latter remains strained to this day. It contrasts sharply with the relationship between the UN Disengagement Observer Force (UNDOF) and Israel. UNDOF is deployed in accordance with a cease-fire agreement between Israel and Syria. There is effective co-operation between the UN force and both countries.

The importance of an agreement about the deployment of a peacekeeping force or a military observer corps is obvious. However, a couple of caveats are in order. First, an agreement may be interpreted differently by the parties, as illustrated by the case of Cyprus. According to Security Council resolution 186 (1964)

UNFICYP should use its best efforts 'to contribute to the maintenance and restoration of law and order, and return to normal conditions'. The Government of Cyprus (exclusively Greek Cypriot since 1964) saw this wording as mandating UNFICYP to disarm Turkish Cypriots and search for hidden arms. The Turkish Cypriots, on the other hand, assumed that the reference to 'normal conditions' meant *status quo ante*. They wanted UNFICYP to deploy force to restore over the opposition of the Cypriot Government the constitutional situation relating to the right of the Turkish Cypriot community. Many of UNFICYP's problems between 1964 and 1974 can be traced to these diverging interpretations of the mandate of the force.

Second, particularly in civil war situations, new groups may emerge and become parties to the conflict, and they may or may not accept the role of the UN. When the Israel Defence Forces expelled PLO from southern Lebanon, new groups entered the scene. There is a fairly good relationship between UNIFIL and the largest of them, Afwaj Al-Muqamah Al-Lubnaniyya (AMAL). AMAL competes with a radical group, Hezbollah, for support among the Shiite population. Hezbollah has declared war on UNIFIL and frequently challenges the force in its area of operations. The Hezbollah leadership is semi-clandestine, and the UN cannot establish liaison with this group.

These examples underline the importance of having an agreement with and among the parties when a peacekeeping mission is initiated, and of establishing a reasonable relationship with new actors as they enter the scene.

Military Capabilities

Having discussed some of the dimensions which may make a peacekeeping mission more or less difficult, I now turn to various aspects of the strength or capabilities of UN peacekeeping. It goes without saying that these capabilities should be at least commensurate with the difficulty of the task.

The Size of the Force

A UN commander recently told me that 'no military commander will ever be completely satisfied with the number of troops at his disposal'. It is particularly difficult to determine the minimum number of troops for a peacekeeping task because it depends critically on the amount of co-operation offered by the parties to the conflict. Most peacekeeping forces have been at peak strength shortly after their establishment. As the situation in the field has improved, the number of troops has been cut back. (During the Congo operation, some national contingents were withdrawn because the troop-contributors were dissatisfied with the alleged political impact of the UN force in the country.) However, in times of crisis it has been necessary to provide reinforcements. This was done during and immediately after the war in Cyprus in 1974.

Crises may also serve as an impetus for reorganisation so as to utilise available resources more efficiently. After the incidents in the French Battalion (FRENCHBATT), in UNIFIL in 1986, the battalion was withdrawn. Additional troops from other troop contributors did not fully balance the reduction; but a rapid deployment force, which, like a fire squad, could be quickly dispatched to trouble spots, was organised in order to maintain the overall strength of the force.

No peacekeeping force or observer corps (with the possible exception of UNYOM) has foundered because it was inadequately staffed. Despite perennial economic problems and ever increasing deficits, UN forces and observer corps have been kept at a level of strength which permitted them to carry out essential functions.

Equipment

For political and economic reasons the UN cannot pre-stock the equipment needed for peacekeeping operations. Most operations have been launched in the midst of a major international crisis and in a great hurry. Under the circumstances the various national contingents have been forced to take with them practically all the national equipment they expected would be needed in the area of deployment. Because it usually takes some time before the UN logistical service operates satisfactorily, many national contingents have been dependent on national supplies of all kinds in the opening phase of an operation.

Contingents from well-equipped national armed forces often find that some of their gear is unsuitable in a different terrain and climate. The Swedes in UNEF II, for example, discovered that some of their footwear had to be changed. Such contingents may also discover that it is desirable to add certain items which are not included in their national inventory. Contingents from armies which are not well-equipped in the first place, may arrive in a peacekeeping area without essential items like vehicles, radios, and so on. It may take quite some time before all contingents of a force are able to function properly.

In some cases special equipment is called for. In the early 1970s UNFICYP wanted patrol boats in order to be able to check the clandestine importation of arms to Cyprus. However, they were never supplied. It has been suggested that UNIIMOG also should have patrol boats on the waterways between Iran and Iraq. The front line between these two countries is very long, and it has been proposed that UNIIMOG should use helicopters. There is a helicopter wing in UNIFIL which is used for transportation, both on a regular basis and in emergencies. In UNIIMOG helicopters are needed for observation. Helicopters are used extensively in this role by the (non-UN) Multinational Force and Observers (MFO) in the Sinai. At present UNIIMOG uses small airplanes for surveillance from the air.

Modern detection devices may be introduced to peacekeeping in the future. They may reduce the manpower required for surveillance and make peacekeeping forces more effective, particularly in sparsely populated areas.

Training and Competence of the Peacekeepers

The methods of peacekeeping differ in several respects from ordinary military activity. UN Military Observers (UNMOs) are unarmed and can neither attack nor defend themselves. They observe, report, maintain communications and negotiate with the adversaries on various levels. Military information is analysed and interpreted at headquarters. Typical military skills are used also for construction of shelters and other forms of passive defence.

Peacekeeping forces are much more similar to regular military units. They have light arms, but as a rule, they are not supposed to use them except in self-defence. Many different military skills are important for the function of the force: guard duty, observation, patrolling, defence, mine-clearing, marksmanship, and so on. Military leadership on all levels is a particularly critical factor.

Soldiers in peacekeeping forces face a double challenge. In order to have the respect of the armed forces of the adversaries, the parties to the conflict, they must demonstrate military competence. Their personal appearance, handling of weapons and vehicles, the quality of shelters and defensive positions, reaction time in crises, firmness of leadership and general behaviour should incite respect. On the other hand non-military methods like dissuasion, persuasion and negotiation constitute the essence of peacekeeping.

It goes without saying that the quality of national contingents differ significantly. They come from countries with different military traditions and very different authority structures in the armed forces. In some national contingents the general level of education is much higher than in others. Differences in language skills is a considerable problem.

Official UN documents are mute on this issue. In my experience officers who have served in peacekeeping forces are also reluctant to talk about them. Disclosures of large variations in competence among national contingents could cause very serious political problems and could easily jeopardize an operation. I know of no systematic and independent research in this field, and it should probably not be encouraged. However, the problem exists, and a discussion of possible remedies is called for.

POLITICAL ASSETS OF UN PEACEKEEPING

Peacekeeping is primarily a political and diplomatic activity. Success or failure depends much more on political conditions than on the military capability of the force, however important. In this section some of the most significant political aspects of peacekeeping will be highlighted. The points of view are not new, but essential, and bear repetition.

The Concern of the International Community

UN peacekeeping represents the concern of a constituency which extends beyond the area of actual conflict. 'The concern of the international community' is both a cliché and a reality. It does not mean that all or most member governments are intensely preoccupied with the conflict and its potential outcomes. However, when the Security Council decides to establish a peacekeeping operation, no major power is directly opposed. The winning coalition represents a formidable amount of political power and influence which the parties to the conflict may find difficult to withstand.

The establishment of UNEF II offers perhaps the best example of this. In the war of October 1973, the US supported Israel and the USSR supported the Arabs, and particularly Egypt. As a consequence of the Israeli progress and the Egyptian retreat in the Sinai, the tensions between the superpowers reached a critical level. After intense negotiations they decided to compel their respective friends to accept the Security Council's call for a cease-fire. Israel, which prevailed in the battlefield, was very reluctant, but had to give in to American pressure.

Again a couple of caveats are in place. First, not all state's groups are equally susceptible to pressure by the Permanent Members of the Security Council. American pressure on Israel in 1978 did not bring about Israeli acceptance of co-operation with UNIFIL. A major power like India, which has participated in several peacekeeping operations, does not recognise any more the need for UN Military Observer Group in India and Pakistan (UNMOGIP) and co-operates no longer with this observer corps. It is a reasonable proposition that large countries are less impressed by the power emanating from the Council.

Second, some non-governmental groups care little about inter-governmental organisations in general and peacekeeping forces in particular. Some of the groups which take hostages in Lebanon, openly challenge the major powers, as well as UN personnel in the area. In contrast to, for example, the PLO, they do not wish to become accepted actors in the international system.

Both these phenomena tend to limit the effectiveness of UN peacekeeping.

An International Stamp of Legitimacy

The political assets of UN military observers and peacekeeping forces cannot be understood only as a derivative of the power of the members, and particularly the Permanent Members of the Security Council. The power of the Council is both more and less than the sum of the power of its members. It is less because the members generally are not inclined to commit themselves fully to implement the decisions of the Council. It is more because the UN has an un-equalled position as an 'authoritative expositor of international values'.[4] The Blue Berets symbolise these values. An attack on a UN force deployed to uphold international values is different from an attack on other multinational forces without this moral clout.

The position of two non-UN forces in the Middle East underlines this point. The Multinational Force in Beirut (1982–86) consisted of contingents from the US, France, Italy and the UK. The MNF fared well at first; but many Lebanese saw it as a manifestation of Western imperialists rather than universalist values. It soon lost whatever legitimacy it might have enjoyed in the beginning and had to be withdrawn.

The MFO is an entirely different story. The Egyptian–Israeli peace treaty of March 1979 (the Camp David agreement) included *inter alia* detailed security arrangements which would be verified through the stationing of a UN peacekeeping force in the area. Soviet and Arab resistance to the idea precluded a Security Council authorisation of a UN force. Therefore Egypt and Israel, with the help of the US, agreed in 1981 to create a substitute organisation to carry out the functions specified in the accord. Violations of the accord are reported to the civilian administration of the MFO. Unlike reports from the Secretary-General to the Security Council, they are classified. The MFO prefers not to be heard or seen by the outside world. The leadership is acutely aware of the fact that the force is not regarded favourably by the states in the region except for Israel and Egypt. The Egyptian government strongly preferred a UN force. It wants the UN Truce Supervision Organisation (UNTSO) to 'maintain a presence' in Cairo and the Sinai in the hope that one day a UN force or observer corps will replace the MFO.

It is of course impossible to measure the importance of the legitimacy factor. It is a fragile asset. The 'authoritative expositor of international values' is full of contradictions. The different organs of the United Nations may pursue different policies. Since 1974 the General Assembly has adopted resolutions with regard to Cyprus demanding the complete withdrawal of all foreign troops and the return of all refugees to their homes. The resolutions may be valid expressions of important values in international affairs, but they are politically unrealistic. They have angered the Turks and the Turkish Cypriots and made both the good-offices mission of the Secretary-General and the work of UNFICYP more difficult.

The recurrent UN condemnation of Israel is another example of how the deliberative organs of the organisation, by upholding international values in a rather selective manner, can impede rather than support UN peacekeeping. The Israelis are certainly able to appreciate the difference between the General Assembly and the office of the Secretary-General; but the latter cannot count on any special goodwill in Israel because he represents the UN.

Finally it should be pointed out that the set of international values implicit in UN resolutions contain many inconsistencies. The UN preaches both sovereignty and self-determination, two values which often dictate quite different solutions to a conflict. Impartiality, a must for peacekeeping forces, is often incompatible with the Charter's concern for the protection of victims of aggression.

Impartiality and the Role of Troop-Contributors

The attitudes of adversaries in a conflict to a UN peacekeeping force may vary. Sometimes they want the force to achieve the objectives which they themselves were not able to achieve in the battlefield. It is often the weaker party which tries to make the UN force an ally. The force would fall out with the other party if it succumbed; but the parties may accept a force also because they are convinced that it is not inclined to, and not capable of, changing the military relationship between them. The Egyptian and Israeli expectations with regard to UNEF II were probably of the latter category.

In either case observing the strictest impartiality is the most important rule in peacekeeping. The standard operation procedures of all peacekeeping forces and observer corps are based on this principle.

It also has implications for the composition of peacekeeping forces. As far as the UN is concerned, it has resulted in two maxims: (1) the Permanent Members of the Security Council should not contribute national contingents, and (2) an equitable geographical representation is desirable. Both of these deserve discussion.

The Permanent Members of the Security Council have been explicitly excluded from some forces (UNEF I), and implicitly from others. In fact there are only two instances of Permanent Members being represented. The UK has had a contingent in UNFICYP since its first deployment in 1964 and there has been French participation in UNIFIL from the start in 1978, although the number of Frenchmen was significantly reduced after the incidents in late 1986.

It seems to me that there are three arguments against the participation of national contingents from Permanent Members of the Security Council. First, these powers tend to have interests in most regions of the world and risk therefore being perceived as biased by the parties to the conflict. However, if two Permanent Members with opposite interests in the same conflict joined a peacekeeping force, they would, theoretically, balance each other. The second argument, then, is that in such a situation friction between contingents from these countries might develop which would immediately weaken the force. Third, major powers are perhaps less likely than smaller nations to respect the international character of the force.

There are also significant arguments for accepting contingents from Permanent Members. More personnel and other resources would be available for peacekeeping. The prestige of the forces would be enhanced, and the major powers would become more committed to the mandate of the peacekeeping operations.

Personally I have doubts about greater involvement of the major powers in UN forces. The role of the French in UNIFIL has done nothing to alleviate this doubt. However, the major powers are represented in some observer corps, apparently without great problems.

An equitable geographical distribution is the second maxim. Only one force, the United Nations Security Force in West New Guinea (West Irian) was recruited exclusively from one country, namely Pakistan. In practice the number of potential troop-contributors is limited. Developing countries and the nations of Eastern Europe are under-represented.

It could be argued, however, that the attitude of the participating countries toward the parties to the conflict is a more relevant criterion than geographical distribution. They should be neutral, none should be strongly negatively or positively inclined toward the parties. To the extent that preferences among the various troop-contributors exist, they should go in different directions and balance each other.

SUMMARY AND CONCLUSION

I have argued above that the essential element in all peacekeeping operations is to sustain a controlled impasse. If this criterion is accepted, the inevitable conclusion is that most UN peacekeeping operations have been successful.

There are certainly some examples of eruption of serious violence despite ongoing peacekeeping; but in no case can the set-back be attributed to inadequacies of the operation. The withdrawal of UNEF I and the subsequent war in 1967 ('the Sinai blunder') was not the result of inefficiency in UNTSO or in the force. The causes of the wars between India and Pakistan (1965 and 1971) cannot be traced to problems along the cease-fire line in Kashmir where UNMOGIP is deployed. The civil war and interventions in Cyprus in 1974 ended a period of very successful peacekeeping by UNFICYP. The war was kindled by a political strife within the Greek Cypriot community which was not within UNFICYP's terms of reference. The Israeli invasion of Lebanon in 1978 was preceded by the least dramatic period of UNIFIL's checkered history. Peacekeeping operations may be a necessary condition for controlling an impasse, but other factors also come into play. No peacekeeping force or inter-governmental organisation can be made responsible for the reckless policies of President Nasser of Egypt or the Greek military government.

The situations that have been controlled have varied significantly. The larger and more complex they have been, militarily and politically, the greater the demands on the military capabilities and the political assets of the force. There are limits to what a UN peacekeeping operation may achieve. Keeping the peace in the Sinai is quite possible, keeping a semblance of peace in an area of southern Lebanon is not impossible. Restoring a semblance of peace to the population of Beirut, however, may be beyond reach unless many parameters change.

I submit that there are trade-offs between the different military capabilities and political assets of peacekeeping operations. The weaker the political support for an operation, the more important it is to be strong on the ground. The more delinquent the members of the Security Council are in supporting its resolutions, the more critical the composition of the force and co-operation among troop-contributors.

In short a force or an observer corps that was actively backed by the Council, properly composed, adequately trained, sufficiently funded, large enough, and so on, could take on more difficult tasks than others, perhaps even Beirut.

REFERENCES

1. *The Blue Helmets: A Review of United Nations Peacekeeping* (New York: United Nations, Department of Public Information, 1985).
2. Cited from George L. Sherry, 'The United Nations, International Conflict, and American Security', *Political Science Quarterly*, IC (1986) p. 759.
3. Ibid., p. 761.
4. Ramesh Thakur, *International Peacekeeping in Lebanon: United Nations Authority and Multinational Force* (Boulder: Westview, 1987) p. 112.

5 Peacekeeping and Peacemaking: The Need for Patience

Günther G. Greindl

THE EXPECTATIONS OF THE UN MEMBERS

> The objective of UN peacekeeping operations is to contribute to the maintenance of international peace and security, which, indeed, is a primary purpose of the UN. Peacekeeping operations are not intended merely to be a guardian of the status quo, but rather, should facilitate efforts towards comprehensive settlement of the regional conflict in which they are involved.

This point of view was expressed by the Permanent Representative of Japan just a few weeks ago. No one will dispute this position because this adequately describes the context in which peacekeeping should be seen. It does, however, indicate an anxiety, which is that peacekeeping might perpetuate the status quo and diminish the chances of solving the problem. Does this perception, which is frequently voiced, reflect the reality?

When looking at the UN peacekeeping operations, one might get the impression that they are all somewhat lengthy. This perception is understandable, because we tend to look primarily at those missions which are still in place. This is compounded by the fact that peacekeeping missions on the surface appear to be similar in nature. The procedure followed by the Security Council when setting up a peacekeeping operation, as well as those followed by the UN Secretariat, are generally the same. The patterns of deployment into the mission areas do not differ much from each other. Once on the ground, the peacekeepers, often coming from the same traditional troop-contributing countries, not only have the same physical appearance, but normally adopt the same operational procedures and peacekeeping techniques.

Looking beyond appearances, however, one will immediately detect that this is where the similarities end. The most important difference between peacekeeping operations is that the political context prompting the intervention of the peacekeepers is in each case unique. A tangible consequence of this major difference is that some missions are terminated within a reasonable time-frame, while others seem to go on for an unpredictable length of time. In fact the duration of a mission is strictly related to the political circumstances and the proposals of peacemaking which go with it.

CATEGORIES OF PEACEKEEPING OPERATIONS

Looking back on UN peacekeeping operations, they can generally be grouped into three categories: peacekeeping operations that are launched as part of a politically negotiated and agreed solution to a conflict; forces that are deployed after a cease-fire agreement negotiated and signed between the nations or communities in conflict; and peacekeeping forces that are interposed with only a broad definition of its mission, but with the consent of the parties in conflict, in order to stop the hostilities.

An example of the first category of peacekeeping missions is the UN intervention in West New Guinea. The deployment of the peacekeeping force took place as part of a politically negotiated and agreed solution to the conflict. The force mandate was clear, and the operation lasted no longer than scheduled. An eventual UN operation in Namibia will hopefully fall into the same category.

When a peacekeeping force is deployed as a result of a prior agreement or treaty, it will probably be used in a supervisory capacity to verify that the terms of the agreement are adhered to. In such cases the size of the organisation deployed will likely be limited, or can be reduced fairly quickly, or even right from the beginning consist of only a small military observer group. The mandate of the missions falling into this category will normally be clearly defined and, as a result, the tasks of the peacekeepers as well as their operating procedures should be relatively simple. The UN Disengagement Observer Force (UNDOF), presently deployed on the Golan Heights in Syria, is a good example of this type of peacekeeping mission: a relatively small force with a well-defined mandate, agreed upon by the two nations in conflict. In cases like this, the presence of the force may also last for a long period, but this fact is more easily accepted by the international community, as it is an integral part of the agreement guaranteeing peace in a particularly sensitive area of the globe. The contributing countries are more agreeable to an extended presence of their troops, and there is more will by the UN members to share the financial burden.

The deployment of a peacekeeping force in a conflict where no prior written agreement has been reached between the belligerents is quite a different matter. Even though the deployment of the force will be with the consent of the authorities concerned, its functions and its short-term objectives differ considerably. Instead of monitoring the adherence to a treaty or to an agreement, the peacekeepers will concentrate their efforts on creating conditions to stabilise a fragile cease-fire. The maintenance of the status quo becomes an overriding goal. The efforts to negotiate a conflict settlement take place in a situation of relative security provided by the presence of the peacekeeping force. If in this circumstance the negotiation of the settlement of the conflict takes more time, the peacekeeping forces may be seen as becoming part of the problem. It is this type of situation which is often referred to critically and where, as is the case in Cyprus, interested parties or troop-contributors from time to time become impatient. This is a dilemma to which there is no immediate solution.

The following are a few thoughts that may help to minimise the negative effects on this type of operation, based mainly on the experience of the UN Peacekeeping Force in Cyprus (UNFICYP).

MINIMISING NEGATIVE EFFECTS

Naturally the public has the impression that as long as a peacekeeping mission is ongoing, the problem is not solved. Therefore the most striking impact of long lasting peacekeeping missions is the global perception that the UN cannot achieve its mission. There is no immediate remedy, but a good public information system could minimise this problem. However, it must be remembered that public information is always a dilemma for the peacekeepers. When the force is successful in maintaining a ceasefire, the interest of the media disappears and as a result the mission is removed from the headlines. This normal reaction is not entirely unwelcome, since it is in line with a basic principle of peacekeeping operations which is to avoid drawing attention to incidents, because inevitably this will complicate their resolution.

To illustrate this quandary better, one could say that the drama of a successful peacekeeping mission is that there is no longer drama!

Nevertheless a well coordinated public information programme would help to maintain public support for long-lasting missions.

In this context visits to the mission area, in particular of delegations from the contributing countries, survey teams from UN Head-quarters and visits from journalists, are welcome. Some considera-tion could also be given to familiarisation tours by members of the Security Council.

An additional problem of long-term UN intervention is the fact that the local governments, and particularly the local media, develop the habit of using the UN as a whole, and the peacekeeping force in particular, as a target to release frustrations arising from their failure to achieve a political settlement. The local population could sub-sequently also become hostile to United Nations presence in their country. The tendency to restrict the force in its functions gradually sets in among the local authorities. In the long run this tendency has a negative effect on the morale of the peacekeepers. As a general rule the UN should ignore unfounded allegations by the local media so as not to be drawn into public exchanges. Only in carefully selected cases may it be useful to issue a press statement to re-establish the facts. The main line of defence is impeccable discipline and the maintenance of total dedication by the peacekeepers. The manner in which they carry out their mission is the best reply in such circum-stances.

The burden that lengthy missions constitute for the participating nations is also a major element to be considered. Here again UNFICYP is a good example of this problem as, since the inception of the force in 1964, several contributing countries have withdrawn their troops on financial grounds. There is no doubt that the longer a mission has lasted, the more the troop-contributors have felt the burden. What must be avoided is that they say goodbye one by one. A pre-planned adjustment of the force's strength and composition may ward off this danger.

The strength of the force is normally decided at its inception and cannot easily be changed even though the need to maintain a large number of troops in the area may no longer be required once the cease-fire is well established. Therefore one should give considera-tion to developing a procedure, allowing a reduction in the strength of a force during periods of relative calm. The capability for a rapid reinforcement, in the event of a sudden deterioration of the situation, must be maintained by developing contingency plans. These quick reinforcement plans should be tested routinely by flying the designated stand-by troops into the theatre of operations. There is a certain element of risk in the conduct of reinforcement exercises. The arrival of additional UN troops in a mission area could be perceived as being prompted by tension, and in itself escalate a situation. This danger could be eliminated by explaining in detail the objectives of the exercises and by providing a schedule of the proposed deployment. In order to train the procedures fully, the additional troops could stay in the mission area for a reasonable period of time, thus making the permanent stationing of a large number of peacekeepers unnecessary.

ALTERNATIVE COURSES

The gradual introduction of military observers into a peacekeeping force is another method of reducing the number of troops required to carry out the tasks entailed in the mandate. For limited periods selected portions of the area of operation could be vacated by the armed peacekeepers and the responsibility to monitor these areas could be given to mobile and static military observer teams. One must keep in mind that military observers are best employed in an environment where cease-fires are strong and very stable. A basic requirement prior to the deployment of observers is therefore an agreed set of rules governing the military activities in the area of operation.

If it is deemed desirable to transform a peacekeeping force into a military observer mission, additional steps must be taken to strengthen the cease-fire further. One of these preliminary measures is the initiation of a system to verify the forces' level of opposing factions. In most missions where such a system exists, its implementation normally lies with military observers. However, it must be remembered that this system cannot be initiated without the consent of the authorities involved. In addition, in sensitive areas, the force can attempt to implement de-confrontation plans aimed at reducing tension in sectors potentially hazardous to the maintenance of the cease-fire prior to the deployment of military observers.

In the case of Cyprus the basic prerequisites for the deployment of military observers do not yet exist, since the necessary agreement between the two sides is lacking.

The use of electronic surveillance equipment, such as cameras, sensors and radars, can facilitate savings in manpower. However, this should be done carefully, as an excessive amount of these sophisticated devices could result in a serious maintenance and financial burden. The reliability of these pieces of equipment is also yet to be proven. Furthermore the introduction of electronic surveillance equipment needs the consent of the parties, and is only possible with success when the necessary agreements have been attained.

It is sometimes suggested in the case of long-lasting missions like Cyprus that a viable option would be the withdrawal of all the peacekeeping forces from the area in order to force the parties to settle their differences. I personally feel that this option would be very dangerous. The most obvious danger is that there is no guarantee that the parties would be able to settle the problem peacefully. It is easy to imagine a possible sprint by the opposing parties to seize the terrain vacated by the peacekeepers. In this event even small clashes could result in the resumption of fighting. Furthermore the international community would perceive that the UN had abandoned a mission before a solution had been reached. It would be an extremely hazardous decision to take and whoever took it would have to bear all the responsibility. The potential to destabilise an area further is too high and the UN cannot afford such a risk.

THE NEED FOR PATIENCE

The static nature of a peacekeeping operation often gives the impression that there is no progress toward a final solution. This perception is due to the fact that the peacekeepers' immediate objective upon deployment is to freeze the existing situation, thereby preventing possible renewed tensions. The prevention of incidents allows the parties to turn their attention to negotiations. At the same time, however, the initiation of negotiations and the calm which has been achieved by the peacekeeping operations on the ground will remove the problem from international attention. This in turn can remove some of the pressure to reach an early negotiated settlement. On the other hand a prolonged negotiating process is not necessarily a negative element, since the chances are better to reach a viable solution as opposed to a settlement hatched up in a hurry.

Alternatives, such as the ones suggested earlier, are not easy to implement. The premature withdrawal of the force would represent a security risk and could be perceived as though the UN had given up before its mission had brought forth a peaceful ending. Military observers cannot operate on their own, unless there is an agreed cease-fire. One might argue that a strong and stable status quo is a sufficient prerequisite for the deployment of military observers. Eventually it might therefore be possible, even in a situation where no cease-fire agreement exists, to introduce some observers with the force.

Although in Cyprus the peacekeeping force is doing very well, and a high degree of stability has been achieved, I do believe there is still a need for the force and for patience.

The safest option remains to keep the peacekeeping force in place and it should direct all its efforts toward the maintenance of a strong cease-fire which is the prime confidence-building measure.

Meanwhile the force can further assist the peacemakers by performing humanitarian functions. The work in this area should be conducted in co-operation with the local authorities and relief agencies, such as the United Nations Development Programme, the United Nations High Commission for Refugees, the International Committee of the Red Cross, and so on. Efforts in this sphere can only enhance the force's image and credibility. The peacekeepers' endeavours to develop common trust can be expanded to art, sports and any type of recreational activity. In this respect they can perform a very active role outside the traditional maintenance of the cease-fire. Together with other agencies they can work as peacebuilders and thus assist the peacemaking efforts of the UN.

6 The Management of UN Peacekeeping
James O. C. Jonah

INTRODUCTION

Recent developments relating to UN peacekeeping, especially the new initiatives by the Soviet Union, have contributed to a convergence of views on the issue of managing of peacekeeping operations. When Security Council members were called upon to approve the arrangements reached in Geneva for setting up the United Nations Good Offices Missions in Afghanistan and Pakistan (UNGOMAP) it became evident that there existed some misunderstanding about procedures for the day-to-day management of peacekeeping operations. The topic of peacekeeping management gained increased attention when the Secretary-General announced on 21 November 1988 that he had decided to make certain structural changes affecting his Executive Office (EOSG) and the Office for Special Political Affairs (OSPA) by which, *inter alia*, responsibility for the conduct of all existing peacekeeping operations would be given to OSPA. More will be said about this latest development below.

The present paper attempts a comprehensive review of all aspects of the management of peacekeeping operations, except for the issue of financial management which will be covered in another paper. Otherwise the issue of peacekeeping management is discussed in terms of its historical evolution.

CONSTITUTIONAL ASPECTS

At the height of the crisis over peacekeeping, from 1963 to 1973, the daily management of peacekeeping operations was one of the controversial items, along with those relating to authorisation and financing, that bedevilled all efforts at formulating appropriate guidelines for peacekeeping. Ever since the UN began its experimentation with peacekeeping, whether in the form of unarmed military observers or the deployment of peacekeeping forces, there was a divergence of views as to who or which organ of the Charter should be responsible for the day-to-day management of peace-keeping. Until recently the Soviet Union and its allies took the position that any use of force by the UN, even in a non-enforcement context, should be the sole responsibility of the Security Council, where each of the Permanent Members had veto power. Any assistance to the Security Council for the management of such forces should rest with the Military Staff Committee, as provided for in the Charter. In accordance with that position, the role of the Secretary-General should be that of Chief Administrative Officer of the Organisation, with no command and control functions.

The United States and most of the Western countries, backed by a large majority of Member States, put forward the contrary argument. Relying on the definition of peacekeeping as a consent-type opera-tion that did not fall under the enforcement provision of Chapter VII of the Charter, they ruled out any major role for the Military Staff Committee. In the view of these Member States, the Military Staff Committee should come into play only when and if the Security Council decided to use military force in the context of collective security. Furthermore, on practical grounds, they could not see any useful role for the Military Staff Committee, as constituted under the Charter, in the day-to-day management of peacekeeping operations. A committee, they argued, particularly one in which the veto power might be utilised, could not respond quickly enough to a critical situation on the ground. Accordingly only the Secretary-General could provide the proper instrument for the day-to-day management of peacekeeping operations.

These divergent concepts concerning how the UN peacekeeping operations should be managed remained unresolved until new life was given to peacekeeping in October 1973, when the Security Council decided to establish the United Nations Emergency Force (UNEF II). In his report containing the guidelines for the new operation, the Secretary-General put forward suggestions on how to reconcile the divergent positions. He recognised that the Security Council retained overall authority over peacekeeping operations, and that any fundamental change in an operation would have to be referred to it. Nevertheless, he proposed, and the Security Council agreed, that the operations would come under the command of the UN, vested in the Secretary-General, but subject to the authority of the Security Council. It was clearly understood, moreover, that the Secretary-General would regularly consult with members of the Security Council. That was how the member states attained an *ad hoc* convergence of views on the management role of the Secretary-General in peacekeeping operations. The recent change in the attitude of the Soviet Union by which it formally accepted the role of the Secretary-General in peacekeeping operations has thus strengthened the position that the Secretary-General should be responsible for the management of peacekeeping operations.

ROLE OF THE MILITARY STAFF COMMITTEE

What has not yet been clarified successfully is the role that the Military Staff Committee can, or should, play in the management of peacekeeping operations. The Soviet Union still suggests that the Military Staff Committee can play a role, but has not specified what type of role it should play. In recent Soviet formulation, the traditional insistence that the Military Staff Committee should take care of day-to-day management has not been emphasised. Nevertheless the majority of Member States are still sceptical about a formal role for the Military Staff Committee.

Those who wish to meet the Soviet Union in the spirit of compromise and accommodation are proposing that a second look be made to determine what useful role the Military Staff Committee can play. As of now, the Committee functions through regular meetings, although it does not take up substantive matters. It is in this context that proposals are being developed to enable the Military Staff Committee to act as an advisory group to the Secretary-General on logistic matters.

Over the years it has been clearly demonstrated that peacekeeping operations are essentially a political exercise rather than a military one. The constant exercise of political judgement is crucial to any successful execution of a peacekeeping mandate. It is doubtful whether this crucial requirement can be met by the Military Staff Committee. On the other hand the members of the Military Staff Committee can provide the Secretary-General with background support on logistic matters. Even though there have been improvements in logistic preparedness in the Organisation, it may prove useful for the Military Staff Committee to be engaged in full-scale logistic planning. A possible role for the Military Staff Committee should not rule out the continuing involvement of the Field Operations Division (FOD) of the Office of General Services. The FOD still requires lieutenant-colonels, majors or captains with logistics and preferably peacekeeping experience to do the detailed staffing of logistic requirements.

HOW THE SECRETARY-GENERAL MAKES ARRANGEMENTS FOR THE MANAGEMENT OF PEACEKEEPING OPERATIONS WITHIN THE SECRETARIAT

Even while there was still controversy about the day-to-day management of peacekeeping operations, the Secretary-General had already assumed that role. Perhaps because of the manner in which the first UN Emergency Force (UNEF I) was authorised by the General Assembly in 1956, Secretary-General Dag Hammarskjöld played a crucial role in formulating guidelines and procedures for the setting up of that force, and consequently played a decisive role in its initial deployment. Hammarskjöld undertook extensive diplomatic contacts with the Government of Egypt as host Government to work out modalities governing the deployment of the force. As a result he was directly responsible for the management of the force. Without a Security Council mandate and with the General Assembly not in session, he devised the procedure of an advisory body composed of troop-contributors to the force to be available for consultations in the management of the force.

Much of the day-to-day management remained with the Executive Office of the Secretary-General, assisted by a small group of senior staff, including one of the Under-Secretaries-General of the Office for Special Political Affairs (Dr Ralph Bunche). This management arrangement was maintained during the critical period of the UN Operation in the Congo (ONUC). Gradually, however, the Secretary-General and his successor, U Thant, delegated the function of the day-to-day management of peacekeeping to the Office of the Under-Secretary-General (USG) for Special Political Affairs. This was a recognition of the long experience of Dr Ralph Bunche in the management of peacckeeping operations as a collaborator of the Secretary-General.

Within the Secretariat, therefore, the Secretary-General remains the overall authority for the management of peace-keeping operations. Relying on the advice of the USG/OSPA and the Military Adviser, the Secretary-General presents to the Security Council detailed plans regarding the implementation of any decision taken by the Council to set up a peacekeeping operation. It is the Secretary-General who recommends to the Security Council the Force Commanders of the forces or Chief Military Observers, as well as the national contingents who will comprise a UN force. The Force Commanders of the forces are appointed by him after endorsement by the Security Council. The Secretary-General relies on OUSGSPA for the day-to-day management. This office exercises on behalf of the Secretary-General the command and control functions of the force. Political and military instructions from Headquarters to the Force Commanders and the Chief Military Observers go from this office and sometimes from the Secretary-General himself. The Commander in the field reports to the Secretary-General through this office; however, military Force Commanders or Chief Military Observers retain the right to report directly to the Secretary-General if the situation warrants it.

The practice has now been fully developed for the Force Commanders to pay regular visits to Headquarters, particularly at the end of a mandate period, to confer personally with the Secretary-General. The regular visits of the Force Commanders also afford them the opportunity for wide-ranging discussions with OUSGSPA and UN officials responsible for management functions.

OTHER ASPECTS OF MANAGEMENT ARRANGEMENTS

Those familiar with the management of peacekeeping operations in the field are aware that management functions go well beyond command and control arrangements at UN Headquarters in New York. Within the Secretariat there is a division between the military command and control functions and the normal administrative functions of peacekeeping operations. At the inception of peacekeeping operations, the purely administrative functions relating to logistics, personnel and financing were located in the Field Operations Division of the Office of General Services. This division is responsible for the management of the field service, which is a major component of all peacekeeping operations and observer missions and the civilian component of peacekeeping operations. The Chief Administrative Officers (CAOs) who work closely with the Force Commanders and the Chief Military Observers in the field are usually appointed by this Division and they report to its Director.

The personalities and management style of the heads of OUSGSPA and the Director of the Field Operations Division (FOD) established a pattern which was widely recognised and known in the field. During the time of Dr Ralph Bunche as well as that of Mr Brian Urquhart's leadership, it was understood that they were responsible under the Secretary-General for the command and control functions of peace-keeping operations. During that time the purely administrative functions were firmly in the hands of the then Director of FOD, Mr George Lanksy. All aspects of the field service personnel and the administrative management functions were controlled by Mr Lansky who had a deep and personal knowledge of all aspects of the operations. He, however, kept in close contact with OUSGSPA, and would hardly have made any major decisions without clearance from OUSGSPA. Apart from that, he was autonomous. Nevertheless it should be noted that this management style was only possible at a time when peacekeeping was in a doldrum (1963–73).

REVIVAL OF PEACEKEEPING IN 1973

When peacekeeping was revived in October 1973 by the creation of UNEF II, and quickly followed by another operation in the Golan Heights (UNDOF) in 1974, certain new management arrangements, mainly in the administrative sphere, were instituted. Command and control functions remained with OUSGSPA; however, it was no longer possible for FOD to control all aspects of logistics, personnel and finance. Prior to 1974 the preparation of the budget on peace-keeping operations rested solely with FOD. In 1974, on the strong advice of OUSGSPA, the Office of the Controller was brought actively into the preparation of the budget. Henceforth the Director of FOD was mandated to work closely with the Controller in the preparation of the budget and its management. During meetings arranged between the Secretary-General and troop-contributing countries at the end of each mandate period, the Secretary-General formally called on the Controller to report on the status of financing. The Controller was also fully engaged in working out guidelines for reimbursement to Governments for their contingents in the peacekeeping forces. Prior to 1974 the methodology for determin-ing the amount to be reimbursed to troop-contributors had been based on the principle of extra and extraordinary cost, but that formula had produced unacceptable imbalances in the amounts reimbursed to high cost countries as opposed to low cost countries.

The Controller's Office played a significant role in working out the new standard rate.

In light of new realities further adaptation was made in the field on the strong recommendation of OUSGSPA. Prior to 1974 the set-up in the field was such that the Chief Administrative Officer (CAO), who reported to FOD, was either perceived as the dominant figure in the force or a co-equal with the Force Commander or the Chief Military Observer. New arrangements instituted in 1974 made it clear that the CAO would operate under the authority of the Force Commander, who reported to the Secretary-General through OUSGSPA.

Between 1982 and 1987 there were adaptations in the management arrangement for peacekeeping within the Secretariat, in an attempt to bring closer together the political and administrative functions. This was done through the establishment of a new office – the Office of Field Operations and External Support Activities (OFOESA). The head of the Office reported directly to the Secretary-General and assumed the leadership of FOD. OFOESA was required to work closely with OUSGSPA.

During this period there were further changes which brought the Under-Secretary-General of the Department of Administration and Management fully into the picture for the management of peace-keeping operations. As mentioned previously, at one time the chief of FOD had operated autonomously; then the Controller was brought into the picture. By the early eighties the role of the Controller had increased to the extent that co-ordination was becoming difficult to achieve. At another stage the Under-Secretary-General for the Department of Administration and Management assumed the right to appoint CAOs, which hitherto had been a major function of the Director of FOD, and later that of the head of OFOESA.

The establishment of OFOESA did not seem to have been fully accepted by all and it was not surprising that on the recommendation of the Group of 18 OFOESA was disbanded in 1987 and the administrative functions returned to FOD in the Office of General Services.

However, before OFOESA was disbanded, that office made serious efforts to put into place arrangements for adequate pre-planning for logistic support of peacekeeping, as well as an enhancement of peacekeeping communications. A Management Study Report of April 1985 gave form to these efforts, particularly by the establishment of (1) a Policy, Planning and Procedures Unit and (2) a

Logistic and Communication Section. These changes were overtaken by the return of FOD to the Office of General Services, and a recommendation by the Group of 18. The general thrust of the 1985 recommendations has been maintained, although with a considerable reduction of staff in the Policy, Planning and Procedures Unit.

The limited number of FOD military/ex-military officers, with or without peacekeeping experience, are located in the Logistics and Communications Section. Additionally throughout FOD there is a very limited number of personnel with the necessary civilian background in both field and Headquarters required to develop policy or contingency plans for mission support. This scarcity, coupled with the need to reduce staff and the restriction on external recruitment means that the only realistic method of policy planning is to incorporate planning within each functional section. During the current Technical Review of the UN Transition Group (UNTAG) it was necessary to obtain military officers from potential troop-contributors and international staff from other UN Headquarters directorates in order to conduct the necessary review of plans and policy. The fact is FOD in general and the Logistics and Communications Section in particular are performing additional functions such as administering additional missions – UN Good Offices Mission in Afghanistan and Pakistan (UNGOMAP) and UN Iran–Iraq Military Observer Group (UNIIMOG) – rewriting logistic directives, and co-ordinating UNTAG with no proportional increase in staff, experienced or otherwise. There is still a valid need for a separate and larger Policy and Planning Cell reporting to the Director.

NEW ARRANGEMENTS FOR MANAGEMENT OF PEACEKEEPING OPERATIONS

It had long been anticipated that upon the retirement of Mr Brian Urquhart and that of Mr George Lanksy, it would be necessary to make some adaptation in the arrangements for peacekeeping management. Even prior to the retirement of Mr Urquhart experience had shown that joint responsibility between the two Under-Secretaries-General within the Office of Special Political Affairs (OSPA) could present difficulties. For most of the 1970s Mr Roberto Guyer (Argentina) and Mr Urquhart, as the two Under-Secretaries-General for the OSPA, jointly assisted the Secretary-General in the command and control functions. Upon the retirement of Mr Guyer in

1978, Mr Urquhart assumed sole control of the management functions again, on the basis of his enormous experience and talent in peacekeeping matters. When Mr Diego Cordovez later joined the Office he played a marginal role in the management of peacekeeping operations, until recently when he helped to broker the Geneva Accords on Afghanistan, which provided for UNGOMAP. However, shortly thereafter, he also resigned from the Secretariat to assume the position of Foreign Minister of his country. As indicated above the Secretary-General has now decided to change the name of OUSGSPA to the Office of Special Political Affairs (OSPA) and to have the Office headed by a single Under-Secretary-General. The current incumbent, Mr Marrack Goulding, will be responsible for the conduct of all existing peacekeeping operations, with the exception of the UNGOMAP, and for the planning and conduct of future peacekeeping operations. The Secretary-General's announcement also noted that Mr Goulding will be associated, at the formative stage, with discussions concerning the possible establishment of new operations, and will be kept informed of all UN activities which have a bearing on existing operations. This arrangement may also help in averting what some have seen as a growing decentralisation of peacekeeping functions in the Secretariat.

In the last few years a tendency has gained ground in the Secretariat which might lead to a greater diffusion of authority in the management of peacekeeping. Those involved, on behalf of the Secretary-General, in peacemaking efforts to resolve a number of regional disputes have assumed that, should a final settlement warrant the establishment of peacekeeping operations, they would then be required to manage such operations outside the purview of OUSGSPA and now OSPA. Concern has been expressed that such a development will prove unacceptable to a number of troop-contributing countries. It would further complicate the task of the Secretariat to deal with the many and varied aspects of peacekeeping and with the use of limited financial resources. Certainly the centralisation of peacekeeping functions in a single office is a goal worth pursuing.

THE ROLE OF THE MILITARY ADVISER

In the last 40 years the role of the military adviser or advisers has evolved and taken different forms. Initially Secretary-General Dag

Hammarskjöld, recognising the difficulties in making the Military Staff Committee operational, decided to assemble a number of military advisers to assist him and his senior colleagues in the management of peacekeeping functions. The Soviet Union and those who questioned the role of the Secretary-General on the management of peacekeeping and who also favoured the use of the Military Staff Committee expressed their opposition to the creation of a group of military advisers to assist the Secretary-General. While the Secretary-General did not abandon his efforts, he reduced the number of military advisers.

Because of the political sensitivity of the post, the military adviser was placed in the executive office of the Secretary-General, rather than in OUSGSPA. In his day-to-day functioning, however, the military adviser worked under the supervision of, or in close co-operation with, OUSGSPA. There was one time when the title 'Military Adviser' was shunned in favour of the more neutral term 'Military Liaison Officer'. After 1974 the military adviser was formally transferred from the Executive Office to OUSGSPA as a clear recognition that the main task was to offer military advice to the office responsible for command and control of peacekeeping operations. Perhaps in anticipation of the erosion of the central control of OUSGSPA in peacekeeping, steps were taken a year or two ago to transfer the military adviser back to the executive office of the Secretary-General. The underlying consideration was that the military adviser in the same capacity as FOD should be available to assist all those involved in peacekeeping management and not necessarily under the auspices of OUSGSPA. This arrangement has complicated the task of the military adviser, and in many instances has confronted him with embarrassing options.

The new change made by the Secretary-General in response to the increasing demand for his Good Offices has now clarified the status of the Military Adviser. He will remain in the Executive Office as the Secretary-General's Military Adviser, but will be available to OSPA and other offices as necessary. Now the Military Adviser performs the role of military adviser in the peacemaking functions of the Secretary-General.

The military adviser's main task is to ensure that proper military advice is made available to OSPA and the Secretary-General when plans are on foot to establish a peacekeeping operation. In addition, when the Military Adviser and OSPA have jointly formulated an operational plan, it is the task of the Military Adviser to approach

FOD with the request that it prepare the necessary logistic and administrative plan for the support of the operation. He normally remains in close contact with the Director of FOD throughout the implementation period of the new mission.

Once the operation has been deployed, the Military Adviser should be the source of continuous military advice and should maintain close co-operation with the Commander in the field. Under present arrangements the role of the military adviser in logistic planning is ambiguous. These arrangements have not led to close and smooth co-operation between the military adviser and FOD which has a primary focus in the field of logistics and administration. The FOD itself has a few military advisers who utilise military expertise in the field of logistic planning and administration. There is a need, however, for devising appropriate arrangements to make use of the military adviser in the work of FOD.

PEACEKEEPING MANAGEMENT IN THE FIELD

Once a peacekeeping force has been deployed in the field the Commander of the force assumes the main management functions. In carrying out his responsibilities he is assisted by military and civilian personnel. The tradition of peacekeeping over the years has produced two separate staffs under the Force Commander. The military staff operates under the immediate supervision of the Chief of Staff, who is assisted by the Chief Operations officer and the Chief Logistic officer. On the civilian side the immediate supervisor is the Chief Administrative Officer (CAO), who is assisted by a civilian Procurement Officer, Transportation Officer, Chief Financial Officer, General Service Officer and Personnel Officer. The practice is for the military staff under the Chief of Staff to concentrate on the command and control functions in the field. That is to say the battalion commanders in the various sectors report to the Force Commander through the Chief of Staff. The daily military activities are closely monitored by the Chief of Operations and the Chief of Logistics ensures that the logistic demands of the force are met to ensure the operational effectiveness of the force. On the civilian side the CAO, under the overall authority of the Force Commander, supervises the civilian staff, which includes both international and local staff. Taking into account the stringent requirements of UN financial rules, the CAO, assisted by the Chief Financial officer, is held accountable for dispensing UN funds in the field. Allusion has already been made to a prior situation when it appeared that the authority of the CAO was greater than that of the Force Commander in the field. Under present arrangements there is no longer any doubt that the Force Commander has the overall responsibility of the field management of peacekeeping.

A common problem in the functioning of separate civilian and military staff is that there is often inadequate co-ordination. This is an area where reform is required. Basically the problem arises as a result of an inadequate career development programme for the field service officers (civilian) and short tours of duty (usually six months) for military personnel. Consequently field service officers are often appointed to senior positions without appropriate cross training in supervision techniques, or experience in all civilian disciplines. Concurrently the military personnel arrive with little knowledge of the unique factors affecting operations and logistics support in international peacekeeping. A six-month tour is inadequate to provide the necessary experience in this area. This common dearth of experience, coupled with a lack of understanding regarding how a civilian or military enterprise functions, understandably creates frictions between the two groups and results in unsatisfactory co-ordination in the administrative and logistics field.

Reforms are being initiated. A comprehensive career development/training programme for Field Service Officers is in the development stage. In addition senior military appointments such as Chief Operations Officer and Chief Logistics Officer are posted to a mission for a minimum of one year and in some instances for two years. Additionally FOD is providing increased direction to the field missions in terms of policy determination, development of common logistic and administrative directives, standardisation of equipment and training of personnel. This Headquarters involvement in management will free mission personnel – both civilian and military – to address local operational or logistics problems instead of debating policy issues.

It may be useful at this point to allude to a potential problem that may adversely affect effective management of peacekeeping operations in the field. There is a growing tendency of some national contingents within a UN force to maintain a back-channel communication link with their home governments. For practical reasons, UN policy has never discouraged communication links between personnel at contingent battalion Headquarters and their home governments for purely administrative matters. However, the rapid development in modern communications technology and the use of this by contingents threaten to complicate reliable operational functions of a peacekeeping force.

There have been instances when home governments were kept informed of operational developments in the field prior to notification of Headquarters in New York. This may be partly due to the less sophisticated nature of UN communications. Nevertheless such occurrences embarrass UN Headquarters. For example, it is often bewildering to UN Headquarters when mission representatives from a particular contingent within a peacekeeping force raise operational matters which have not yet been reported formally to Headquarters in New York. A more serious occurrence is when, owing to close communication links between a contingent's headquarters and its home government, operational orders are proposed to contingents that may not be in line with the wishes of the Force Commander or Force Headquarters. Such a situation destroys the concept of an integrated UN command. It is, therefore, of the utmost importance that efforts be made to minimise this potential danger to the administrative management of peacekeeping operations in the field.

UNIFICATION OF PEACEKEEPING MANAGEMENT

The recent structural changes instituted by the Secretary-General have come a long way toward improving the methodology and framework for the management of peacekeeping operations. They have not, however, resolved all outstanding difficulties. As noted previously, even though OSPA now has the responsibility for the day-to-day management of peacekeeping operations, UNGOMAP is now outside its authority. The potential threat of a diffusion of management responsibility of peacekeeping operations has thus not been eliminated. Perhaps the intention of the Secretary-General is to prevent such diffusion by centralising peacekeeping functions in one office; but the exclusion of UNGOMAP, even though that exclusion is understood in terms of the Geneva Accords, may encourage others responsible for other peacemaking functions to seek exclusion of their operations from OSPA. Within the spirit of the Secretary-General's new restructuring, such attempts must be firmly resisted.

Another aspect in the centralisation of peacekeeping management, and one which has been muted in the new restructuring arrangements, is the current division of responsibility between the new OSPA and FOD in the Office of General Services. As has been demonstrated, it is possible for full co-operation between these two sections of the Secretariat; nevertheless this division has often caused confusion among troop-contributing countries and others. For example, there are times when troop-contributing countries seek consultations or seek remedies from OSPA on matters essentially within the purview of FOD. As a result they could not obtain proper satisfaction because OSPA may not be familiar with the subject matter raised; nor can it by its own means meet the requested demands. In addition it might baffle officials in FOD who might misunderstand why OSPA is consulted on matters that are within FOD's responsibility.

Unfortunately the division of responsibility within OSPA and FOD has not promoted in the field smooth co-operation between the military and the civilian components of peacekeeping. The fact that they report to different offices at Headquarters in New York has complicated matters. Furthermore, even though there is now a clear line of authority between the Force Commander and the CAO, there remains the potential for conflict because the two officers are not reporting to the same superior at Headquarters. It is, therefore, of some urgency that this matter be clarified.

The best solution would be the full consolidation of FOD into the new OSPA. Such consolidation would ensure that all aspects of peacekeeping, particularly command and control, administration and logistics, would be under the responsibility of one office and a single executive head. It would make for better co-ordination among the various branches of peacekeeping operations in the field, and foster a singleness of purpose in the day-to-day management of peace-keeping operations.

This approach has long been sought by many practitioners of peacekeeping in and out of the Organisation. Although it is a rational approach, it has been strongly resisted in many quarters. One surprising recommendation of the Group of 18 was to disband OFOESA and to return FOD to the Office of General Services. Those with long experience in peacekeeping both at Headquarters and in the field could not understand such a recommendation. It would have been more practical if there had been a recommendation for the consolidation of FOD into what was OUSGSPA and now OSPA. It has been argued that much of what is undertaken in FOD is primarily administrative and should therefore be within the administrative structure of the Secretariat. This, however, does not seem to be the true picture. Even within FOD there is a separate personnel and financial section, an expression of the fact that the administrative functions relating to peacekeeping are not in the same class as those of the normal administrative responsibilities of the Secretariat.

There is yet another objection to the consolidation of FOD into OSPA. There is a strange perception that it is somehow unseemly for the head of OSPA to dabble in administrative matters. However, anyone thoroughly familiar with the day-to-day management of peacekeeping in the field readily understands the importance of a single line of authority for the entire military/political operation that is peacekeeping. In actual fact, after an initial period, perhaps up to nine months following the deployment of a new peacekeeping operation in the field, most of the activities of the Force relate to day-to-day administrative matters. As has been pointed out on many occasions the situation prevailing in UNIFIL, where political factors dominate day-to-day operations, is not typical of peacekeeping operations. The UN Disengagement Observation Force (UNDOF) represents a typical peacekeeping operation; therefore it makes practical sense that the office responsible for command and control of peacekeeping should also be responsible for the day-to-day administrative functions. One should not minimise the fact that certain decisions relating to day-to-day administration may require sound political judgement; for example, when and where to procure fresh fruits, or from what source spare parts and equipment should be obtained, may require political judgement since a wrong move may affect the smooth running of the operation.

There is no doubt that the consolidation of FOD into OSPA will foster greater *esprit de corps* in the day-to-day management of peacekeeping operations. The entire field service personnel, which remains the backbone of peacekeeping, may obtain greater satisfaction knowing that they are responsible to a single office at Headquarters. Such a consolidation may have its immediate impact in the field, in that it may enhance the clout of OSPA in tackling its peacekeeping responsibilities within the Secretariat. The executive head of OSPA will be able to speak with one voice in dealing with troop-contributors, who themselves will find much satisfaction in knowing that in seeking clarification on peacekeeping matters they merely have to approach one single office. Finally such a consolidation may enhance the role of OSPA to undertake pre-planning for future peacekeeping.

NOTE

The views expressed in this paper are those of the author and do not necessarily represent the position of the United Nations Secretariat.

7 The Financing of UN Peacekeeping Operations: The Need for a Sound Financial Basis

Susan R. Mills

The increased international attention which was given during 1988 to the successes of UN peacemaking and peacekeeping has served to focus attention as well on the grave financial situation of the UN. Not since the early 1960s, when peacekeeping operations precipitated a financial crisis for the UN, has the world community shown more than cursory interest in its financial stability.

SUMMARY OF FINANCING METHODS

Contrary to the general perception, not all UN peacekeeping operations are financed by special arrangements separate and distinct from those of the Organisation's ordinary expenses under its regular budget. In fact, of the 15 peacekeeping operations initiated by the UN during its 43-year history, six were or are being financed from the UN's regular budget. If only for that reason – but there are other reasons as well – the Organisation's capacity to maintain its peacekeeping operations is profoundly affected by the financial 'health' of the UN in respect of the regular budget.

Two of the other nine peacekeeping operations initiated by the UN over the past 43 years, namely, the UN Yemen Observation Mission (UNYOM) and the UN Temporary Executive Authority/UN Security Force in West New Guinea (UNTEA/UNSF), were financed by the parties most directly concerned. For UNYOM, the costs were borne by Egypt and Saudi Arabia, while the costs of UNTEA/UNSF were shared by Indonesia and the Netherlands. One peacekeeping operation, that is, the UN Force in Cyprus (UNFICYP), has been financed, since its inception in 1964, from voluntary contributions. The remaining six peacekeeping operations were or are being financed by special assessments on all member states.

91

Put another way, of the seven UN peacekeeping operations which are currently operational, three – the UN Truce Supervision Organization (UNTSO), the UN Military Observer Group in India and Pakistan (UNMOGIP) and the UN Good Offices Mission in Afghanistan and Pakistan (UNGOMAP) – are financed from the UN regular budget; one – UNFICYP – is financed, as indicated above, from voluntary contributions; and three – the UN Disengagement Observer Force (UNDOF), the UN Interim Force in Lebanon (UNIFIL) and the UN Iran–Iraq Military Observer Group (UNIIMOG) – are financed through special assessments.

The history of peacekeeping operations, with its interplay of financial and political considerations, as well as the basic legal arrangements for UN financial operations, serve to explain how and why this mixed system of financing peacekeeping operations has developed.

LEGAL REGIME GOVERNING ASSESSMENTS

Article 17, paragraph 2, of the Charter of the UN provides: 'The expenses of the Organisation shall be borne by the members as apportioned by the General Assembly.' The apportionment of expenses is normally made on the basis of a scale of assessments, approved by the General Assembly on the advice of the Committee on Contributions, a group of experts elected by the General Assembly. Each member state is assessed on the basis of its capacity to pay, measured essentially on the basis of national income. Under the scale which applies to the period 1986–88,[1] assessments range from 0.01 per cent for 78 Member States, to 25 per cent for the largest contributor, the United States.

Under the Financial Regulations and Rules of the UN, member states have the legal obligation to pay their assessed contributions, whether for the regular budget or for peacekeeping operations assessed on a special basis, in full within 30 days of receipt of a letter from the Secretary-General informing them of the amount of their assessment. Throughout the Organisation's history, however, most member states have not fulfilled that legal obligation, either in terms of the completeness or the timeliness of their payments.

Article 19 of the Charter of the UN provides that a member state which is in arrears in the payment of its financial contributions to the Organisation shall have no vote in the General Assembly if the amount of its arrears equals or exceeds the amount of the contributions due from it for the preceding two full years. This is the only sanction which can be applied for failure to pay assessed contributions.

Over the years this sanction has been applied from time to time to various member states. The General Assembly has also chosen *not* to apply this sanction, by avoiding any votes at all (see discussion below). Experience has shown that the threat of the application of Article 19, or the actual use thereof, has not constituted an adequate incentive to pay to those member states who do not wish to do so.

FIRST PEACEKEEPING OPERATIONS

UNTSO and UNMOGIP

The first UN peacekeeping operation to be established was UNTSO, created by decision of the Security Council in 1948. As the UN regular budget was, for all practical purposes, the only method in use at the time to finance the activities of the Organisation, the General Assembly decided that provision for the costs of UNTSO should be made in the regular budget and thus should be shared among all member states on the basis of the regular scale of assessments. The same approach was followed in 1949, when UNMOGIP was formally established.

No other UN peacekeeping operation was established until 1956. Even before that time, beginning in the early 1950s, the Secretary-General had been obliged to draw the attention of member states (then totalling 78) to the fact that the Organisation was encountering financial difficulties caused by the late payment of assessed contributions as well as the high level of unpaid contributions to the regular budget.

UNEF I

On 30 October 1956, when the Security Council was unable to agree on a call for a cease-fire between Egypt and Israel owing to vetoes by some permanent members of the Security Council, it transferred consideration of this matter to the General Assembly, in accordance with the procedure envisaged in General Assembly resolution 377(V) of 3 November 1950, the 'Uniting for Peace' resolution. The first emergency session of the General Assembly was convened on 1 November 1956. On 4 November 1956, the General Assembly, in resolution 998 (ES-1), requested the Secretary-General to submit, within 48 hours, a plan for the setting up of an emergency international UN Force.

A first report on the matter was submitted by the Secretary-General on the same day; on 6 November, he submitted a second and final report on the plan.[2] In that report, the Secretary-General indicated, *inter alia*, that the question of how the Force should be financed required further study, but he suggested the application, provisionally, of a basic rule that a State providing a Unit to the Force would be responsible for all costs of equipment and salaries, while all other costs should be financed by the UN *outside its normal budget*.

The Secretary-General did not give a reason for this proposal, but it may be inferred that the difficulties already encountered in collecting regular budget assessments might have led him to propose this arrangement. Another reason may have been the expectation that the eventual costs for this Force would be much higher than the costs previously experienced for other peacekeeping operations. In its resolution 1001 (ES-1) of 7 November 1956, the General Assembly, *inter alia*, provisionally approved the basic rule concerning the financing of UNEF, thus endorsing the proposal that such costs should be financed outside the regular budget.

The first emergency session of the General Assembly was closed on 10 November 1956 and was immediately followed by the eleventh regular session of the General Assembly. On 21 December 1956, by its resolution 1089(XI), the General Assembly decided that the expenses of UNEF, other than for such pay, equipment and supplies and services that member states might supply without charge, would be borne by the United Nations and that such expenses, up to $10 million, would be apportioned among all member states on the basis of the regular scale of assessments for 1957.

Almost immediately a number of member states refused to pay their share of such assessed contributions, on the basis of what they characterised as positions of principle, the primary reason given being that only the Security Council could authorise a peacekeeping operation. The practice of deliberately withholding assessed contributions is not envisaged in the UN Charter or in the Financial Regulations and Rules. It is, rather, in contravention of both.

The amounts that these member states were called upon to pay, but refused to, were not large enough to precipitate an *immediate* cash crisis, nor to trigger the application of Article 19. Their action did, however, lead to the adoption, in February 1957, of General Assembly resolution 1090(XI), by which the General Assembly authorised commitments above the $10 million already approved and invited voluntary contributions to cover the additional costs, thus postponing until later that year a decision on how any costs over $10 million which were not covered by such voluntary contributions would be met.

These withholdings of assessed contributions also led to the beginning of a practice that has, unfortunately, continued to the present time – namely, delays in payment by the UN, because of lack of resources, of amounts which the Organisation owes to troop-contributing countries.

ONUC

The first genuine *cash* crisis precipitated by peacekeeping operations started in 1960. On 14 July 1960 the Security Council, in its resolution 143 (1960), authorised the Secretary-General to take whatever steps were required to give the Government of the Congo military assistance. This constituted the authorising resolution for the UN Force in the Congo (ONUC), the largest peacekeeping operation the UN has ever mounted to date.

Since the General Assembly was not in session, the Secretary-General immediately sought and obtained, under the annual resolution on unforeseen and extraordinary expenses, the concurrence of the Advisory Committee on Administrative and Budgetary Questions[3] to meet the costs of the Force, up to $40 million, from the Working Capital Fund (then at a level of $25 million) and then by borrowing from other funds in his custody, pending necessary action by the General Assembly in the autumn of 1960.

In October 1960 the Secretary-General submitted to the General Assembly budget estimates for ONUC for 1960, totalling $66.6 million. The Secretary-General stated that he recognised the heavy burden that costs of this magnitude would place on member states. He expressed the hope that Governments would accordingly make generous voluntary contributions to defray part of the costs and that other means would be found to mitigate the effect of additional assessments on those having the least capacity to pay.

An extensive debate on this matter took place in the General Assembly from November to December 1960, in the course of which a number of member states stated that they would not contribute to any expenses of ONUC because its establishment ran counter to decisions of the Security Council and the General Assembly. There was also wide disagreement on how the costs of ONUC should be financed, ranging from those member states which considered that the expenses should be included in the regular budget and apportioned on the usual scale of assessments, to those member states which believed that the costs should be financed entirely from voluntary contributions. Some member states proposed a number of different financing arrangements between these two opposing positions.

Ultimately, on 20 December 1960, the General Assembly adopted resolution 1583(XV) on the financing of ONUC, in which it decided that the costs of ONUC should be met from an *ad hoc* account established outside the regular budget, that the amounts appropriated for the costs of ONUC would be apportioned among all member states on the basis of the scale of assessments, with the proviso that voluntary contributions which had been received would be used to reduce by 50 per cent the assessments of those member states assessed at the minimum (at that time, the minimum was 0.04 per cent) and then would be used to reduce the assessments of other member states receiving technical assistance[4] from the UN, in increasing order on the scale of assessments until all voluntary contributions had been fully applied. (This variant had been applied in 1959 for the first time to the costs of UNEF.) In this resolution the General Assembly specifically indicated that the expenses of ONUC constituted 'expenses of the Organisation' within the meaning of Article 17, paragraph 2, of the Charter and that these assessments were therefore a binding legal obligation on member states to pay.

Notwithstanding this statement of principle the member states which had indicated they would not pay the expenses of ONUC did not pay their assessments. The legal and constitutional aspects of the issue were put to the test, when the General Assembly requested, received and accepted in 1962 an advisory opinion from the International Court of Justice, which held that the expenses of both UNEF and ONUC constituted 'expenses of the Organisation' within the meaning of the Charter. The member states that had withheld their contributions still would not pay.

Indeed, beginning in 1960, member states have overtly acknowledged many times that the financial problems of the UN are, in fact, only the symptoms of a political crisis. Though symptoms, they have nonetheless been real and acute.

The Bond Issue

At the end of 1961, having been warned by the Secretary-General that the Organisation was facing imminent bankruptcy, the General Assembly found a temporary solution to the financial crisis precipitated by UNEF and ONUC. It authorised the Secretary-General to issue bonds, beginning in 1962, up to an amount of $200 million, and to use the proceeds therefrom to cover the cash-operating requirements of the Organisation, essentially those of the peacekeeping operations.

Ultimately only $169 million of such bonds were actually sold. The interest and principal of the bonds have been repaid, over a 25-year period, beginning in 1963, by including provisions for that purpose in the regular budget of the UN.

The bond issue, in turn, precipitated a new kind of financial crisis for the Organisation. A number of member states, including but not limited to those which had refused to pay their assessed contributions for the UNEF and ONUC peacekeeping operations, began also to withhold a portion of their assessed contributions to the regular budget, in amounts which they considered represented their proportionate share of the repayment of the bond issue. The member states concerned also characterised these withholdings as 'withholdings on the basis of positions of principle'. While initially the amounts so withheld were cumulatively relatively small, over the years such withholdings (together with withholdings of amounts for other activities to which certain member states have objected) led to a substantial shortfall in the payment of assessed contributions under the regular budget as well.

The Article 19 Crisis

By 1964 the total withholdings of the Union of Soviet Socialist Republics, both under the regular budget and for specially assessed peacekeeping operations, had exceeded the equivalent of two years' assessed contributions; accordingly the provisions of Article 19 should have been applied. When the nineteenth session of the General Assembly convened in September 1964, it became apparent that the membership was unwilling to risk 'the ultimate confrontation'.

As a result, it was decided, by a 'gentlemen's agreement', that the General Assembly would transact no business that would require putting a question to a vote. Among the consequences were that no scale of assessments for the following year was adopted; nor was it possible to approve either a regular budget for 1965 or a budget for UNEF (ONUC having been phased out in 1964). The General Assembly did, however, adopt by consensus a decision to the effect that the financial difficulties of the Organisation should be solved through voluntary contributions by member states.

Coping with the Cash Shortfall

The Working Capital Fund is a mechanism to enable the Secretary-General to meet operating expenses under the regular budget until sufficient assessed contributions have been received. The Working Capital Fund is designed as a form of cash reserve to enable the Secretary-General to meet the Organisation's day-to-day expenditure obligations. The Working Capital Fund is also intended to be used to meet unforeseen and extraordinary expenses, such as those for peacemaking or peacekeeping operations for which provision has not previously been made, until such time as the General Assembly can convene and decide how such expenses should be met. Over the years, the Working Capital Fund has been increased, from some $20 million in 1947, to its present authorised level of $100 million, to which it was raised in 1982.

The Special Account is another mechanism that has been used to cover the cash shortfall. In 1965 and again in 1972, the General Assembly requested the Secretary-General to establish a Special Account, into which member states were encouraged to make voluntary contributions 'so that the future may be faced with renewed hope and confidence',[5] such contributions to be used for 'clearing up the past financial difficulties of the United Nations and especially for resolving the short-term deficit of the United Nations'.[6] These euphemistic descriptions mean, in plain language, that the Special Account was intended to allow those member states which had withheld their assessed contributions to peacekeeping operations to maintain their positions of principle but, at the same time, to make voluntary contributions which could be used to meet some of the expenses incurred for assessed peacekeeping operations which other-wise could not be paid.

Initially a number of member states made substantial contributions to the Special Account, a portion of which was used to finance the costs of UNEF in 1965. Although the General Assembly has appealed annually since 1965 to member states to make voluntary contributions to this account, no substantial contributions were received between 1974 and 1982. In 1982, however, China contributed $5 million and in 1986 the Union of Soviet Socialist Republics made a contribution of $10 million to this account. Over the years, the interest accumulating on the contributions received has allowed the resources in the Special Account to grow to some $109 million in 1988.

The cash flow difficulties of the UN over the same period have obliged the Secretary-General to use this Special Account as if it were an additional Working Capital Fund, a purpose for which it was *not* intended. Using both the Special Account and the Working Capital Fund together as reserves, the Organisation has just barely managed to meet its day-to-day cash commitments in the face of extremely high levels of unpaid assessed contributions.

MEMBER STATES SEARCH FOR SOLUTIONS

From 1956 to the present day member states have attempted, largely without success, to reach a consensus on the issue of how expenses for peacekeeping should be met and apportioned. When debates in the General Assembly have failed to produce agreement, the General Assembly has periodically established committees or working groups to study all aspects of the issue. None of these groups has ever reached a genuine consensus, but at varying times, when a large measure of agreement was reached among most of the membership of the Organisation, particular approaches have been adopted, at least for a while.

One approach, adopted for the very first peacekeeping operations in the late 1940s, for three other small peacekeeping operations conducted in the 1950s and 1960s, and adopted once more in 1988 for UNGOMAP, has been to include the costs of the particular operation in the regular budget of the UN and to apportion the costs among all member states on the basis of the regular scale of assessments.

A second approach, used initially for UNEF I, was to meet the costs outside the regular budget but to apportion the costs on the regular scale of assessments.

A third approach, used at a later stage for UNEF I and then for

ONUC, was to meet the costs outside the regular budget, to apportion a part of the costs on the regular scale of assessments, and then to apportion the remainder on a sliding scale which reduced the assessments on some member states (generally the less developed), the difference to be made up by voluntary contributions from other member states. One variation of this approach, used from the mid-1960s on, was to make up the reductions given to less developed countries by additional assessments on economically more developed member states. Still another variation was to meet part of the costs directly from other special measures, that is, voluntary contributions or the bond issue, used for UNEF I and ONUC, and the Special Account, used for UNEF I.

A fourth approach, which has been used only once, for UNFICYP, was to decide that all costs should be met from voluntary contributions. At the time this decision was taken (1964), no other avenue may have seemed capable of commanding support. The difficulties inherent in ensuring continued operations on such an uncertain financial basis are, with the benefit of experience, now so widely understood that this type of approach is unlikely to be used another time.

In 1973, after more than 15 years of inconclusive debate in special committees and in the General Assembly on a wide range of criteria that might be brought to bear in meeting and apportioning the costs of peacekeeping operations, the General Assembly adopted a resolution on the financing of UNEF II, which has been the model followed, in its essential features, for financing all peacekeeping operations established thereafter except UNGOMAP.

General Assembly resolution 3101 (XXVIII) of 11 December 1973 requested the Secretary-General to set up a special account *outside the regular budget* to cover the costs of the Force. The General Assembly appropriated the full amount required for the operation of the Force and apportioned the total among member states as follows. The 135 member states then constituting the membership of the UN were divided into four groups: (A), the states which are Permanent Members of the Security Council; (B), economically developed member states which are not Permanent Members of the Security Council; (C), economically less developed member states; and (D), economically less developed member states which were specifically named. (By enumerating which member states would constitute Group B, the General Assembly also defined by exclusion which member states would constitute Group C.)

The General Assembly also decided that: (1) 63.15 per cent of the total appropriated (which was expressed as a total dollar amount) should be apportioned among the five Permanent Members of the Security Council (Group A) in proportions determined by the regular scale of assessments then applicable; (2) 34.78 per cent of the total appropriated should be apportioned among the 23 economically developed member states not Permanent Members of the Security Council (Group B) in proportions determined by the scale of assessments; (3) 2.02 per cent of the total cost should be apportioned, in proportions determined by the scale of assessments, among the 82 member states characterised as economically less developed (Group C); and (4) 0.05 per cent should be proportionally apportioned among 25 specifically named least economically developed member states (Group D).[7]

Over the years since 1973 the relative shares of the total costs have shifted a bit among the four groups, but overall, these basic arrangements remain. Using the current membership of the UN and the assessments for UNIFIL as an example, the proportions are as follows:

Group A (5 member states): 57.88 per cent
Group B (22 member states): 39.51 per cent
Group C (85 member states): 2.56 per cent
Group D (47 member states): 0.05 per cent

The proportions of the total peacekeeping costs currently assigned to each of the four groups are compared in Table 7.1 below with the proportions of regular budget assessments (comparable data at the time of the first UNEF II assessment are given in parentheses).

TABLE 7.1   *The Peacekeeping Budget*

	Peacekeeping (per cent of total)	Regular Budget (per cent of total)
Group A	57.88 (63.15)	47.22 (54.64)
Group B	39.51 (34.78)	39.51 (34.78)
Group C	2.56 (2.02)	12.78 (10.08)
Group D	0.05 (0.05)	0.49 (0.50)

The significant differences in the apportionment of costs are due to several factors. The first is that the methodology by which the General Assembly divides the total cost of peacekeeping operations among the four groups is consciously designed to produce a sub-stantial reduction in the dollar amounts to be borne by the less and least economically developed member states. Thus, even though the number of member states in Group D has virtually doubled since 1973, the part of peacekeeping costs to be shared by that group has been maintained at 0.05 per cent. Another factor is that some member states which have been characterised by the General Assembly as 'economically less developed' for the purposes of special peacekeeping assessments, may actually have a greater 'capacity to pay' when the relatively more objective criteria utilised by the Committee on Contributions to establish the scale of assessments are applied.

Table 7.2 shows, in descending order, the 30 member states which pay the largest percentage assessments to the regular budget. It also shows the percentage share of total costs paid by the same member states for specially assessed peacekeeping operations and the group to which they are assigned for that purpose. From that Table it can be seen that:

(1) the five Permanent Members of the Security Council pay a higher percentage share, in some cases, a significantly higher share, of peacekeeping costs than of regular budget costs;

(2) of the 22 member states considered by the General Assembly as 'economically developed' for the purposes of sharing peace-keeping costs, only 16 are among the top 30 contributors to the regular budget;

(3) in contrast, nine member states are among the top 30 contribu-tors to the regular budget of the UN, yet are deemed to be 'less economically developed' in the context of special assessments for peacekeeping. For these member states the application of this arrangement significantly reduces, that is, by 80 per cent, the percentage of peacekeeping costs they are called upon to carry.

CURRENT FINANCIAL STATUS OF PEACEKEEPING OPERATIONS

As indicated above three current peacekeeping operations are financed under the regular budget of the UN. Since 1985, for reasons mostly unrelated to peacekeeping operations, the UN has been coping with a financial crisis of unprecedented dimensions with respect to the regular budget, a crisis which has forced the Secretary-General to implement drastic economy measures to avert bank-

TABLE 7.2   *The 30 main contributors to the United Nations regular budget listed by size of contribution*

Member state	Regular budget assessment* (per cent)	Peacekeeping assessment (per cent)	Group
United States of America	25.00	30.65	A
Japan	10.84	10.84	B
Union of Soviet Socialist Republics	10.20	12.50	A
Germany, Federal Republic of	8.26	8.26	B
France	6.37	7.81	A
United Kingdom of Great Britain and Northern Ireland	4.86	5.96	A
Italy	3.79	3.79	B
Canada	3.06	3.06	B
Spain	2.03	0.41	C
Netherlands	1.74	1.74	B
Australia	1.66	1.66	B
Brazil	1.40	0.28	C
German Democratic Republic	1.33	1.33	B
Ukrainian Soviet Socialist Republic	1.28	1.28	B
Sweden	1.25	1.25	B
Belgium	1.18	1.18	B
Saudi Arabia	0.97	0.19	C
Mexico	0.89	0.18	C
China	0.97	0.97	A
Austria	0.74	0.74	B
Denmark	0.72	0.72	B
Czechoslovakia	0.70	0.70	B
Poland	0.64	0.64	B
Iran (Islamic Republic of)	0.63	0.13	C
Argentina	0.62	0.12	C
Venezuela	0.60	0.12	C
Norway	0.54	0.54	B
Finland	0.50	0.50	B
Yugoslavia	0.46	0.10	C
Greece	0.44	0.09	C
Sub-total	93.67	97.74	
Other	6.33	2.26	
Total	100.00	100.00	

* Scale of assessment for 1986–88

ruptcy. Although no programme financed from the regular budget has been immune from the effects of these economy measures, every effort has been made to reduce their impact on the peacekeeping operations so financed.

The financial status of the peacekeeping operations financed from special assessments has also continued to be precarious. The level of unpaid assessments, whether due to 'withholdings on the basis of positions of principle' or otherwise, remains extremely high, as shown in Table 7.3.

In this connection it should be noted many of the member states which had withheld contributions to the regular budget and to

TABLE 7.3   *Unpaid Assessments to the Budget*

	Cumulative assessments through current mandate	Outstanding contributions as of 31 December 1988	Percentage of contributions unpaid
	(millions of US dollars)		
UNEF/UNDOF*	843.0	35.7	4.2
UNIFIL†	2 169.0	304.0	14.0
UNIIMOG‡	35.2	15.5	44.0

* Assessments through 30 November 1988
† Assessments through 31 December 1988
‡ Assessments through 8 November 1988

peacekeeping operations have shifted their positions since 1973 and have paid up amounts previously withheld, some in full and others in significant part.

The decision to pay past withholdings and arrears which has attracted the most publicity has been that of the USSR, which announced in April 1986 that it would begin to pay its current peacekeeping assessments in full and would take steps to liquidate its arrears, both for specially assessed peacekeeping operations and for the regular budget, over the next few years. To date the USSR has reduced the level of its arrears under current peacekeeping operations[8] to $151.4 million, as of 31 December 1988, from some $164.5 million at the end of 1985; it has also reduced its arrears under the regular budget to $7.2 million at 31 December 1988 from some $40.8 million at the end of 1985.

At the same time, that is, since late 1985, the US, which is assessed at the highest rate for the regular budget and for specially assessed peacekeeping operations, has fallen significantly behind in its payment of assessed contributions to both. At the end of 1985, US unpaid contributions to UNEF/UNDOF and to UNIFIL totalled only $31 514. At 31 December 1988, US unpaid assessments for those operations totalled $83.2 million and for UNIIMOG, $10.9 million. Over the same period, US outstanding contributions for the regular budget, which had been minimal prior to 1985, rose from $85.5 million at the end of 1985 to $307.7 million by 31 December 1988. These shortfalls, particularly for the regular budget, are far greater than the previously outstanding contributions that have been paid by other member states.

On average about 42 per cent of the budget of each specially assessed peacekeeping operation is devoted to operating costs (the costs of civilian personnel, housing and rations for troops, and so on) and the other 58 per cent represents the reimbursements to be made to governments for the troops and equipment they supply to the operation. As mentioned earlier, peacekeeping operations financed from special assessments are able to continue in spite of very high levels of unpaid contributions only through the forbearance of the countries to whom the Organisation owes reimbursements. In other words the troop-contributing countries have been willing to wait for the moneys owed to them, which the UN pays as and when enough contributions are received for each operation. With the rising level of unpaid assessed contributions for current peacekeeping operations (from a total of some $262.1 million at the end of 1985 to some $355.2 million at 31 December 1988),[9] the patience of troop-contributing countries may be tried even more in the future.

Unpaid assessed contributions to the regular budget have increased from $242.4 million at the end of 1985 to $394.9 million in December 1988. In contrast to the situation for specially assessed peacekeeping operations, shortfalls in payment of regular budget assessments result in an immediate cash shortage in respect of the UN day-to-day operating requirements, since most of the regular budget is devoted to payroll and payment to vendors. It is for this reason that the UN has been obliged to use the Working Capital Fund and the Special Account as cash reserves. By so doing the Organisation has been able to avoid bankruptcy so far – but just barely.

Thus, just as the UN is being called upon to assume new and expanded roles in peacemaking and peacekeeping, its very viability

– not to mention its capacity to fulfil its roles in relation to peace – is seriously jeopardized once again.

ISSUES CURRENTLY UNDER DEBATE IN THE GENERAL ASSEMBLY

During the forty-third session of the General Assembly (which was suspended near the end of December 1988 but was expected to resume in February 1989), member states began to grapple with a number of issues which directly concern the financial aspects of peacekeeping operations. To date it is still not certain whether agreements will be reached – and whether any such agreements will constitute solutions or merely palliatives.

The General Assembly debate, while focusing primarily on the financing of UNIIMOG and UNGOMAP, was initiated and will be continued in a wider context, in full awareness of: (a) the problems of past operations which are outlined above; (b) the imminent launching of a new operation in Namibia that, in scope and cost, will exceed any operation undertaken heretofore; (c) the possibilities of new operations in the Western Sahara and Kampuchea, perhaps in 1989; and (d) lastly, but of overriding concern, the precariousness of the financial situation of the UN overall.

Four of the many issues being discussed deserve particular mention. The first of these is the question of voluntary contributions of goods and services, also referred to as 'contributions in kind'. Throughout the Organisation's history a number of member states have made contributions in kind to peacekeeping operations. Virtually every peacekeeping operation has benefited from such contributions. Most often, such contributions have consisted of major equipment (for example, medical equipment and supplies, ground transport equipment and the use of aircraft) or of services (for example, airlifting of troops and equipment to the site of the peacekeeping operation). Contributions in kind have normally been made by member states at the very beginning of an operation and have therefore been taken into account before the budget for a peacekeeping operation was developed and submitted to the General Assembly for approval. Contributions in kind have thus been excluded from the costs to be apportioned among member states and have constituted, in real terms, additional resources provided to the operation.

Some member states are now proposing that contributions in kind be accepted not as *additional* resources but as offsets to the assessments of the member state making the contribution, or as an element to reduce the budget of the particular peacekeeping operation. Such a proposal raises both political and financial problems. Among the political aspects are whether the specific contribution (equipment, supplies or services) would be suitable for the particular operation or acceptable to the countries which are the focus of the peacekeeping operation. Among the financial problems, one is the method of valuing the contribution in kind (if it is an item for which it is difficult to make market comparisons). Another is the question of how, if this approach were to be widely used, adequate cash would be obtained to meet the other costs of the peacekeeping operation.

A second issue, related to the first, is that of voluntary contributions in cash. The use of voluntary contributions in cash to cover part of the costs of a peacekeeping operation, in lieu of assessments on member states, was abandoned after UNEF I and ONUC (see above). Beginning in 1973 with UNEF II, voluntary contributions in cash have been treated as advances to provide working capital to meet the start-up costs of a particular peacekeeping operation until sufficient assessed contributions are received to maintain the operation. At that time they are repaid to the donor(s).

Proposals are now being made that voluntary contributions in cash be used to reduce the costs of the operation to be assessed on all member states. As with contributions in kind, these proposals raise political as well as financial problems. The political problem is that such an approach would tend to weaken the principle, now generally accepted after many difficult years, that the entire membership of the UN has the collective responsibility to share the costs of peacekeeping operations. Among the financial problems is the fact that so long as a significant portion of assessed contributions for peacekeeping remain unpaid, the cash shortfall will continue to threaten the Organisation's capacity to carry out the operation. Reducing the overall assessment on member states by treating voluntary contributions as income may actually exacerbate the cash shortfall, if it leads some member states to conclude that the timely and full payment of their assessed contributions is no longer essential for the financial viability of peacekeeping operations.

This leads to a third issue, namely, the absence of cash reserves for peacekeeping operations. Unlike the Working Capital Fund, which has been formally established by the General Assembly to serve as a cash reserve for the regular budget, there is no officially sanctioned mechanism to serve the same function for peacekeeping operations in general. The Working Capital Fund may be used, as described above, to meet very early expenses of a new peacekeeping operation until the General Assembly can decide how the costs can be met; but this constitutes a very limited resource. Similarly it has become the practice, since UNEF II, to appeal for voluntary contributions as cash advances for each new peacekeeping operation. Additionally, by suspending the application of certain Financial Regulations for UNDOF and UNIFIL, the General Assembly has enabled some cash to be retained, temporarily, that would otherwise be returned to member states (and must be eventually).

None of these mechanisms provides, however, a satisfactory solution for two problems: (a) adequate cash to meet substantial start-up costs for a large peacekeeping operation before the General Assembly can authorise assessments and member states pay them in sufficient amounts; and (b) adequate cash to meet significant shortfalls when such assessed contributions are paid with substantial delays or not at all. Given the precarious cash situation of the regular budget, its resources do not constitute the reserve or buffer required. While member states have increasingly come to recognise that this is a major problem, it is not certain that they are ready to address it and solve it.

A fourth issue – equally unlikely to be resolved by the General Assembly in the near future – is the relationship of the UN regular budget to peacekeeping operations. Apart from the direct costs of the three peacekeeping operations financed from the regular budget, many indirect costs for specially assessed peacekeeping operations are met from the regular budget. Such indirect costs include, *inter alia*, the infrastructure of the Secretariat which oversees the political and military aspects of peacekeeping operations; the political offices engaged in the peacemaking operations which precede, and frequently also accompany, peacekeeping operations; as well as the wide range of administrative activities (financial, personnel, logistical) which are required in support of such operations.

Until very recently no effort was made to attempt to quantify all these indirect costs. However, pressure to do so is mounting because of the keen attention focused on the level of the regular budget, accompanied by strong pressure to reduce that level, as well as the awareness that starting in 1988, UN peacekeeping operations are once more growing in number and size after some ten to fifteen years of relative stability. How to meet these dramatically increasing requirements for the support of peacekeeping operations in the light of current regular budget resources and of demands to reduce them, is a question that must also be faced. In this area, too, the outcome cannot be predicted.

In summary UN peacekeeping operations are growing in number and importance. Member states have yet to agree, however, on how to meet the costs of these activities without provoking repeated financial crises. Until and unless agreement is reached and all parties unreservedly abide by such an agreement, UN peacekeeping will continue to be placed in jeopardy.

NOTES AND REFERENCES

1. A new scale of assessments for 1989 and 1990, and possibly 1991, was adopted by the General Assembly in December 1988 at its forty-third session (General Assembly resolution 43/223 of 21 December 1988). The new scale, which was recommended to the General Assembly by the Committee on Contributions, does not vary significantly from the scale for 1986–88.
2. A/3302
3. An expert group elected by the General Assembly to provide advice to it on administrative and budgetary issues.
4. That is, development assistance.
5. General Assembly resolution 2053(XX) of 15 December 1965.
6. General Assembly resolution 3049 A(XXVII) of 19 December 1972.
7. In introducing the draft resolution that ultimately became General Assembly resolution 3101 (XXVIII) on behalf of the member states which sponsored it, the representative of Brazil stated that the intent of the sponsors, in establishing the total amounts assigned to each group, was to ensure that the vast majority of member states would receive a more favourable treatment with regard to their share in the financing of the Force than they did under the scale of assessments for the regular budget. The methodology was intended to produce the following results: the member states in Group D would pay 10 per cent of the assessment rate they paid for the regular budget; the member states in Group C would pay 20 per cent of the assessment rate for the regular budget; those in Group B would pay the same rate – that is, 100 per cent – as their regular budget assessment; and the member states in Group A

would pay 100 per cent of their regular budget assessment rate plus the amounts not otherwise apportioned.

8.   Excluding unpaid assessed contributions for UNEF I and ONUC.

9.   These figures *exclude* unpaid assessed contributions for UNEF I and ONUC.

8   Support and Limitations: Peacekeeping from the Point of View of Troop-Contributors

Johan Jørgen Holst

THE NATURE OF UN PEACEKEEPING

We need at the outset to determine the specific character of UN peacekeeping operations. They differ from regular military operations in many important respects. They constitute a special kind of operation with unique characteristics. Most important, UN peacekeeping operations do not aim at imposing an external will on warring parties or civilian populations. Hence they are different from intervention by expeditionary forces. The great powers have often resorted to such intervention throughout history in order to protect or expand their own interests or in order to constrain those of their competitors or adversaries. States with a history of intervention or harbouring a colonial legacy may find it difficult to adjust to the non-interventionist nature of UN peacekeeping and, equally important, they may find it difficult to be accepted by the warring parties as disinterested intermediaries. Hence the small and medium powers have enjoyed a comparative advantage in regard to peacekeeping.

UN peacekeeping operations constitute a confidence building measure. They seek to assist the parties to a conflict in holding their fire or to disengage, provided they prefer cease-fire and disengagement to continued fighting, but do not trust their opponents to do so unaided. They may assist the parties by providing credible evidence and assurance to all sides that the others are not breaking the rules. They may build confidence among parties with a shared interest in maintaining the peace, but caught in the vicious spirals of mutual mistrust. They facilitate such confidence-building by adding international authority to the condemnation of violations.

UN PEACEKEEPING: THE INTERNATIONAL CONTEXT FROM A NORWEGIAN PERSPECTIVE

The Second World War contained for many the lesson that, in the future, nations would have to solve their disputes by peaceful means, rather than resort to the use of force. The carnage of that war seems to have demonstrated the folly of past practices. The invention of nuclear weapons and the means to deliver them over long distances had eliminated the very foundation on which the international system of nation states rested. The roofs had been blown off the nation states which could no longer provide shields for protecting their citizens. Novel methods were needed. However, the objective imperative of a common security approach to national security did not translate into subjective action. After five long years of occupation it was self-evident that Norway should sign the UN Charter in which the maintenance of international peace and security constituted a key objective. The Charter contains the guidelines for a collective security system that was intended 'to save succeeding generations from the scourge of war which twice in our lifetime has brought untold sorrow to mankind', as it was stated in the preamble.

The UN has become both a dream and reality. The dream is still that the nations will unite in a collective responsibility to preserve the peace and secure for everyone a life worthy of human beings. The reality, as we all know, is unfortunately quite different. Nations have continued to fight each other. Some peoples have not seen peace in their lands since the Second World War. Millions of people are starving and living under unworthy conditions. We have a very long way to travel before we reach the world which was envisaged in 1945, a world where people live in peace with each other and in harmony with their environment, a world characterised by sustainable development. The UN is an imperfect organisation in an imperfect world. We cannot, however, think of our world without the UN; without this vital pressure chamber in international politics; without the network of special organisations which transcends national borders and carries the proof of true solidarity among the peoples of this planet; without peacekeeping operations in complex conflicts which threaten to ignite international conflagration.

Every armed conflict in the present world carries a challenge and threat to the peace everywhere. The linkages and conveyor belts which obtain in the international system combine the destinies of nations in unprecedented ways. The means of communications have altered perceptions of distance, the media creates the conditions for instant awareness and involvement, the means of destruction provide the potential for rapid escalation and unprecedented destruction, the means of production provide potentials for unprecedented wealth and welfare as well as for undermining the future well-being of the coming generations. The 'global village' is more than a captivating phrase.

Norway's engagement in UN peacekeeping is predicated on the following considerations.

First, the prevailing constellations of political interests and distribution of military power in the international system contain the risk that local conflicts could spread very rapidly or become more intractable as a result of the competitive involvement of outside powers. Owing to its exposed position in an area which is dominated by the strategic interests of the major powers, Norway is particularly concerned about the possibility that distant conflicts could impact on the environment in northern Europe. It is important, therefore, to create options and instruments which provide viable alternatives to great power intervention in local conflicts.

Secondly, in the international division of labour, small states frequently have comparative advantages for the task of international peacekeeping, as they are more easily accepted as disinterested parties whose engagement reflects an international mandate rather than partisan interests. This does not mean that it may not be desirable to bring in the great powers in addition when they are able to join actively in supporting the consensus upon which must rest such operations. Great power participation could lend legitimacy and authority to the operations. However, it would still seem desirable that the small states continue to play the leading role. For Norway, participation in UN peacekeeping is a contribution to burden-sharing in the global security context, a contribution which is fully consistent with its position as an aligned nation in the context of East–West conflict in Europe.

Thirdly, Norway's engagement in peacekeeping is based on its interest in upholding certain basic principles of international conduct which are of vital importance to small states everywhere, particularly those that find themselves in exposed positions in the geometry of international power relations. One of those basic principles is that territorial conquest by military force is unacceptable. Might does not make right. Borders can only be changed legitimately by agreement. If that principle be violated and weakened anywhere the security of small states will be weakened everywhere.

Fourthly, we have seen some 150 wars – international and internal – in the Third World since 1945 and the incidence has increased over the last decade. On average about twelve wars were being fought every single day since the end of World War II. The casualty statistics are incomplete and highly uncertain. The numbers are, however, horrendously large. At the level of interstate relations we have today more than 70 territorial and border disputes which could erupt into physical violence, and some of them already have. An increasing number of states will be unable to provide for their own security, even in the most provisional and minimal sense. In the Third World there are more than 60 states with populations of less than a million and almost 40 of those have less than 200 000 inhabitants. We can envisage a growing need for UN peacekeeping in the years ahead. Peacekeeping is likely to become an essential element in the maintenance of minimum world order. Norwegian security depends on that order.

For purposes of classification and analysis we may distinguish among five partly-overlapping categories of armed conflict in the contemporary world: (1) conflicts over national borders; (2) conflicts with or among ethnic groups; (3) conflicts relating to issues of self-determination; (4) conflicts about the distribution of wealth within or among states or regions; and (5) conflicts concerning the norms and rules of international relations. Those are not neatly distinct categories. In the real world many conflicts exhibit elements of several of the categories suggested. However, they indicate the spectrum involved. UN peacekeeping seems particularly relevant to the first three categories of conflict.

Boundary disputes are perhaps the most obvious category for which UN peacekeeping can become a relevant instrument. A large number of the boundary disputes in the Third World form a legacy of colonialism. The arbitrary drawing of lines divided many nationalities and artificially amalgamated others. Ethnic divisions have been compounded by religious divisions. Attempts to create homogeneous states out of ethnically diverse regions have exacerbated the intensity and pervasiveness of armed struggles, and at times produced human disasters of immense proportions. It is difficult sometimes to establish clear distinctions between minority issues and issues of self-determination. They merge to exercise considerable pressure on the legitimacy and efficacy of fragile national institutions. The geometry of centripetal and centrifugal forces which operate in all nation states is particularly unstable in developing countries.

Many conflicts which have dominated international relations since World War II have been discussed in the Security Council. However, the Council has but on rare occasions been able to agree on pressures against those that have broken the peace or threatened to do so. It has failed to create expectations that the UN will intervene to stop those that do not abide by the established code of conduct.

The Security Council has proved itself a more valuable organ for international crisis management as demonstrated in the conflicts of the Middle East in 1956, 1967 and 1973. The Security Council can meet on an hour's notice and constitutes a permanent readiness instrument making it possible to convene both the great powers and the parties to conflicts which arise on short notice.

In the reform efforts that are now under way in the UN, Norway has supported strongly initiatives to strengthen the apparatus of the Secretary-General for early warning of international situations which may develop into armed conflicts, and the organs which are currently available for calling the conflicting parties to the negotiating table, if necessary, through direct mediation by the Secretary-General.

UN peacekeeping has proved most successful when the troops have been committed following an agreement by the conflicting parties which defines the area of operations and other issues of importance for the fulfilment of a peacekeeping mandate. A typical example here is the UN observer force on the Golan Heights between Israel and Syria (UNDOF). In instances where such agreement is absent or when the parties are unable to conclude and adhere to such agreements the task of peacekeeping is infinitely more difficult. This has been the predicament of UNIFIL from the very beginning. Instances may arise in which it is possible to reach rapid agreement on committing a UN force but where the international consensus may not extend to all the details of operational significance for the force. Speedy commitment is necessary in order to contain the danger of explosive escalation. In such instances working out the rules of engagement on the ground becomes an integral part of the peacekeeping operation.

A UN force does not maintain the peace as a result of the armed power it represents but rather as a result of the authority it represents, that of the only universal world organisation we know, the UN. It cannot and it should not impose an external will on the parties to the conflict at hand. It must not become a party to or participate in that conflict. Its legitimacy is to a large extent a function of its reputation for impartiality and objectivity, as well as its reputation for effectiveness. Here the UN force often gets entangled in vicious circles. The contending parties may not trust the UN force to control its area of operations and hence take measures to insert their own control, thus degrading the possibilities for the UN force to prove its efficacy. Hence a UN force can only solve its task if the conflicting parties want it to succeed. Its presence makes it easier for those parties who prefer not to fight, but who are incapable of agreeing on the terms, to observe a *de facto* cease-fire. A UN force can help in creating the modicum of trust which the parties are incapable of creating themselves.

Peacekeeping has many faces. It has been applied to quite different situations and under dissimilar conditions. It is possible to talk of peacekeeping techniques and tactics but hardly of *the* peacekeeping technique or tactic. Until now peacekeeping has hardly involved enforcement, although the UN Congo operation (ONUC) did come close. It is certainly possible to envisage that a stronger element of enforcement action in the mandate for future peacekeeping operations provided by present consensus among the Permanent Members of the Security Council be upheld. Most of the peace-keeping operations to date, and certainly those which have given rise to the rudiments of a theory of peacekeeping, have taken place in the Middle East. It would be fallacious to conclude that we have the makings of any general theory – we probably never will. It is necessary, on the threshold of a possible geographical and functional expansion of the UN peacekeeping effort, to explore new options and possibilities. The UN Angola Verification Mission (UNAVEM), which was established in January 1989, is a case in point.

SOME LIMITS OF UN PEACEKEEPING OPERATIONS

There is always the danger that UN forces contribute to freezing and preserving patterns of conflict rather than resolving them. The reduced danger of escalation tends to reduce the priority of the conflict on the agendas of the great powers. It is important therefore to develop further effective strategies for exploiting the potential synergisms between military peacekeeping and diplomatic peace-making. However, the roles should be kept quite separate. The UN forces could indeed jeopardize their reputation for impartiality and objectivity if they were to engage in exerting diplomatic pressure on the contending parties.

Very often the conflicts are so complex that the contending parties themselves lose control and thus are incapable of negotiating authoritatively or delivering on promises. UN forces in such circumstances very easily move into the role of a substitute government, performing the essential functions of protection and ensuring basic supplies. Therefore the troop-contributing countries must always be prepared for a long haul. All peacekeeping operations tend to last a long time. The UN forces become supporting elements for a fragile and volatile status quo. The troop-contributing countries therefore assume the responsibility not to jeopardize a tenuous stability by threats of pull-out. Such threats have little impact on the weak parties which are incapable of exercising independent control and they tend to play into the hands of the stronger parties who would prefer to translate their upper hand into decisive influence. They tend to undermine the authority of the UN and its mediating efforts, particularly if the threats are communicated publicly.

As already observed, peacekeeping has tended to freeze conflicts rather than move them towards solution. That is not the fault of the peacekeepers but rather of the statesmen and diplomats who have settled for containment rather than peacemaking. More could probably be done at the level of peacekeeping tactics to transform situations rather than preserve them. The established tactics of observation posts, checkpoints and patrols tend to create a static pattern to which the contending parties adjust and which they frequently exploit for unilateral advantage. UNIFIL has started to move in the direction of a more dynamic pattern by the formation of a Force Mobile Reserve. Such trends could perhaps be further developed by increased exploitation of technology for surveillance, releasing manpower for highly mobile rapid reaction.

When coping with opposing forces of greatly divergent military force, UN peacekeeping operations have tended to peg their level of military power lower than that of the superior party and above those of the weaker ones, thus giving rise to suspicions that they are neither effective nor objective. Since the peacekeepers are not there to force the contestants to lay down their arms or to retreat, they must instead develop tactics designed to constrain the superior party from exploiting its superiority in arms. Thus peacekeeping is also about the diffusion of power and the neutralisation of military force. It cannot substitute for prudent national defences, but it provides a unique supplement which is particularly well suited to dampen regional conflicts in the context of superpower *détente*.

Participation in UN peacekeeping constitutes an exercise in reality-testing for small and medium powers which tend to view distant conflicts from rather abstract points of view. They very often relate to such conflicts in terms of principles rather than facts, in terms of analogies rather than analysis. Distant conflicts are always infinitely more complex up close. Lebanon is a case in point. In many ways UNIFIL is the most complex of all peacekeeping operations to date. In part this is a function of the nature of the Lebanese conflict, in part it is a result of its international context.

LEBANON: THE DOMESTICATION OF REGIONAL CONFLICT

Lebanon, the spectacularly beautiful country of the Levant, has been made into a substitute arena for nearly all the contending forces at work in the Middle East. It has been torn asunder by its penetration of external forces linking up with the many indigenous parts of the Lebanese mosaic. The volume and multiplicity of imported conflict have greatly surpassed the carrying capacity of the Lebanese polity. In addition complex constitutional compromises were under indigenous pressure as demographic trends eroded the factual basis for the constitutional compromise, and the politics of clientelism, family clans, and privilege eroded the normative basis for the social contract. The politics of fission have severed the institutional links between society and the state, depriving Lebanon not only of effective governmental authority but also of most legitimate governmental authority. Instead, competing authorities with powerful foreign sponsors continue to vie for power and influence by means of violence. The pattern of conflict is fluid and volatile, as the various factions and movements change allies and are courted by outside sponsors. The latter, more often than not, seek engagement in order to contain or defeat rival states. The Lebanese crisis is tied by the strings of proxy wars and surrogate confrontations; but inside the crisis we find a unique resilience which defies all theories of politics and economics. Herein resides the Lebanese enigma.

Dismemberment has been repeatedly predicted, but always postponed. The intermingling of confessional groups in the Lebanese mosaic protects the polity against cantonisation. Movements for social reform and redistribution contain a potential for nation-building across confessional divisions and against the traditional patterns of privilege. The links with outside sponsors are often weak and ambiguous, forming marriages of convenience rather than durable coalitions. Minimum consensus could only be reached for an independent Lebanon. Other constructions would exclude movements powerful enough to demand representation. An independent Lebanese state would also seem to constitute the minimum consensus solution for the outside powers, although some of them may prefer other solutions. Both of the superpowers prefer an independent Lebanese state and their *détente* enables them to promote their preferred solution largely unencumbered by competitive considerations, and increasingly in *de facto* coalition with Syria. American support of Syria's role in Lebanon reduces possible fears lest a Greater Syria be in the making. Syrian disengagement will not take place as long as the Maronite Lebanese Forces are not contained by indigenous forces in Lebanon, nor is it likely to ensue as long as the Israeli Defence Forces remain in South Lebanon in symbiotic coalition with the so-called Southern Lebanese Army (SLA). The Israelis are caught in a dilemma. If they withdraw the SLA may disintegrate as the lines of supply and the money dry up. If they remain, the SLA may grow strong enough to turn against their Israeli sponsors as that sponsorship serves to delegitimate the SLA in the eyes of the Lebanese. We do not know, of course, to what extent the fear of revenge will nevertheless move the SLA to stay with their Israeli sponsors. The end of the Iran–Iraq war has brought Iraq into the Lebanese quagmire, not so much in order to continue the war against Iranian sponsored fundamentalism represented by the Hezbollah, but as an extension of the intra-Ba'ath rivalry and an attempt to constrain Syrian hegemony in Lebanon. Iraqi support of the Maronite forces could offer the latter an alternative to their Israeli connection. The political bazaar in Lebanon never closes.

The Israelis are caught in further contradictions. Their continued presence serves as a focal point for Lebanese resistance; for the moderate Afwaj Al-Muqamah Al-Lubnaniyya (AMAL), for the more radical Hezbollah and, of course, for the Palestinians. They become the unwilling victims of the self-fulfilling prophecy. Invoking the need to maintain a security zone in southern Lebanon in order to protect Israel's border against infiltration and assault stimulates opposition to the presence of foreign troops in Lebanon. Such opposition is viewed in Israel as proof of the imminent threat to the Israeli border.

The Israelis have an alternative, namely, to permit the UN Interim

Force In Lebanon (UNIFIL) to deploy down to the international border in consonance with UN Security Council Resolution 425. Israel claims that UNIFIL would be incapable of stopping infiltrators. It is, however, a contention which has never been put to the test, simply because Israel has never allowed UNIFIL to deploy in all of the stipulated area of operations. UNIFIL has in fact proven to be a rather effective screen, and the majority of infiltration attempts take place in the corridor where the Israeli security zone separates the UNIFIL area of operations into two parts.

UNIFIL has acquired credibility and local support as it extended protection to the population of the south against the arms of the Israelis and the various other armed elements. Since the governmental authority UNIFIL should assist in restoring in the south continued to disintegrate in Beirut, UNIFIL has become in many ways a substitute government for South Lebanon, making it the safest part of the country as witnessed by the immigration into the area. However, the prolonged absence of constitutional government in Beirut could weaken the legitimacy of UNIFIL's continued presence. Renewal of the mandate could become increasingly difficult. Hence the authority and legitimacy of UNIFIL requires the restoration of a constitutional national government in Lebanon.

As we have noted, the power of UNIFIL does not grow out of the barrels of its guns, but rather from its international mandate and identity. Superpower *détente* has led to a renewed interest in UN peacekeeping as an alternative to unilateral intervention, and, for the first time, both the United States and the Soviet Union actively support UN peacekeeping. The role of UN observers in Afghanistan and along the Iran–Iraq front, the preparations for a major operation in Namibia and exploration of similar options for Kampuchea and other areas suggest that UN peacekeeping may become more credible as it commands expanding international support. The Nobel Peace Prize provides additional salience to a unique mechanism for conflict resolution. The UNIFIL option could come to loom larger in Israeli policy on Lebanon as Israel concentrates its attention on the Palestinian issue which has come to a boil through the *intifada*.

PAYING FOR PEACEKEEPING

Peacekeeping is not cheap. However, compared to the costs and burdens of dangerous conflict the bills do not seem so awesome. The financing of UN peacekeeping operations which is approved by the relevant organs of the UN is allocated among the member nations in accordance with an agreed formula. If a member country should fail to pay its share, a gap will develop between the running costs and the economic means of the UN to meet the expenses.

According to the UNIFIL budget, the participating countries shall receive the same amount per soldier per day. This implies, not unreasonably I might add, that countries with a high level of wages will have to defray a part of the wages by their own means, while countries with a lower wage level may even earn money on the basis of the refunds received from the UN.

Norwegian expenditures exceed the amount refunded by the UN. Norway receives at present refunds for only about one quarter of its expenditures. In addition some countries are delinquent in paying their share of the financial burden. The UN has not been in a position therefore to refund the expenditures of the troop-contributors at the agreed levels, thus adding to the burden of the troop-contributing countries.

We must wish for an early settlement of the difficult financial situation of many UN operations, particularly UNIFIL. All member countries, including the great powers, share in the collective responsibility for UN peacekeeping operations. By paying their share they strengthen the authority of the UN peacekeeping operations; and conversely, by failing to pay their share they weaken the legitimacy and authority of peacekeeping operations which depend on the consensus in the Security Council.

The Soviet Union now pays its assessed dues for peacekeeping. However, the US Congress has constrained the American government from contributing its assessed share. Since peacekeeping has become the primary responsibility of smaller states, the failure of the great powers to pay adds immeasurably to a burden which has been carried by states with small economies. It could exclude the small countries of the developing world from participation.

PEACEKEEPING AND NATIONAL DEFENCE

In the debate in small countries on how to allocate resources for defence in the most productive manner, the proposals may emerge to withdraw from peacekeeping operations after some time. Since all peacekeeping operations tend to last a long time such debates constitute a recurring phenomenon.

In Norwegian policy participation in UN peacekeeping operations form a part of the established tasks of the national defence forces. Such participation demonstrates the importance Norway attaches to the UN as an organisation and its role in the efforts to preserve international peace and security. I have referred already to the ways in which instability and conflicts in distant areas, particularly in the Middle East, could escalate horizontally to encompass also the Nordic region. Competitive interventions by the major powers would almost certainly affect tensions in the Nordic environs. UN peacekeeping operations constitute preventive defence policy from the point of view of an exposed small nation.

Norway's contribution to peacekeeping operations therefore cannot be measured with the same scale as its own defence effort at home. It is neither a substitute for its national defence effort nor an alternative to that effort. It constitutes an addition which involves bonus effects. Peacekeeping operations reduce the risk that local conflicts will spread in a manner that becomes a threat to peace in the Nordic world. By containing and defusing the conflicts peacekeeping operations contribute to war prevention also in a more immediate sense. It is basically a matter of widening one's perspective.

A peacekeeping force operates in an environment which in some respects is more realistic and complex than can be simulated during initial service or refresher training in one's own country. It has to cope with different challenges from those presented to ordinary military units during peacetime conditions at home. Leadership is tested in a more direct way than is possible in a peacetime army.

Even if a peacekeeping force is committed to action in accordance with agreements with the parties concerned, great demands are made on the UN force. The personnel must be able to use weapons in self-defence. On certain conditions the force must be prepared to use limited armed force in order to accomplish its mission. The peacekeeping mission involves significant challenges to the skills of each soldier, to leadership, and to discipline. It is significant that all our commanders who have participated in peacekeeping operations agree on this. The sceptics are those who did not share in that experience.

Reports from UNIFIL show that almost all participants are of the opinion that service in the force is of great, and even very great, value for service in their national defence establishment. The personnel have been serving in an environment which is as close as one can come to real war during peacetime. Fortunately Norway's armed forces have not seen actual combat since the Second World War.

UNIFIL personnel therefore have been able to accumulate experience which could not have been given them in any other way. UN service contributes to sharpening the sharp edge of one's defences. Most of the soldiers are reservists who will add to the competence of the mobilisation army. UN service cannot, of course, replace the training in bigger formations and the regular army tactics which are needed for the defence of Norway. It does not include all the skills needed in its national defence establishment, but it contributes a valuable complement.

Participation in UNIFIL then provides the troops with experience which is of great benefit to Norway's mobilisation forces. By the end of this year about 20 000 Norwegians will have served in UNIFIL. They constitute a reservoir of experience which Norway must put to the best use possible. Individual experiences will be studied and assessed by the defence establishment and reflected in the manuals for education and training.

Norwegian units have carried out their mission in UNIFIL in a way that has earned them respect in the area of operations. From this we may conclude that the education and training of Norway's defence forces are basically sound and that they form a good basis for integrating the experiences gained at individual and unit level in UNIFIL into Norway's national defence ethos and approach.

Participation in UN peacekeeping does not only provide military experience and proficiency of considerable value to Norway's national defence establishment. It conveys a greater understanding also of the relationship between military force and social stability, of the need for basic protection if social life is to flourish and develop. Military power is not an end in itself but a means to an end. That relation, I believe, is more comprehensible and tangible to soldiers who have served in UN peacekeeping operations than those who have not shared in that experience.

CONCLUDING REMARKS

The UN peacekeeping operations constitute an important contribution to the preservation of peace in a world of turmoil and conflict, inequity and underdevelopment. They provide no substitute for diplomacy or for mutual restraint on behalf of the great powers. They provide no substitute for a credible defence of one's own country. They provide a valuable bonus to one's mobilisation forces. They can provide a marginal contribution to the prevention of great power involvement and horizontal escalation. Thus they can contribute also to preventing such conflicts from reaching one's own shores. Norway has a special interest in that relation due to its vulnerable strategic position. Participation in UN peacekeeping operations therefore is a contribution also to preserving the peace in the Norwegian part of the world. In a broader context, UN peacekeeping contributes to maintaining the UN as a framework and mechanism for promoting collective security. It contributes to maintaining the concept of a world based on international law instead of the authority of weapons, on the collective will of the UN instead of the partial interest of the most powerful of nations.

9 Peacekeeping and the Parties
Alan M. James

INTRODUCTION

In keeping with its non-forceful nature, the device which has become known as international peacekeeping rests on the consent of the state or the states on whose territory the peacekeepers operate. If any such operation is to maximise its contribution to the maintenance of peace, it must also have the co-operation of all the relevant disputants, whether or not they happen to be host states. It is, in other words, the parties who provide the context for peacekeeping – and without that context there will be no peacekeeping. There are, of course, other requirements. Someone or somebody has to make the necessary arrangements and take the appropriate decisions, for peacekeeping represents the involvement in a dispute of a third (and impartial) party. Among these arrangements will be the provision of personnel, almost always military. This means that some states have to volunteer such people. Some states, too, have to finance the affair, and while the parties are not to be excluded from this role, it is unlikely that they can usually be looked to as exclusive paymasters.

However, generally speaking, it is the parties who play the crucial role, not only in respect of the success of a peacekeeping mission but also in its creation. If they are agreed on the desirability of such a mission it is highly probable that, in one way or another, it will be provided. If, on the other hand, it is outsiders who are pressing for such a body, it can only move to the area of dispute with the consent of the host states, and can only operate successfully with the co-operation of all disputants. Pressures of various kinds may be employed to achieve these ends; but ultimately this is a matter over which the disputants, and more particularly the potential host(s), possess a veto.

Even a very impressionistic glance at the post-1945 period reveals that conflicting parties have not been falling over themselves to solicit the help of peacekeeping missions. During this time there have been numerous international disputes, or disputes with a strong international flavour: when figures are given it is not unusual to be offered

125

a number of between one and two hundred. Yet no more than about 20 peacekeeping operations have been established in all (about 15 by the UN) and nearly half of them relate to various aspects of the Arab–Israeli conflict. One should not be too quick to draw critical conclusions from this situation. Peacekeeping offers help in the calming, containing, or composing of a quarrel,[1] and not all quarrels have reached the stage where the parties are ready to embark on any of these directions. Alternatively they may have been able to do so without the assistance of a third party, for there is no basis for the assumption that an impartial or non-forceful third party is essential, or even always desirable, in the winding down or containment of conflict. It would, in any event, be surprising if resort had always been made to this useful device in appropriate-looking circumstances.

There are three broad grounds on which the parties may have reservations about involving a peacekeeping body in their conflict. Moreover these reservations may be equally valid in respect of the actual presence of a peacekeeping mission, for it is by no means the case that the existence of such a mission implies that the parties are entirely happy with it. Even if they had been so minded at the start of its work, problems may have developed later on. One reason for disputants not welcoming peacekeepers is that their presence could have undesirable international repercussions, not just for the host state(s) but also for any non-host parties. A second set of reservations arises from the fact that there could be adverse international consequences of a kind which affect the host(s) alone. The third set is also applicable only to hosts, but is distinguished from the second in that it relates to the possibly unhappy domestic repercussions of having peacekeepers on one's soil. Each of these categories will now be explored. To avoid undue speculation, examples will generally be given only from situations in which peacekeeping bodies (including non-UN groups) have actually operated, or where they currently exist. It must be remembered, however, that the factors being discussed also apply to other situations, and may have resulted in states deciding not to ask for the help of a peacekeeping mission.

INTERNATIONAL REPERCUSSIONS I

This section deals with factors which are not just applicable to a state which plays host to a peacekeeping group but which also apply to non-host disputants. The latter fall into two categories. In the case of an operation which focuses on a border (whether an established international frontier or a cease-fire or armistice line), the non-host will be the state on the other side of the border from the one on which the peacekeepers operate. In the case of an operation which operates partly or wholly in a general way within a single jurisdiction (a 'law and order' rather than a 'barrier' group), the non-host parties will be those who might have a strong perceived need to intervene within the host state. With regard to this second group, the co-operation which is required for the success of the peacekeeping operation is negative in character: the states concerned must refrain from intervening. With regard to the first group, co-operation of a more positive kind is called for, although it may well be of an informal and unofficial nature. The absence of such positive co-operation does not necessarily undermine the whole *raison d'être* of the peacekeeping operation: it may still be able to make a contribution to the maintenance of peace; but it may also be less successful in this respect. Its continuation in these circumstances may come to look more like an exercise in finger-pointing than an attempt to assist in the maintenance of calm.

The Existence of an International Issue

Almost by definition, an international dispute is one in which there is an imbalance of satisfaction. If the side which is less dissatisfied feels sufficiently well placed to do so, it may take the line that there is really nothing to argue about, that the situation is essentially settled or is at most only of bilateral concern, and that the other side is doing a disservice to their potentially good relationship by striving to keep the issue alive at a wider international level. In these circumstances the first state would almost certainly resist the suggestion that the dispute should attract the attention of the peacekeeping group, and if such a group is already in place it may well try to diminish its importance or even seek its withdrawal. The dispatch of such a group or its activity on a border would be a clear sign that in the view of the parent body there was a live international dispute.

The best example of this approach is that of India to the UN Military Observer Group in India and Pakistan (UNMOGIP) – that is, in Kashmir. After the third bout of fighting between these two states in 1971, India ceased to co-operate with UNMOGIP. The Group continues to exist and India continues to provide it, 'as a matter of courtesy' with administrative facilities. India, however, no longer complains to the Group about incidents along the Line of Control in Kashmir nor invites the Observers to investigate incidents. In India's view, Kashmir is no longer a matter which should concern the UN; rather, India believes that the dispute should be exclusively handled by the two states concerned. No doubt it was much earlier on that India began to regret the UN's involvement in the issue, and now it has done as much as it deems prudent to minimise that involvement – to the inconvenience and frustration of the Observers posted on the Indian side of the line.

There is perhaps some echo of this approach in Israel's denunciation of its Armistice Agreement with Egypt in 1956 and of the Armistices with its other Arab neighbours in 1967. Much of the activity of the Jerusalem-based UN Truce Supervision Organization (UNTSO) was initially geared to the Mixed Armistice Commissions which had been provided for by the Agreements. Israel, however, was never happy about the presence and work of the UN Observers, and was also at this period emphatic about the desirability of bilateral discussions with each of its neighbours: anything which undermined the UN's local role was therefore welcomed. However, the Commissions had never assumed great importance, and most of UNTSO's activity had instead become based on certain Security Council resolutions of 1948 and 1949 calling for the maintenance of a ceasefire. Israel did not wish to challenge this, so the situation on the ground was not greatly affected.

Two further cases should be noted. They both bear on the way in which peacekeeping operations relate to an issue's internationalisation, but in different ways from that which has just been discussed. South Africa's agreement to discussions on the future of Namibia (South West Africa), which led to the UN's 1978 scheme for a Transition Assistance Group (UNTAG), was a sign that it had abandoned its view that the Territory's future was not a matter for outsiders. In Cyprus, the Turkish Republic of Northern Cyprus (TRNC), promulgated in 1983 but recognised by no state other than Turkey, is trying to gain something of an international foothold for itself on the back of discussions concerning the UN Force in Cyprus (UNFICYP). It refuses to accept the resolutions extending UNFICYP's mandate because they do not mention the TRNC. Meanwhile, it says, UNFICYP is its guest – and on the ground the matter gives rise to no problems.

The Limitation on a State's Freedom of Action

Peacekeeping missions are neither intended nor equipped to act forcefully. The members of an observer group are customarily unarmed, while those serving in a force carry only light arms for purposes of self-defence. Accordingly such missions are no physical obstacle to a state which is determined on a particular course of action. Nonetheless the presence of a peacekeeping mission does add a diplomatic and psychological dimension to the scene, which changes it in a subtle and perhaps not insignificant way. At the very least a state which intervenes in one playing host to a peacekeeping body, or which marches across a border watched over by peacekeepers, knows that a report on its activity will quickly be furnished and given wide coverage and considerable credibility. Moving up a notch, such a state must also take account of the possibility that its standing may suffer to some degree if it acts in a cavalier way toward international peacekeepers. If any of the latter comes to physical harm this could give rise to some embarrassment between the state which has effected the injury and that from which the injured come. All of which does not amount to very much, but it is an imponderable something. It means that the introduction of a peacekeeping mission leaves interested states with rather less effective freedom of action than hitherto. Some states may be concerned about this, or come to be so.

If, for example, (as was widely suggested at the time but which even then could be viewed as most unlikely)[2] the Soviet Union had been contemplating intervention in the Congo in the early 1960s, the presence of, by UN standards, a large peacekeeping force must surely have presented a complicating consideration. Likewise, one assumes that Turkey, when deciding to invade Cyprus in 1974, would much have preferred the UN not to have had a peacekeeping force spread throughout the island (which, in an unusual turn of events, succeeded in preventing the Turkish capture of Nicosia Airport). The presence in Yemen of a UN Observer Mission to watch, *inter alia*, over the withdrawal of Egyptian (or United Arab Republic as that state was then called) troops in 1963 made things even more awkward for President Nasser when he decided that he must *renege* on his promise to depart. When, in 1958, the UN Observer Group in Lebanon failed to substantiate Lebanese claims of intervention from the (then) Syrian province of the United Arab Republic, President Chamoun was exceedingly annoyed. All these cases are a reminder that one's hand is somewhat less free in the presence of international peacekeepers.

There are a number of similar instances in the various phases of the Arab–Israeli conflict. Egypt found itself inconvenienced by the UN Emergency Force (UNEF) in 1967, and the demand for its withdrawal set off a series of events which culminated, chronologically if not causally, in the Six Day War. It may have been for more than legalistic reasons that Israel refused to co-operate with UNTSO's observer activities in South Lebanon which began in 1972, and Israel has always been opposed to the idea that UN observers be posted along the River Jordan where it forms the post-1967 cease-fire line between Jordan and Israel. Mr Khrushchev is said to have regarded UNEF I as a restraining influence on Israel,[3] and in 1982 Israel's decision to send an invading force through the lines of the UN's Interim Force in Lebanon is said to have been taken only after careful consideration of its political costs.[4] When the invaders reached Beirut, Israel at first refused a Security Council demand that the ten UNTSO Observers already in the city be increased to 50, and did not back down until it found itself in great embarrassment over the massacres in the Sabra and Chatila refugee camps. It might also be noted that when the establishment of a UN peacekeeping mission on the Israeli–Syrian front was being discussed in 1974, Syria – the party with a large territorial grievance to rectify at some future date – wanted an observer group rather than a force. There may well have been reasons for this other than the greater problem which a force might later present to the Syrian Army, but that consideration may not have been absent from Syria's calculations.

Moving away from the Middle East, it might be noted that at the end of 1971, India resolutely opposed the idea that UN observers be posted on its border with East Pakistan, and made it clear that it would not co-operate with any who were sent to East Pakistan alone. The situation there was fast deteriorating, and India, preparing to intervene, had no desire to be inconvenienced or even internationally observed. A contrasting point may be made regarding southern Africa, to the effect that South Africa is only likely to agree to UNTAG operating in Namibia when it decides that there is no danger of its having to interfere with its activities.

The Creation of a Bad Impression

Quite apart from the possibility of official reports putting an imprimatur on already known facts, an additional consequence of an international presence is that its senior officials and ordinary members may develop a firm view about the merits of the dispute and the behaviour of the parties. If that view inclines markedly in one direction it may be thought to work to the international disadvantage of the state concerned. It ought not, of course, to manifest itself in the official workings of the peacekeeping mission – although it may do so; but the letters home of the mission's members, the tales they tell on their return, and the impressions of visitors may not embellish the reputation of at least one of the parties. It is possible that at a later date a few members of the mission may go damagingly into print. If such individuals come from a democratic state which has traditionally had sympathetic ties with the criticised party, it is not impossible that some complications might ensue in the relations of the two states.

The available examples of this phenomenon almost all relate to the same state: Israel. The first Chief of Staff (that is, the head) of UNTSO (an American) seems to have had poor relations with the Arab states, and a later Acting Chief of Staff (also an American) fell out with Jordan. However, UNTSO's second Chief of Staff, General Bennike of Denmark, was publicly charged by Israel with one-sidedness in his reports; a later Chief of Staff, General von Horn of Sweden, incurred Israel's severe hostility during his last year in office; and his successor, General Bull of Norway, although he succeeded in retaining the confidence of both sides, later wrote his memoirs because he found that public opinion in his country 'regarded the Palestine problem almost entirely from the Israeli point of view'.[5]

With the establishment of the UN's Interim Force in Lebanon (UNIFIL) in 1978, many ordinary soldiers from Western European and Scandinavian states, among others, found themselves exposed to both Israel and her critics. On the latter aspect of the matter one Israeli academic has written that:

> many soldiers in the UNIFIL troops were meeting Palestinians for the first time and learning about their cause and their sufferings. The Palestine Liberation Organization (PLO) propagandists were very active in trying to spread PLO ideas among the UNIFIL units. Indeed, not only were these soldiers influenced by PLO propaganda, but they communicated it in various ways to their respective homelands. Finally, the occasional clashes between UNIFIL units and Israeli soldiers only intensified this trend of opinion in UNIFIL.[6]

Another analyst, who served for 30 years in the Israel Defence Forces, has made an almost identical assessment, adding that the 'empathy' of UN soldiers 'towards the Palestinian population and its "freedom fighters"' also came to be shared by 'the long line of newsmen and politicians who came from countries friendly to Israel such as Holland, Norway and Ireland, to see at close hand the contribution of their countries' soldiers to peace in the Middle East'.[7] He concluded that Israel should therefore 'exert whatever influence she can to assure that countries friendly to Israel do not send troops to Israel'. Indeed Israel should in this context argue for troops from states which were 'neutral . . . in relation to the Arab–Israeli conflict, and who are not too active in international politics'.[8]

The withdrawal of the Netherlands contingent from UNIFIL in 1985, which was said to be influenced by the very anti-Israeli comments of returning Dutch troops, is in keeping with this line of comment.[9] Clearly, whatever the positive returns, Israel has suffered in several ways during the last decade from its policy toward and behaviour in Lebanon.

INTERNATIONAL REPERCUSSIONS II

In addition to the consequences which have been discussed in the previous section, host states may well find that the involvement of a peacekeeping mission has some adverse international repercussions which are special to them. Three such repercussions will be identified and considered in this section. As with the ones discussed earlier, the awareness of these factors may not only affect a state's readiness to act as host to peacekeepers but may also result in some tension in those cases where a state has invited a peacekeeping body to operate on its soil.

The Underlining of a State's Weakness

There is no necessary reason why the establishment of a peacekeeping body should reflect weakness on the part of the host state. In principle, two states could amicably agree that it would be good for their relationship if a group of impartial and non-forceful soldiers patrolled their border, and even if the soldiers were posted and operated on only one side of the border, that need not carry the implication that the host was in a relatively weak position. The establishment of the non-UN Multinational Force and Observers (MFO) in Sinai in 1982, in consequence of the 1979 Peace Treaty between Egypt and Israel, provides a fair amount of support for this point.

However, it is a readily understandable fact of political life that states rarely extend an unqualified welcome to foreign troops, even those who come on the basis of close ties between the states concerned. Peacekeepers are very definitely two or three notches below allies, it not being possible to depict them in the warm context of international friendship. It may well be that their arrival can be presented by the host as serving some important national purpose, and it may even be possible to work a tone of triumph into the announcement. However, in the cold light of international relations it is hard to get away from the usually fairly evident fact that the presence of peacekeepers, especially in the shape of a force, is an indication that the host state has in some important way been unable to cope on its own. Other states, generally in the name of the UN, are having to bail the host out, and they stay on with a view to making it less likely that on some future occasion the host will again be subject to such embarrassment.

The impression of weakness which this gives to the world is something that is only acceptable as the lesser of two evils. There is little doubt that it is a powerful disincentive to any state which might be contemplating the issue of an invitation to a peacekeeping mission. Thus, on the one hand, it is no coincidence that the world's more powerful states have never played host to a peacekeeping mission; and that middle powers – India and Israel – have become very edgy about the presence of even small observer groups. Nor, on the other hand, is it surprising that all seven of the UN's peacekeeping forces have been established in situations of international crisis in which the potential host has been in a particularly awkward jam.

The very first peacekeeping force, the UN Emergency Force, it must be remembered, was not just born out of an urgent need to save British and French faces by providing them with an acceptable avenue of withdrawal; it was also a means of relieving Egypt's considerable humiliation. The second force with this name set up in 1973, also had this local purpose as well as being a means of defusing a very dangerous looking confrontation between the superpowers. The UN Security Force, sent to West New Guinea/West Irian in 1962, was a way of allowing the Dutch to leave without too much indignity. The UN's Congo force was a response to the total break-down of that state. Cyprus was in serious disorder in 1963–64, so that the UN's offer of a force was the least unacceptable way forward. The creation of UNIFIL in 1978 was at bottom a response to the collapse of the Lebanese state. Finally the appearance on Golan in 1974 of the UN Disengagement Observer Force (UNDOF) can very plausibly be seen as the way in which Syria achieved a partial Israeli withdrawal.

Most of these forces stayed for some time, and three of them are currently in place; but their presence was not without some embarrassment for the host. UNIFIL still testifies to Lebanon's huge misfortunes; UNDOF is something of a reminder of Syria's inability, as yet, to regain its lost territory; and UNFICYP is certainly a continuing testimony to Cyprus's weak and exposed position in relation to Turkey. UNEF II became less of an incubus to Egypt on account of its early and continuing association with the idea and practice of Israeli withdrawal; but UNEF I's presence between 1957 and 1967 resulted in President Nasser being 'subjected to periodic criticism and ridicule from other Arab countries for hiding behind UNEF in Sinai instead of confronting the Israeli enemy'.[10] King Hussein of Jordan asked 'why did Nasser cower behind the shield'[11] of UNEF, while 'the Syrians sneered at his failure to come to their aid and advertised his delinquency to the Arab nations'.[12]

The Damaging Effect of International Watchdogs

A different kind of inferiority – moral rather than physical – can all too easily be suggested by the presence within a state's boundaries of international observers. They are there to keep an eye on something, and it is but a small step from that premise to the conclusion that the state in question needs to have an eye kept on it. Naturally enough, this implication of doubtful probity is something which states dislike, and gives rise to an apprehension that other states are going to think less well of them. This judgement regarding the demeaning effect of observing peacekeepers combines with the instinct of privacy and resentment at its breach, which results in a reluctance to play host to such persons and, when they have actually been admitted, to their often being given a hard time.

In the UN's earlier days the colonial states' refusal to permit international observers into the territories they controlled was a very clear reflection of this approach. Thus they were very unhappy when, in 1965, New Zealand broke ranks by inviting the UN to observe an election in the Cook Islands, and went on record to say that this was not to be regarded as a precedent; but of course it was. Fifteen years later Britain's 'wariness of being observed'[13] during the elections which were to lead to the independence of Rhodesia/Zimbabwe has been recounted by a member of the secretariat of the co-ordinated Commonwealth Observer Group which emerged, to Britain's chagrin, out of its agreement that individual Commonwealth governments might send observers.

From time to time, most recently in 1988, tension has developed between Rwanda and Burundi on account of the massacre of Tutsis by the ruling Hutus in Rwanda and of Hutus by the ruling Tutsis in Burundi; but there has been no inclination at all on the part of either state to admit UN observers to see what was going on, try to provide some protection, and encourage reconciling moves. When such an event first happened – in Rwanda at the end of 1963, shortly after both states had become independent – the UN Secretary-General did send a special representative on a peace mission; but he was unwelcome in Rwanda, and got nowhere.

Another case of the UN being spurned occurred at the end of the Cuban Missile Crisis of 1962, when the United States and the Soviet Union agreed that the removal of Soviet missiles from Cuba should take place under UN supervision. The Secretary-General and a party of officials immediately flew to Cuba, but all concerned had reckoned without the Cubans. President Castro flatly refused to have UN observers on his soil, or indeed, international observers under any auspices, so the inspection had to be done bilaterally, and at sea. As an Egyptian delegate put it at a very early stage of UNTSO's activity, 'No one wants outside supervision if it can be helped'.[14] As it turned out, however, it was the Israelis who have always been particularly cool about and sometimes obstructive towards the work of UNTSO's observers, so much so that when the idea of a UN force was raised during the Suez crisis, Secretary-General Dag Hammarskjöld was at first unenthusiastic, pointing out that 'Ben Gurion considered even the present UN observers to be intruders'.[15]

Sometimes the reluctance to play host to international observers reflects a more specific concern than the feeling of suffering some humiliation in the eyes of other states (which is not to underestimate the potency of hurt international pride). Jordan, for example, has long held the view that for UN observers to watch over the post-1967 cease-fire line between itself and Israel would give an air of legitimacy to the River Jordan as the appropriate international frontier. Thus it rejected a 1968 proposal by Secretary-General U Thant for such observation, and subsequently did not alter its view on the matter. Whether, in the light of its 1988 renunciation of the West Bank, it will now change its opinion, remains to be seen.

An even more specific concern which not a few states almost certainly entertain in connection with the presence, or possible presence, of foreign military men has to do with the damaging intelligence which they might gather. The equipment and disposition of a state's military forces and its defence arrangements are matters which may be of particular interest to certain other states, and the possibility cannot be ruled out that they may acquire some valuable information from those who have been inside the state in question in a peacekeeping role. The likelihood of this often happening in a significant way is perhaps not very great, and there are other and probably more effective ways of trying to get hold of secrets than by suborning peacekeepers; but states are very sensitive in this area, and will go to some lengths to keep informed foreign eyes at bay.

Worries about Sovereignty

On account of the variety of ways in which it is used and its rich emotional resonance, the term sovereignty has considerable rhetorical potential. Anything which restricts a state's freedom of action – whether internationally or domestically and whether in formal or practical terms – is liable to be presented, by those who wish to make political capital out of it, as a limitation on sovereignty. Peacekeeping activity offers clear scope for charges of this kind. An observer group or a force may be watching over an agreement which places restrictions on how a state may behave at its border. Also, a peacekeeping force will almost certainly arrange for its military personnel to remain subject to the criminal jurisdiction of their various national states, and perhaps for them to be exempt from the civil jurisdiction of the host state as well. The force as a whole and the bases from which it operates will doubtless be subject to certain jurisdictional immunities and enjoy certain privileges. It may also have the right to the exclusive occupation, or at least the exclusive military occupation, of certain areas; and so on.

If any ill-disposed person or state (not excluding the host state) wishes to make trouble for a peacekeeping group it may couch its remarks at least partly in terms of the loss of sovereignty suffered by the state in question. A potential host may need to be reassured that its sovereignty is not in danger of diminution. In 1956, for example, Egypt's concern about the impact of the UN Emergency Force on its sovereignty led to the Secretary-General instructing the Force Commander 'to point out that cooperation with the United Nations ... would not infringe on Egyptian sovereignty'.[16] However, Egypt was not immediately reassured, and the arrival of UNEF was in fact held up pending the settlement of Egypt's claim that the Secretary-General was interpreting their agreement in a way which 'would be an infringement of Egyptian sovereignty.'[17] Seven years later, in West Irian, Indonesia's urgent desire to get the UN Temporary Executive Authority and its UN Security Force out of the territory at the earliest possible moment may well have had something to do with the feeling that their presence cast doubt on its right to sovereignty over the area.

Of course in any such discussion everything depends on what is meant by sovereignty. It can be shown that, in its most basic sense of that which makes a territorial entity eligible for full participation in international relations, sovereignty is totally unaffected by the presence of a peacekeeping mission.[18] On a less comprehensive definition, however, a state may have a real worry on this score, or about what others may say on the matter. It is very hard, even in a particular case, to put a weight on it; but in a general sense it may contribute to a state's unease about the presence of peacekeepers, and when added to other considerations may have a significant effect on policy.

DOMESTIC REPERCUSSIONS

This section considers the domestic complications which may ensue for a state which acts as host to a peacekeeping mission. Besides actually being a source of tension, an awareness of them may influence a state's decision whether or not to play the role of host, and they could be very influential. For a government sits, as it were, between the majesty of the state, in whose name it speaks, and the pressures of national life, to which it must perforce respond. Anything which threatens to upset a government's political base or position will immediately give rise to acute concern. The impact of peacekeeping on the domestic scene will therefore be watched very closely by the government of the host state.

Relations with the Populace

Peacekeepers are usually relatively thin on the ground and often geographically out of the way; but sometimes a peacekeeping force may be widely spread throughout a state, as was the case in the Congo and in Cyprus until 1974. In any event soldiers will from time to time take local leave. So at least occasionally and perhaps even frequently there is likely to be some contact between the people of the state and the peacekeepers.

Three sorts of problem may then arise. First, there is a probable cultural gap, with at least some of the peacekeepers being unattuned to local ways; but it would be a poor peacekeeping mission which did not issue clear advice on the matter and take firm action to remedy any particular troubles. Second, there is the licentious soldiery problem. That too, however, is something which all peacekeeping forces will be very anxious to minimise and can therefore be kept under control – even to the point, as happened with one UNIFIL contingent (at least at one time) – of declaring tours of duty to be 'dry'. Third, there is the 'bad apple' problem. Some soldiers may get involved with anti-government groups, organise a little smuggling, or even arrange a modest amount of gun-running; but here again any peacekeeping mission will be alert to the possibilities and crack down strongly on malefactors.

All told, therefore, these problems are unlikely to be of much practical significance; in fact, peacekeeping bodies seem to have coped extremely well in these respects. One or two cases have come to public light; but on the reasonable assumption that they are not the tip of the proverbial iceberg, host states would seem to have little need to worry about the theoretical possibilities. Certainly it is most improbable that important decisions about peacekeeping are going to turn on this issue.

Peacekeeping in National Politics

If the presence of, or the issue of, an invitation to a peacekeeping mission becomes a controversial matter in national politics, in the sense that the state's policy elicits strong opposition, warning bells will soon be ringing with the government of the day, perhaps to significant effect. It is not hard to imagine such a scenario. If it became known that the United Kingdom and the Republic of Ireland were contemplating a joint request to the UN to provide a peacekeeping force to secure their frontier, there could well be political ructions in both states. Likewise, an Israeli initiative to invite the UN, or even another international body, to help maintain order on the West Bank would hardly be quietly received; but in fact peacekeeping has not given rise to much controversy of this kind within disputing states. In part this is because such missions have not been sought or accepted in contexts which would have been politically troublesome. The question remains, however, as to why such peacekeeping bodies as have been established have been received with such relative quiet by the parties.

In two situations which, on the face of it, could well have given rise to problems – the Congo in the early 1960s and Lebanon since 1978 – the entire life of each country was in such disorder that there was little scope for a coherent response through established political mechanisms to the presence of foreign peacekeepers. Yemen did not enjoy the degree of participatory democracy which might have produced a lively political debate, and the same is broadly true of Egypt and Syria. In respect of the operations in these last two countries, the fact that the peacekeepers were and are confined to a border area may also have helped to keep them from the political limelight. The observer groups in Kashmir and on the Arab–Israeli borders have not generally had a high political profile, and the group in Lebanon in 1958 pleased the opposition rather than the government, and was soon upstaged by American intervention. The group sent to the Indo–West Pakistani frontier in 1965 was there for too short a time to make a political impression.

Three democracies which withdrew from interventionary or colonialist positions in favour of peacekeeping bodies – Britain and France from the Suez in 1956 and the Netherlands from West New Guinea in 1962 – were moving with rather than against the tide of domestic opinion, and those who might normally have raised strong objection to what was happening were very aware that the international cards were stacked against their states. Indonesia only allowed the Act of Free Choice to go ahead in West Irian in 1969 in the sure knowledge that this UN-supervised event would produce the 'right' result, and hence cause no domestic problems.

That leaves Cyprus – a vibrant democracy which for ten years had a UN Force spread throughout her land, and which since 1974 has agreed to that Force playing a buffer role in circumstances which keep it to the political fore, in that the buffer zone runs right through the capital city. Here, if anywhere, are opportunities for political

argument about the presence of a peacekeeping mission; but the
opportunities have not been taken. Doubtless the value of the Force
– on economic as well as on security grounds – is sufficiently evident
to undercut any such developments. Their lack is also a tribute to the
conduct of the Force.

Politics, however, is not a one-way process, nor is it only to be
found in participatory democracies. A regime always needs to justify
itself, and if not to the people at large, to those individuals and
groups who could provide alternative leaders. Accordingly the state
authorities will from time to time very probably want to show
peacekeeping groups that they, the authorities, are in charge, and
that the peacekeepers are there on sufferance. While it may seem
folly to outsiders for the host to demand a mission's withdrawal,
nonetheless some moves may be made in that direction to remind the
peacekeepers that the host's pleasure must not be taken for granted.
Some of this, of course, may be no more than the working-out of a
natural bureaucratic imperative in a relatively favourable environment; and some of it may be directed to the outside world. However,
it would be surprising if it was wholly unrelated to a regime's wish and
need to cut a dash in its local political context.

The awkwardness which peacekeeping missions sometimes
encounter in their dealings with host officials may be partly explained
on this ground. So may the occasional difficulties over the extension
of a mandate – as happened in the early days with UNDOF and also
to some extent with UNEF II. The absence of a status of forces
agreement with Syria in respect of UNDOF may also have something
to do with a Syrian desire to be able to put the force on occasional
tenterhooks. However, none of this has been taken to such an extent
as to make life intolerable for a mission (and it could be politically
very difficult for the UN or any other parent body to justify its
withdrawal on this ground). Nor has any host government had such
urgent domestic needs that it has demanded a mission's withdrawal.

Over-strong Peacekeeping

One thing a host side wants to feel very sure about, however, is that if
it does ask a peacekeeping mission to go, that wish will be immediately respected. In most circumstances a host state will probably be
able to enforce such a desire, by making life hard for the mission as
well as by making representations to the contributor states; but no
host wants to be put in that position. Thus, if there is even the hint of a

suspicion that a peacekeeping body might make difficulties about going when asked, problems are likely to occur; and if such a suspicion arises at the invitation stage, the invitation will probably be unforthcoming. The importance of this matter was widely overlooked in 1967 by those who poured buckets of criticism over U Thant for agreeing to Egypt's request for the withdrawal of UNEF I. Had U Thant refused or even prevaricated, it would, quite apart from any more immediate consequence, have made potential hosts far more reluctant to invite peacekeepers on to their soil.

There is one exception to the argument just advanced, but as befits its nature it occurred in very exceptional circumstances. That was the agreement of Egypt and Israel, in their 1979 Peace Treaty, to invite the UN to watch over their border (almost entirely from the Egyptian side), and their undertaking 'not to request [its] withdrawal'. Any withdrawal was only to occur on the authority of the UN Security Council 'with the affirmative vote of the five Permanent Members'[19] (which went beyond the Council's practice of not regarding an abstention as a veto). As it happened, this idea fell through, but the provisions regarding its replacement – the non-UN Multinational Force and Observers (MFO) – made it clear that withdrawal could be effected 'only by mutual consent of both parties'.[20]

Generally, however, a host wants to ensure that there are no legal obstacles to its getting rid of a peacekeeping body if it wishes to do so, and to have confidence that the peacekeepers will in fact go. If the large Syrian force which has been in Lebanon since 1976 is regarded as a peacekeeping body,[21] then a bad example has been set. For although Syria lost its Arab League mandate in 1982, and its authority from Lebanon in 1983, its troops are still very much in place; but fortunately, most commentators do not regard the Syrians as fulfilling a peacekeeping role. Their behaviour, however, is a reminder to potential hosts of the risk of having large numbers of foreign troops on one's soil, especially if they come from just one state which is also a next-door neighbour.

It happens that Lebanon provides a more appropriate warning about the imaginable perils, for a host, of peacekeeping activity. The non-UN Multinational Force (MNF) which went to Beirut in August 1982 did a very good job and left within a month; but on its almost immediate return as MNF II, it had, within a year, slipped away from a peacekeeping to a very different kind of role. Instead of trying to hold the ring, two of its contingents moved, in effect, into combat on behalf of one of the local contestants – a development which led to the breakup of the Force and the rather ignominious departure of the Americans and the French. In this particular case they had taken up arms on behalf of the government which had invited them; but potential hosts cannot have failed to reflect that a peacekeeping body which moves beyond peacekeeping will not always necessarily do so in favour of the inviting government. They might also note that the temptation to behave in this way is much more real for some contributory states than for others: if the United States is crossed it has the wherewithal to try to exact retribution; that privilege is not open to, say, Fiji.

The behaviour, or misbehaviour, of MNF II is somewhat reminiscent of what happened to the UN Force in the Congo (ONUC) in the early 1960s. For here, too, a body (still the biggest peacekeeping force to date) which went in with one mandate ended up by taking forceful action which had the effect of ending the secession of the rich Congolese Province of Katanga. It is also very arguable that that was the intention. As the Secretary-General at the time said later, large sums of money had been expended by the UN in the Congo 'primarily to prevent the secession of Katanga'.[22] It happened that that was exactly what the Government of the Congo, and virtually all other states, wanted; but it caused much concern among some West European states; and it was a general reminder that a peacekeeping operation can be the thin end of the wedge with no guarantee that the wedge will be palatable to the host.

In one or two respects, ONUC's activity was in fact very unpalatable to the Government of the Congo, and left unhappy memories in a number of other states, particularly in Africa, which to this day colour their attitude to international peacekeeping. This had both a general and a specific aspect.

The general anxiety was that at various times, and in a number of eyes, the UN was seen as acting in a high-handed way towards the Congo – as if it were trying to take over authority in the country. Particularly in the early months of 1961, several of the UN's efforts were ill-received: the activities of its Conciliation Commission; the authorisation given to ONUC to use force, if necessary, to prevent civil war; and the appointment of a commission to inquire into the death of the former Congolese Prime Minister, Lumumba. Alongside these perceived improprieties, there was often an assumption that what was going on was the use, by the United States, of the UN for its own purposes, and the emergence in August 1961 of a legitimate Government which was sympathetic to the West was seen as an endorsement of this analysis. As an Indian scholar has written, 'From beginning to end, the shadow of the greatest Power on earth, the United States, loomed large in the UN operations in the Congo.... The result was that [they] could not help becoming an instrument to achieve United States' foreign policy goals'.[23]

The more specific and very chilling worry was that the UN had been instrumental in the overthrow, early in September 1960, of Lumumba, the very left-wing Prime Minister. Certainly ONUC's action when both the President and the Prime Minister announced the deposition of the other worked to Lumumba's considerable disadvantage. Within a week the Canadian Ambassador to Germany was writing that 'Already the United Nations has demonstrated in the Congo that it can in Africa act as the executive agent of the free world.'[24] Others saw it this way too, but drew very different conclusions. A few years later, in connection with a crisis in his own country which was not totally dissimilar to that which had occurred in Congo, the President of Yemen was said to be 'fearful of a United Nations "presence" on Yemeni soil similar to the one in the Congo'.[25] Towards the end of the decade, during the Nigerian civil war, the Secretary-General's Military Adviser asked the President of Nigeria if he had considered inviting the UN to involve itself in some way in the problem. The response was negative on the grounds that the President did not want to be removed.[26] Clearly, although its exact significance is difficult to gauge, the UN's behaviour in the Congo made a very adverse impression in Africa, and elsewhere. The chance of something of the same kind happening again may well be in the minds of potential and actual hosts as they contemplate the possible domestic repercussions of having a peacekeeping force on their soil; and the way in which MNF II comported itself in Lebanon during 1983–84 does nothing to provide reassurance on this score.

REMEDIES

Many of the problems which have been analysed above are, to some extent, of an in-built kind. It is in the nature of peacekeeping that there are going to be some difficulties between the visitors and the hosts. Internationally, too, peacekeeping has certain repercussions which cannot be wished away; but it should be possible to minimise the problems, and in that connection four brief concluding points will be made.

The first is that the problems must be seen in perspective. Nothing has been said directly in this paper about the advantages of peace-keeping operations – both for the parties and the whole international society; but they do have very considerable advantages. Put most generally, what peacekeeping offers is help with the maintenance of stability, and possibly with its creation. That is often seen as of considerable value, and may have more than local significance. The potential customers, as it were, should be left in no doubt that this is something of which, very probably, they can avail themselves. The goods should be prominently displayed in the shop window.

Second, it should be emphasised at every opportunity that there is nothing demeaning in accepting the help of an impartial third party. Neither conceptually nor practically is a state diminished by involving peacekeepers in its affairs. Indeed it can be argued that, as in the case of individuals, a willingness to do so is a sign of maturity. One remains in control, but is sufficiently aware of the problem to recognise that it would be sensible to get some assistance of a non-directive kind. The point may even be made that international matters are often so important that it is a mark of responsibility to take advantage of all such help as is available. There is nothing 'unmanly' in buying these particular goods.

Third, in fairness to both the hosts and the peacekeepers, it is important that a 'contract' be set out as clearly as possible. This is not so much a call for full and unambiguous mandates, as the political situation in which peacekeeping operations are launched may make those very hard to obtain; but in one way or another – for example, through the UN Secretary-General's initial report on how an opera-tion might be arranged – the way in which the peacekeepers are to operate should be fully understood by the states concerned. On the other hand the obligation of the host to respect the mission should be emphasised very firmly, and in this connection it might also be helpful if a commitment to negotiate and sign a status of forces agreement was sought at the very outset from any potential host.[27] The terms and conditions on which the goods are provided must be very clear to all concerned.

Finally it must also be made abundantly evident that these goods are of sound quality. There must be no hidden dangers involved in buying them, no 'catch' in the transaction. What this means is that there must be complete and unquestioned respect for the principle that a peacekeeping body operates on the basis of impartiality and non-forcefulness (except in self-defence – and that must be strictly defined). There must be no suggestion at all that such a body might incline in one direction or the other, or that it might try to impose itself on the situation. It must also be clear, unless it has been specifically and freely agreed to the contrary, that the peacekeepers will only stay for as long as they are wanted. Only in this way will hosts develop confidence in the compatibility of peacekeeping with their very basic concern about the independence and integrity of their states. Talk of toughening-up a peacekeeping operation, of the need to implement the will of the international community, can only damage this process. There may well be a place for action of this tougher sort; but there is a fundamental distinction between it and the activity which has become known as peacekeeping. There is no real half-way house between them, and it is in everybody's interest that that fact is widely recognised.

NOTES AND REFERENCES

1. For a general discussion of peacekeeping, see the writer's 'Unit-Veto Dominance in United Nations Peace-keeping', in L. Finkelstein (ed.), *Politics in the United Nations System* (Durham: Duke University Press, 1988) pp. 75–105.

2. See, for example, the writer's 'UN Action for Peace. II Law and Order Forces', *The World Today*, vol. 18 (1962) no. 12, pp. 505–7.

3. See H. C. Lodge, *The Storm Has Many Eyes* (New York: Norton, 1973) p. 137, referring to *Khrushchev Remembers* (Boston: Little, Brown, 1970) pp. 450–1.

4. See N. A. Pelcocovits, *Peacekeeping on Arab–Israeli Front* (Boulder: Westview, 1984) p. 24.

5. O. Bull, *War and Peace in the Middle East* (London: Cooper, 1976) p. xv.

6. Y. Evron, *War and Intervention in Lebanon* (London: Croom Helm, 1987) pp. 81–2.

7. A. Levran, 'UN Forces and Israel's Security', *The Jerusalem Quarterly* (1986) no. 37, p. 65.

8. Ibid., p. 74.

9. See the writer's *Interminable Interim: The UN Force in Lebanon* (London: Centre for Security and Conflict Studies, 1988) p. 13. In this connection it is interesting to note the observation that a 'survey of Norwegian soldiers who had served with the first UNEF suggested that partiality on the side of one party might be fostered by *not* [emphasis added] having contact with that party': C. Moskos, *Peace Soldiers* (University of Chicago Press, 1976) p. 165, fn. 6. Moskos refers to a paper by S. Witgil, 'Neutrality and Partisanship of the Impartial

Soldier', which was presented at the Seventh World Congress of Sociology, Varna, Bulgaria, 1970.

10. B. Urquhart, *A Life in Peace and War* (London: Weidenfeld and Nicolson, 1987) p. 211.

11. W. Burdett, *Encounter with the Middle East* (London: Deutsch, 1970) p. 194.

12. Ibid., p. 208.

13. S. Chan, *The Commonwealth Observer Group in Zimbabwe* (Gweru: Mambo Press, 1985) p. 15.

14. UN Security Council, Official Records, 435th Meeting, p. 10.

15. L. Pearson, *Memoirs, Volume II 1948–1957* (London: Gollancz, 1973) p. 247.

16. B. Urquhart, *Hammarskjöld* (London: Bodley Head, 1973) p. 186.

17. Ibid., p. 188.

18. See the writer's *Sovereign Statehood* (London: Allen and Unwin, 1986); in particular Chapter 9.

19. Treaty of Peace, Article IV.2, quoted in R. C. R. Siekmann (ed.), *Basic Documents in United Nations and Related Peace-Keeping Forces* (Dordrecht: Nijhoff, 1985) p. 229.

20. M. Tabory, *The Multinational Force and Observers in the Sinai* (Boulder: Westview, 1986) p. 107.

21. One writer who does so regard it, when enjoying the support of the Arab League, is I. Pogany, *The Arab League and Peacekeeping in the Lebanon* (Aldershot: Avebury, 1987) p. 96.

22. Quoted in *UN Monthly Chronicle* , vol. VII (1970) no. 2, p. 36.

23. K. P. Saksena, *The United Nations and Collective Security* (New Delhi: D.K. Publications, 1974) p. 272.

24. Quoted in E. Reid, *Time of Fear and Hope: The Making of the North Atlantic Treaty 1947–1949* (Toronto: McClelland and Stewart, 1977) p. 251.

25. C. V. McMullen, *Resolution of the Yemen Crisis, 1963* (Washington, DC: Institute for the Study of Diplomacy, Georgetown University, 1980) p. 46.

26. I. J. Rikhye, speaking at the Royal Institute of International Affairs, London, 28 September 1976.

27. In this connection it is interesting to note that the Secretary-General's report on the modalities for the establishment and operation of the UN Iran–Iraq Military Observer Group (which was approved by the Security Council in Resolution 619) states that status of forces agreements should be concluded 'without delay'. UN Document S/20093, 7 August 1988, para. 5(c).

10   Peacekeepers and Local Populations: Some Comments on UNIFIL

Marianne Heiberg

INTRODUCTION

Although peacekeeping operations share many common elements, experiences from past operations can never provide a full blueprint for present or future operations. However, some operations are clearly less complicated than others. Arguably the most straightforward are those operations, such as the UN Disengagement Observer Force (UNDOF) and Multinational Force and Observers (MFO), set up to monitor a buffer zone – usually demilitarised and frequently sparsely populated – between former combatants, ideally two sovereign states, and established as a result of peace treaties or disengagement accords negotiated between them. However, in a completely different category are those operations launched often, although not necessarily, in densely populated areas in order to contain and stabilise a crisis in which the destructiveness of regional confrontation and the violence of civil war have become enmeshed. Such operations, which include UNIFIL and the Multinational Force (MNF) in Beirut, present severe political and military challenges. There is nothing straightforward about them. The appropriate agreements and encouraging political symmetries are absent. However, a cursory glance at the entangled political geography of areas such as Afghanistan, Kampuchea, Central America and Namibia suggests that such operations may increasingly come to represent the rule, rather than the exception. The challenges involved require a rethinking of peacekeeping both on the military and political levels.

With this in mind, this paper will focus on the relationship between UNIFIL and the culturally complex local populations with which it deals. It should be noted that this aspect of peacekeeping has received very little attention in the literature. Yet it can be convincingly argued that the nature of the relationship a peacekeeping force achieves with the population within its area of control is a decisive element in determining the operation's success or failure. Stated in a nutshell: a relationship to local civilians built on communication and confidence is a necessary factor for success; a relationship characterised by mounting hostility, suspicion and lack of communication is a sufficient cause for failure. Critically, however, the local population concerned is not a homogeneous, seamless or indeed self-evident entity. The human and political equations involved are multilayered, highly intricate, often contradictory and shifting, and not necessarily fully visible.

This paper will proceed in two parts. First, I shall discuss certain general political and economic characteristics of the relations between UNIFIL and local Lebanese, focusing on their implications for a UNIFIL withdrawal. An implicit theme in this section is that the presence over time of a peacekeeping force probably inevitably and usually unintentionally helps restructure the society in which it operates. The analysis will then move to a more detailed examination of certain specific features of UNIFIL and its impact on local attitudes. It must be noted that whereas the southern Lebanese are ethnically and culturally differentiated, the same holds true for the multinational forces of UNIFIL. Each national battalion brings with it its own particular cultural complex and set of assumptions, the distinctiveness of which is not erased by a UN uniform. Some of the material presented in this article is highly controversial, sensitive, possibly provocative and quite possibly inadequate. Therefore it must be stressed that responsibility for the observations, judgements and faults of this article are solely mine.

The Security Zone

The background to UNIFIL and the major events that have shaped its evolution are well known and need not be repeated here; but perhaps a short description of Israel's security zone, initially established in 1985 after the partial Israeli withdrawal, might nonetheless be useful.

The security zone, which comprises the old enclave together with parts of UNIFIL's western Area of Operation (AO) and all of its eastern AO, is the central military feature of south Lebanon and has implications for all aspects of the daily life of the area's inhabitants. Moreover for the foreseeable future the security zone will remain part of the military and political landscape of southern Lebanon and will continue to constitute the major challenge to UNIFIL's authority and mandate.

Sketched briefly, the security zone is based on a chain of heavily fortified compounds situated on high-lying ground and weaves some 2 to 10 kilometres into Lebanon. The wadis and valleys in the areas lying below and to the front of these compounds are treated as free fire zones. Several reports indicate that the Israelis are involved in a deliberate effort to depopulate certain villages immediately surrounding the compounds in order to make this free fire zone easier to control.

The present policy of the Israel Defence Force (IDF) is to base the static defence of the compounds on the South Lebanese Army (SLA). Recently the training, tactics and discipline of the SLA have been greatly improved and, currently, Shiite Muslims seem to comprise the majority of SLA's foot soldiers. The eventual success of the SLA in managing and defending the compounds will be decisive for the human and financial costs Israel must sustain in order to maintain the zone. Mobile defence remains largely the preserve of the IDF. In addition to the 1000 to 1500 Israeli soldiers assigned to Lebanon on a rotating basis, the compounds can be quickly reinforced from Israel and can also be used as forward command posts for an all-out attack on the area, if and when required.

Like all forces of occupation, the IDF has enhanced its effectiveness through an extensive network of local informers. Local collaboration is obtained through a series of both positive and negative sanctions. Positive sanctions include the right of family members, especially those who reside in the enclave, to work in Israel, provision of free medical care and coverage of family education expenses. These advantages frequently mean the difference between family survival and family destitution. In addition recruits to the SLA receive a monthly payment of approximately $120 to $150 per month, a salary which is roughly equivalent to the current salary of, for instance, the deputy director of the Central Bank of Lebanon. Negative sanctions include the withdrawal of the right to work in Israel, and so on, for all family members as well as the risk of detention, interrogation and eventual confinement in the prison at El Khiam in which the widespread use of torture is sweepingly and convincingly documented. Over the years the IDF has also built up extensive genealogical charts of the inhabitants of southern Lebanon which, in particular, note the family relationships between those who live in the enclave and those who reside outside of it.

From an Israeli point of view the security zone is regarded as highly successful. It can be maintained on a level of financial and, very importantly, human, costs that are considered acceptable. It also satisfies certain critical domestic political requirements. Arguably because of Israel's domestic constraints, a full withdrawal in 1985 was not attainable. Regardless, the policy is not controversial. The wide-spread consensus is that the security zone works and, therefore, experimentation with alternative solutions – such as UNIFIL deploy-ment down to the international border – is unnecessary.

A critical aspect of the security zone in relation to this paper is that the attitudes of the local population toward UNIFIL vary according to where people live in reference to the zone. Currently, for those who live in proximity to its boundaries, the prime value of UNIFIL is the protection and safeguard from abuse the Force offers. Indeed UNIFIL is the only protection they possess. For those who live further removed, UNIFIL is viewed more ambivalently. Possibly as a reflection of UNIFIL's success, the function of the Force is less understood. Its interference with daily life – for instance, movement control – is less accepted. The area seems peaceful. The disturbances that do occur are often due to the local Lebanese themselves, for instance, Afwaj Al-Muqamah Al-Lubnaniyya (AMAL) and, as such, are regarded as internal Lebanese affairs.

PART 1

General Observations

In examining UNIFIL's interaction with local Lebanese, the first and indeed most obvious point to note is that UNIFIL is an alien element in the area. The 6000 UNIFIL personnel are drawn from eight different nations, none of which, with the exception of France, have historical connections to the region. Ironically, perhaps, the Lebanese often have a much better insight into the distant national cultures of the various UNIFIL battalions – or at least into the ways in which these cultures are manifested in Lebanon – than the battalion members have of their Lebanese hosts. Only a small minority of UNIFIL personnel receive satisfactory political or cultural training about the area prior to their arrival. Nonetheless imported UNIFIL has been in the area for over ten years. Inevitably during this period the Force has been sucked into the economic and political fabric of the wider society in which it operates and of which it has become an integral part.

Some Political Aspects

Without doubt the most important aspect of the relation between UNIFIL and local residents is the much needed security and physical protection the Force has provided. Despite the Israeli invasion of 1982, southern Lebanon has been one of the most stable areas in the country. Currently some 300 000–400 000 people reside within UNIFIL's AO. The exact number varies according to the season and the degree of violence and disruption occurring elsewhere in Lebanon.

UNIFIL has also been critical for rebuilding a local political infrastructure in the south. At the time of UNIFIL's deployment in 1978, legitimate political leadership in the area had all but disappeared. The new leaders were brash young men, often Palestinian or Lebanese from outside the area, who based their claims to power and authority on the magnitude of their firepower. Following its mandate, UNIFIL insisted upon upholding Lebanese legality (albeit in a manner the Lebanese themselves rarely practised) and, therefore, conducted its relations with the local population strictly through the official local leaders, in particular the Mouktars and the village mayors. UNIFIL brought the Mouktars new resources, including important financial ones, prestige and, because of UNIFIL's protection, independence. This renovated political infrastructure provided the south with a significant degree of stability and local citizens with a viable option for political neutrality. Notably, until recently many Mouktars mounted considerable political resistance to the Israeli occupation, staunchly refusing to deliver pro-Israeli militias. Instead they viewed their interests and loyalties better served within the context of UNIFIL.

However, UNIFIL increasingly has come to function as a pseudo-government for the south whose chances of being replaced by the appropriate authorities in the foreseeable future seem remote. This fact – together with the considerable military and, not least, economic resources UNIFIL commands – means that the Force has become a powerful agent of legitimation in the area. This has had a range of implications, among which are the following.

First, the present set of Mouktars were elected early in the 1970s and for the most part are products of a political society that has largely ceased to exist and which some authors have described as semi-feudal. During the last ten years the south has been transformed by sweeping economic and political changes. The traditional political system based on landownership and certain forms of clientelism has to a large extent broken down. Hence most Mouktars currently represent neither the population under their jurisdiction nor the political trends and forces that are reshaping southern society. Instead they are often viewed as codicils of an ossified, increasingly irrelevant, political structure now bordering on collapse.

However, UNIFIL continues to extend to the Mouktars the exclusive legitimate right to represent the requirements of local residents and mediate between them and the Force. Therefore, the Mouktars and the system of patronage and clientelism, through which they traditionally gained and exercised influence and power, are now largely sustained through the Mouktars' continued relationship to UNIFIL and, crucially, through access to UNIFIL's resources.[1] As a result and in contrast to its previous experience, UNIFIL may inadvertently become instrumental in delaying development of the political process in the south.[2]

Second, UNIFIL does, of course, recognise that new types of political leaders have emerged in the south. In the western part these leaders are usually connected to the Shiite AMAL and have genuine local support. In the eastern part of UNIFIL's AO – enclosed in the security zone and monitored by the Norwegian battalion, NORBATT – they are connected to the SLA and to the much feared and somewhat obscure organisation called the General Security Services, or GSS.[3] The GSS is composed mainly of renegade Lebanese who collect information for the Israelis and coerce locals into submission on various levels. Its support is mainly built on intimidation.

However, UNIFIL has had much more difficulty in identifying precisely who these new leaders are and the nature and character of the leadership they offer. Thus, in the Western AO UNIFIL occasionally accepts as AMAL 'leaders' individuals whose claims to such positions are not fully justified by either their relation to a political following or to AMAL. Liaison with UNIFIL provides a local leader and his faction with authoritative stature in relation to the wider political balance and in relation to rivals. Extending recognition, through liaison, to the wrong faction or wrong faction leader not only may lead eventually to a violent correction of the resulting distortion in the status quo by the aggrieved party, but also to an increasing manipulation of the battalion to serve sectarian gains.

In the eastern AO, NORBATT has accepted the claims of the GSS – many of whose members in a normal society would be dismissed as dangerous psychopaths – legitimately to represent the IDF and, thus, unwillingly has abetted this organisation in its disagreeable endeavours. Unlike the SLA which can only enter the AO unarmed unless accompanied by the IDF, NORBATT permits the GSS, fully armed, free access to its territory.

Finally, in order to protect civilians and prevent a possible escalation of confict, UNIFIL often moves in quickly to contain armed confrontations between local political factions. By so doing, however, the Force has to some extent prevented political re-adjustments – a process of fine tuning between political competitors – from taking place. This is one reason, among many, why the political constellation of forces in place in the south at times does not correspond to the real political and military resources these forces control. In south Lebanon such a state of affairs is inherently unstable.[4] In this context Lebanon can be compared to a tribal society in which the amount of territory a tribe commands corresponds to the amount that can directly be defended.

The implications of the above three points are discussed below.

Some Economic Aspects

The traditional economic system of the south was based on agriculture with an overlay of commerce of both the legal and illegal varieties. Currently agriculture is disappearing as a means of gaining a livelihood. The decline of agriculture is, of course, a general phenomenon throughout the Mediterranean area; but in south Lebanon it has been accelerated by a range of special factors.

First and foremost has been the effects of more than 15 years of social disruption and violence beginning in the early 1970s with Israeli bombing raids on southern villages in retaliation for Palestine Liberation Organization (PLO) attacks on Israel. Second, the current political and military situation in the south makes access to traditional markets difficult and, at times, impossible. In the AMAL-controlled west, produce must go through several check posts, which also often operate as customs posts, before reaching the urban markets in Tyre, Sidon or Beirut. At each check post 'taxes' are demanded and collected. In the SLA-controlled areas, in addition to the payment of 'taxes' at check posts, individuals are required to seek special permits in order to leave the area, permits which generally are not granted to persons under suspicion. Occasionally entire villages are placed under suspicion. For instance, the village of Chebaa, near the Syrian border, is forced to sell its entire crop of high quality cherries to an approved SLA middleman who buys the crop locally at Leb £50 a kilo (spring 1988) and resells the cherries the next day in Beirut for Leb £150 a kilo. Third, incomes from agricultural work, which average only some $30 to $50 per month, have fallen considerably below the average household income required for subsistence, which has been estimated at approximately $70 to $80 per month.[5] Moreover, because of the availability of more attractive and lucrative employment opportunities, agricultural labour at key points in the agricultural cycle is difficult to obtain in any case.

Not surprisingly, throughout the south there is evidence not only of a dramatic decline of agriculture, but also of a move away from cash cropping to subsistence farming, the surplus of which, if any, is sold locally.

Yet despite the erosion of the south's traditional economic base, the area, which historically has been one of the poorest in Lebanon, is experiencing an unprecedented prosperity. A construction boom – largely in the form of vast private houses – together with a considerable expansion of commerce is taking place. Although pockets of poverty do exist, people on the whole are well fed, clothed and housed; but the prosperity of the south bears little, if any, relation to its productivity.

One source of employment is the militias. As mentioned previously, a member of the SLA receives about $120 monthly – paid in dollars. Until Iranian funding ceased, foot soldiers in the Hezbollah received a similar level of remuneration. AMAL is also reported as paying its members reasonably although levels of remuneration seem to vary considerably between the different AMAL factions.

However, most other important sources of the south's new found prosperity are all contingent on UNIFIL. First and very importantly, the protection and stability UNIFIL affords means that the area has become an investment target for Lebanese expatriates as well as wealthy Beiruti businessmen. Money is usually invested in property, new houses and commercial establishments of various sorts with substantial multiplier effects for the regional economy as a whole.

Second, and perhaps more importantly – exact figures for comparison are, of course, unavailable – UNIFIL injects some $35 to $45 million annually directly into the regional economy.[6] It must also be remembered that the area involved is a very small one indeed. This sum is injected in four forms. First are the purchases made by UNIFIL soldiers while serving in Lebanon, purchases which have been largely responsible for the mushrooming of commercial establishments throughout the area. Second, UNIFIL purchases locally most of its fresh produce, such as vegetables and fruit, as well as a good deal of building materials; for instance, cement blocks and sand for sandbags. Third, UNIFIL provides employment for several hundred local civilians who work as cooks, gardeners, translators, cleaners and so forth. Fourth, certain battalions, such as the Finnish and Norwegian, provide considerable funds for humanitarian and development assistance. This assistance ranges from food to destitute families, sewage systems and medicines to the construction of Muslim prayer shelters and Christian Churches.[7]

The multiplier effects of all these transactions have been enormous and to a large extent have replaced agriculture as a fundamental pillar of the south's economy. Arguably, UNIFIL currently represents the biggest, single financial resource the south possesses. Moreover, it is a financial resource that carries few social overheads. Tellingly, much of the southern economy, in particular the commercial sector, is now operated in American dollars rather than Lebanese pounds.

Implications for Withdrawal

It must be stressed that the issue of whether or not UNIFIL should have been deployed in 1978 – and many argued that it should not have been – is quite distinct from the issue as to whether UNIFIL should now be withdrawn. As mentioned earlier, UNIFIL has become an integral part of the south. In a wide range of ways the residents of the south have become directly or indirectly dependent on the Force for their protection, political influence and economic livelihood. Hence UNIFIL's removal would carry the risks of highly dangerous, radical surgery. From just brief consideration of the economic and political dimensions summarised above, certain conclusions, although, of course, speculative, seem to emerge.

At the political level withdrawal would probably provoke an intense and complex civil war. The legal political system based on the Mouktars and the remnants of central authority present in the south would disintegrate. The political and military vacuum left by UNIFIL would be ferociously contested by the numerous over-armed and over-eager political factions and militias that inhabit the area. Old scores between neighbours would be settled and new political leaders and militia groupings would be brought down to size or simply eliminated. One result would be a massive dislocation of civilians.

A UNIFIL withdrawal would also compel Israel to make major reinforcements to the security zone which would involve a significant escalation of costs both financially and in terms of human lives. The zone itself would probably be extended northwards and the areas used as free fire zones greatly expanded. The possibility of direct confrontation with Syria would also be increased. On the economic level the prosperity so visibly evident would simply vanish.

In broad outline, therefore, the results of a UNIFIL withdrawal could well be three-fold: (1) because of endemic violence and economic collapse, southern Lebanon up to the Litani River would be largely depopulated; (2) the dangers of a regional conflagration between Israel and Syria would be augmented; and (3) the international attention and spotlight UNIFIL represents would be turned off. The personal involvement of the international community in the fate of Lebanon would to a large extent cease.

PART 2

'Each Battalion a Kingdom'

So far UNIFIL has been discussed as if the Force were a uniform entity. However, this is not the case and local Lebanese both in their attitudes and behaviour clearly distinguish between UNIFIL's different national components.

Unlike a regular military unit which represents one military culture under a unified national command, UNIFIL contains eight different cultures under a mixed command structure. Although formal command over the national units is transferred to the UN, in practice this does not really occur. Because national military commands and political authorities remain ultimately responsible in the eyes of sensitive, domestic public opinion for the fate of their UNIFIL contingents in the field, not surprisingly they in practice retain ultimate control. One result is that commanding officers enjoy an autonomy on the battalion level with regard to the Force Commander far in excess of that found in regular armies. Therefore the discontinuities are considerable between the instructions UNIFIL headquarters issues and the actions of national battalions on one hand and between the national battalions themselves on the other.

The variations, so apparent to the outside observer, between the various national battalions on the ground stem from a wide array of factors. Needless to say, motivation for peacekeeping duty in general is quite different in those units in which service in Lebanon is voluntary – such as the Irish, Norwegian and Finnish – and those units which, regardless of the preferences of their soldiers, are simply ordered to the country – such as the Ghanaians and Nepalese. Other factors relate to historical experience. Ireland's domestic situation, for example, has meant that the Irish army is extensively instructed in techniques relevant to internal security. Many of these techniques are very appropriate to UNIFIL's peacekeeping role. In contrast, French military training is heavily influenced by French experiences in Vietnam and, especially, Algeria. Not surprisingly, French military behaviour in Lebanon often carries clear vestiges of these prior ordeals. In Lebanon, the French are frequently chided for acting as if they were surrounded by enemies and, therefore, becoming overtly provocative, a military style which often tempts local Lebanese militias to competitive exhibits of pugnacity.

Military culture also varies between those battalions – such as the French and Fijian – recruited from countries with professional armies and those – like the Finns and Norwegians – which come from countries with conscript armies. In the first case the units tend to be comprised of professional combat troops. In the latter most of the soldiers are civilians. Along with a rudimentary military training, the personnel of these battalions also come equipped with a host of civilian skills ranging from journalism and architecture to animal husbandry and gourmet cooking.

The cultural diversity between the battalions is most readily illustrated by the diversity of religious affiliation. This ranges from the secular Lutheranism of the Nordic battalions, through the Catholicism of the Irish and the fundamental Methodism of the Fijians, to the Hinduism and Buddhism of the Nepalese. Notably, although GHANBATT has a smattering of Muslims among its soldiers, only SENBATT (Senegalese battalion), which has been dismantled, shared the same religious conviction as the majority of the Lebanese host population.

Cultural diversity also serves as a source of frequent misunderstandings inside UNIFIL. I shall take the example of the Nepalese Battalion (NEPBATT) in some detail, not because it is in any way extreme, but because it illustrates so clearly the cultural discrepancies that occur.

In Nepalese culture ritual distance is a critical organising concept in social relations. In NEPBATT the significance of the ritual distance between officers and men is manifested in a range of ways which particularly alarm baffled Western UNIFIL personnel. The startlingly low level of maintenance at Nepalese positions is one example. Rubbish is discarded immediately outside kitchen windows and dining rooms. Kitchens tend to be dark with accumulated grime. Many doors hang limply on their hinges or have fallen off entirely. At one position the five toilets available were used until each in turn overflowed and the unusable cubicle simply closed. No attempt had been made to unblock the toilets or clean up the human spillage.

In addition to the lack of routine maintenance in NEPBATT it is the apparent lack of all initiative, particularly among the lower ranks, to ameliorate the accruing discomforts that most bewilders outsiders. The most common example cited is the case of two dormitory prefabs located adjacent to each other. One prefab had been without doors and several windows for the entire winter, which in southern Lebanon is icily bitter. The adjoining prefab had both doors and windows. The one without doors was occupied, the one in adequate repair was not.

Because they collide with commonplace Western notions concerning, for instance, cleanliness and individual welfare, these situations are difficult to understand unless the attitudes and the assumptions of the Nepalese themselves are used as a starting point. Many factors are involved, but the Nepalese caste system and the concepts of ritual distance and occupational hierarchy are common to several of them.

One factor involves what is dirt or dirty. Whereas Western culture contains a ritually neutral definition of dirt,[8] for instance, rancid cooking fat on kitchen walls, in Nepalese culture the definition of dirt is ritually laden. What matters is not so much the rancid fat, but whether the fat is vegetable or animal based. The critical opposition is not between the clean and the dirty, but the pure and the polluting. Purity and pollution are spiritual states rather than physical ones. Excrement spilling from clogged latrines is not *per se* dirty. It is the act of cleaning up the mess that is polluting and thereby ritually dangerous. Such activity can only be performed by those castes that are already polluted and defiled.

The notion of purity and pollution involves a stratified relationship between people or rather groups of people, the castes. Indeed the notion provides the essential legitimation for the caste system. Castes are ranked in terms of relative purity and purity is defined in terms of distance from those individuals who deal with polluting or low status things. Leather workers and toilet cleaners form the bottom of this ritual hierarchy. Brahmins who deal solely with the spiritual form its apex.

It is also very important to note that each caste constitutes an occupational grouping and consequently all occupations are also ritually ranked. Street cleaners form one caste, woodworkers form another and all jobs are seen as highly specialised. People do not move from one to another. Hindu culture has no place for the general handyman.

With these considerations in mind, it becomes fairly clear why routine maintenance is not and, because of the cultural assumptions that obtain, cannot be carried out in NEPBATT. Soldiers are soldiers – a relatively high status occupation. They are not meant to be sweepers, carpenters or plumbers. Crafts in general are of low status. The removal of human wastes can only be performed by members of the lowest caste.

Within this context, the concept of human welfare is anchored in, among other things, the preservation of ritual hierarchy upon which harmonious social order depends. Welfare is much more concerned with protection from pollution and loss of status than with, for example, provision of warm sleeping quarters and three course lunches, the lack of which so distresses UNIFIL logistics.

In addition to contrasts in culture and military training, the varying levels of economic development of the troop-contributing countries are critical for understanding the dissimilarities between the UNIFIL battalions. While Norway and Finland have a Gross Domestic Product per capita in excess of $10,000, Ghana and Nepal have a GDP per capita of $520 and $154 respectively (1983–84 figures).[9]

These economic differentials seem to have serious implications for UNIFIL's military coherence on a range of levels.

All UNIFIL troop-contributors are reimbursed at the same rate in the same manner. Full-rate reimbursement is $1000 per person per month. (Currently, because of the shortfall in the UNIFIL Special Account resulting from the non-payment of assessed contributions by certain member states, reimbursement to troop contributors is at a reduced rate of $600 per month.)

Although UN reimbursement is similar for all troop-contributing countries, the salaries which these countries in turn pay their UNIFIL contingents differ radically. French officers are by far the best paid. In addition to the free board and lodging all UNIFIL personnel are entitled to, a French officer earns just under $9000 per month. The Norwegians are the second best off. An officer receives a net monthly salary somewhat in excess of $4000, while an enlisted solider, who on the average is in his early twenties without dependents, can count on a net monthly pay cheque of approximately $1800.[10] These rates in turn are about 30 to 40 per cent higher than those which other Nordic UNIFIL personnel earn. The Ghanaians and Nepalese occupy the bottom end of the scale. A high-ranking Nepalese officer earns approximately $300 per month. The salaries of Nepalese enlisted men are far below this.

These salary differentials have far-reaching effects. Local Lebanese attitudes are certainly coloured by the spending power of the various UNIFIL battalions. Particularly in the areas outside of the artillery range of the security zone compounds, the various UNIFIL battalions are ranked in value according to the economic benefits local civilians can obtain from them. Such discriminations form a constant theme when local Lebanese discuss UNIFIL.

The economic disparities between the battalions also seem to contribute to the marked differences in their military performance. Many of those who receive least pay claim that dissimilarities in pay are a source of notable dissatisfaction. Because of low pay, many Ghanaians and Nepalese soldiers say they have little motivation to carry out their duties when risk is involved. Over-armed local militiamen are more than ready to counter perceived insults or improprieties on part of UNIFIL by opening fire. However, the relation between low pay and reluctance to face risk is not a simple one, nor is it always present. The Fijians behave with a fearlessness and courage that have captured the admiration of their UNIFIL colleagues and the awed respect of local Lebanese.

Salary differences also help produce a social hierarchy and reinforce separation between the battalions. Leisure activities that are readily affordable by, for instance, Norwegian soldiers – such as dining in local restaurants or a weekend holiday in Israel – are beyond the economic resources of, for example, a Ghanaian soldier. During my last visit to UNIFIL, a group of Ghanaian soldiers petitioned the Commanding Officer (CO) of NORBATT for permission to spend the entirety of their leave in NORBATT since they had no possibility of paying for a holiday. In contrast, three Norwegian soldiers had just returned from a stay in Tel Aviv where they had managed to spend $3000 to $5000 each in just under five days of lavish living, a not uncommon occurrence among the Norwegians. A nominal part of this money apparently went to 'hire' Ghanaian UNIFIL soldiers as bodyguards in order to protect the Norwegians from local Israeli reprisals when their alcohol-induced exuberance eclipsed all limits of the tolerable. In the words of one Norwegian:

> The Ghanaians, they were very happy. They sat there at our table (in the restaurant), didn't say much, and when they went dry, we bought them more drinks. But the Israelis, that was different! Whenever one of them came over and tried to complain, we would just snap our fingers. Then these two gigantic, black Ghanaian fellows – one was almost 2 meters tall – would stand up, lean over and growl fiercely. That pacified the Israelis alright.[11]

The relationship between economic remuneration and motivation for service in UNIFIL has another dimension which places severe strains on the internal solidarity of the Force. Economic remuneration is a core motivation for many UNIFIL soldiers. However, the manner in which this motivation is manifested differs from battalion to battalion according to culturally relative norms. Norwegians are motivated by high salaries and cheap Lebanese gold, Finns by the possibility of exporting a duty-free Mercedes Benz back to Finland. Without such fringe benefits it is doubtful that service in UNIFIL would be as popular as it is among Norwegians and Finns. Among certain battalions this dimension involves the pilfering of UNIFIL equipment and supplies on a large scale.

Pilfering can by no means be viewed only as a way to compensate for low salaries. It seems also to reflect a confluence of additional factors which include motivation and training for UN peacekeeping service, deficiencies in military leadership and, very importantly, cultural variations concerning what is or is not acceptable behaviour.

To take the case of GHANBATT: Ghanaian soldiers do not seek duty in Lebanon. Their units are assigned to UNIFIL. In Ghana training of the new contingent is conducted to a large extent by the new CO whose experience with UNIFIL is often limited to one short prior visit to the area. The encounter most Ghanaians have with Lebanon is not agreeable. Among other reasons, throughout the Middle East, Africans in general are allocated an exceedingly low status, an aspect of Arab culture of which the Ghanaians are fully aware.[12] One compensation – for many, the only compensation – for this enforced sojourn in a society regarded as disagreeable as well as dangerous is the opportunity to acquire goods which in Lebanon are cheap for later sale in Ghana where they are expensive or unavailable. While in UNIFIL the Ghanaians try to accumulate as many goods as possible from tape recorders and expensive liquor to refrigerators and other large domestic appliances. The money used for this end is taken from UN salaries as well as from cash resources brought from Ghana. Frequently Ghanaian soldiers come to Lebanon with resources pooled from their extended families who consider their kinsman's tour of duty with UNIFIL a profitable investment opportunity.

However, a significant portion of the items used in these exchanges are in fact UNIFIL property. Upon each rotation UNIFIL logistics has to undertake a major resupply of GHANBATT. The figures quoted for missing property ranged from 50 to 90 per cent of all moveable items and include toilet paper, clothes lockers, generators, air conditioners, spare parts and tools of all sorts. A member of UNIFIL's military police reported that a former high-ranking officer of GHANBATT had on one occasion been apprehended in Haifa attempting to load a four-wheel drive UN estate car for shipment back to Ghana.

The items pilfered from UNIFIL are either included in the general accumulation shipped for sale in Ghana or else are sold directly to Lebanese merchants. In fact, local traffic in UNIFIL goods has to a certain extent become institutionalised. Local merchants operate with standard prices for most stolen UNIFIL equipment although some bargaining is permitted. One local merchant claimed that, especially for construction tools, GHANBATT was the cheapest local supplier.

Needless to say, it was very difficult to assess how the Ghanaians themselves viewed this illicit trade. What I observed was that the comparative resale prices of, for example, generators, in Lebanon and Ghana respectively, provoked enthusiastic, detailed discussions among the Ghanaians. The impression I gained was that this activity was viewed as part of accepted procedure and, indeed, replicated patterns of behaviour common to the military inside Ghana. Although possibly illegal, trade in official property was certainly not judged as immoral.

The situation in NEPBATT is similar to that in GHANBATT but with significant cultural variations. Like the Ghanaians, the Nepalese are poorly trained for peacekeeping service in Lebanon.[13] Before arrival in UNIFIL, their instruction in peacekeeping techniques and on the situation in Lebanon is slight. Moreover few Nepalese have an adequate command of either English or French. Thus communication with other UNIFIL contingents is inhibited and communication with local civilians often impossible. Yet many Nepalese officers eagerly seek assignment to UNIFIL. Their motivations are numerous, but one, in common with the Norwegians and Finns, appears to be financial.

Unlike the Ghanaians, the Nepalese do not seem to conduct any significant trade in UNIFIL equipment. Also unlike the Ghanaians, the illicit trade that does occur seems to involve mainly Nepalese officers. What they principally trade in is foodstuffs destined for consumption by NEPBATT's enlisted men. Thus, while at NEP-BATT headquarters a typical lunch for officers will consist of a wide array of delicious Nepalese hot dishes together with an assortment of salads and desserts, the lunch served enlisted men is comprised mainly of a sparse portion of rice with possibly some vegetables and occasionally some meat or fish. On the one logistics inspection tour of NEPBATT AO which I accompanied, the food supplies of all the positions visited, with the exception of headquarters, were judged inadequate by UN standards and most of the food supplies delivered to the battalion were simply unaccounted for. The Norwegian captain in charge of supplies said that the inadequacy of food supplies was an unvarying feature at NEPBATT positions. Despite repeated admonitions to the Nepalese officers responsible, the situation never seemed to improve.

From the Nepalese viewpoint this situation might involve some irregularities, but it does not involve breaches in accepted norms and practices. Features of Nepalese culture and the rigid ritual and social distance that exists between individuals of high and low rank should again be noted. In Nepalese society notions of individual equality or common human dignity are not particularly germane. UN food rations are scaled to the appetites of hungry Americans and not to the more austere consumption patterns of Nepalese soldiers. Nepalese officers ensure that the men under their command receive food supplies that, by Nepalese standards, are regarded as sufficient both in terms of quantity and variety. The rest is viewed as surplus exchangeable on the local market for cash or bartered items.

Like in GHANBATT, trade in UN commodities is semi-institutionalised. Local merchants operate with more or less fixed prices for UN foodstuffs. Until 1986, when the Force Commander closed them down, three local shops – where Nepalese officers could exchange food for more durable consumer items – had established themselves at the entrance of NEPBATT Headquarters. The first was established as a concession to the widow of a local civilian employed by UNIFIL, who had been killed by Christian militias. The second was as a concession to a local merchant who argued that the widow's shop represented unfair competition. The third was owned by the man who owned the land upon which the previous two shops had been built.

That Nepalese officers sell foodstuffs and the Ghanaians abscond with large amounts of UN equipment is well known in UNIFIL. However, the subject is a source of intense embarrassment and is rarely discussed openly. Perhaps unfortunately for UNIFIL, it is also well-known among the Israeli Defence Forces, who use the alleged deficiencies of certain UNIFIL battalions as one argument against permitting UNIFIL deployment down to the border. For their part local Lebanese militiamen clearly recognise the possibilities of entrapping the UNIFIL personnel involved in illicit trade in a web of manipulation in order to serve sectarian purposes.

The effects in the field of the variations between the battalions already discussed are further exacerbated by their systems of rotation which, among other things, can cause severe problems of continuity between battalion contingents. There is no standardised UN system for rotating the battalion contingents in the field. Since in general UNIFIL's mandate comes up for renewal every six months, most battalions rotate on a six-month interval. Indeed this term of rotation is one of the unfortunate side-effects of UNIFIL's 'interim' nature. As one officer stated, 'It takes us at least four months to learn something about Lebanon so we can be effective, and then we use the remaining two months to pack up and go home.' Only FIJIBATT and FINBATT rotate on a different schedule.

In FIJIBATT the basic period of duty is one year; 50 per cent of the contingent is rotated in June, the remainder in November. Because Fiji's three infantry battalions also rotate in serving with UNIFIL, at any one time at least 50 per cent of the battalion has been in Lebanon for at least six months and most of the battalion's personnel have served with UNIFIL on prior occasions. In FIN-BATT normal service is also one year. Moreover only one-third of the battalion is rotated at a time so that two-thirds of those in the field are familiar with the area. The continuity of operational practice is further reinforced by the Finnish military's peacekeeping school which provides all Finnish UNIFIL personnel with extensive training in peacekeeping techniques.

In contrast GHANBATT and NEPBATT practise close to 100 per cent rotation every six months. The rotation period lasts from two to four weeks, but critically the units are moved intact so there is no overlapping at positions. This means that there is little operational continuity between the contingents. Indeed the only contact many arriving units have with those they are replacing in UNIFIL service is a hurried exchange of experiences at Ben Gurion airport.

NORBATT and IRISHBATT, both of which are based on voluntary service, also rotate on a six-month interval and as a result also suffer difficulties with consistency in operational practice. In the case of NORBATT this problem is partly dealt with by permitting some 10 to 15 per cent of the battalion to serve two consecutive six-month terms and applications for 'recap' are never lacking due to, among other things, the high salaries paid. In IRISHBATT full rotation takes two weeks, but many officers in particular have served previously with UNIFIL and thus provide for a certain continuity.

The effects of rotation and the resultant discontinuities are many. In those battalions which practise abrupt rotation, rather than a gradual rotation as in the case of FINBATT, the discrepancies between succeeding contingents can be large. Upon arrival in Lebanon they are inevitably greeted by the local militias with 'the welcoming ceremony'. Rotation is often marked by an increase in violence as the strengths and weaknesses of the new contingents – their ability to respond to fire, manage and diffuse confrontation, show courage, withstand manipulation and so forth – are tested and assessed by local Lebanese militiamen. Although much depends on the qualities of the Commanding Officers, in general those battalions in which lack of continuity is most marked are those who tend to perform worst in this critical phase. The rules for proper peace-keeping procedures are complicated and require experience combined with a finely tuned sense of balance and judgement. For example, the failure to return fire when appropriate can be as detrimental to security and the ability of a battalion to control its area of operation as a return of fire when not called for. The first reaction undermines the battalion's military credibility and the respect extended to it by the local population, civilian as well as militia. The second can quickly degenerate into a contest for military deference, the outcome of which will probably not be in UNIFIL's favour. The precedents established during 'the welcoming ceremony' seem to create a framework of mutual reference and thus are often determining for the battalion contingent's performance throughout its term of service with UNIFIL.

An effective system of local liaison is one of the most important resources that a contingent must transfer to its successor. Lack of sufficient continuity between contingents also can undermine the delicate system of liaison upon which a battalion depends for carrying out its duties with regard to the local population, such as gathering information, and critically, communicating with the various military factions in the area; but an initial and vexing task for any Commanding Officer is to figure out who is who. In the shifting political and military topography of southern Lebanon, this task is not straightforward and the consequences of misjudgement can be serious. Additionally the failure to maintain an adequate network of liaison means that the battalion is deprived of knowledge of local events and access to local people. Thus it becomes isolated and is forced to operate as an enclave unconnected to and thereby unable to exercise control in the local society.

CONCLUSIONS

The observations made in this paper must not be misunderstood. UNIFIL's achievements have been considerable. The Force has been required to do a difficult job in impossible circumstances and has performed very well indeed. The relative stability of the area – one of the more potentially volatile areas in the Middle East – is in large part a measure of UNIFIL's success. Particularly since few of the elements conventionally regarded as essential to successful peacekeeping have been present in southern Lebanon, UNIFIL also provides an opportunity to learn more about both the possibilities and restrictions involved in the peacekeeping instrument.

Part of the difficulties UNIFIL confronts relate to its 'interim' nature. The force has been in place for about ten years and could well remain in the area for ten more. Inevitably its long-term presence in the south will create even longer-term effects on the social, political and economic character of the area. Inadvertently some of these effects may unduly complicate the process of an eventual UNIFIL withdrawal. Although much of the effect of UNIFIL on local society, particularly in the economic sphere, is probably unavoidable, it nevertheless requires attention and evaluation as to its long-term implications. Indeed more emphasis and continuity of political planning and monitoring in the field might be helpful. In this context the establishment of certain types of development programmes in the south designed to strengthen local political and economic institutions in order to help them sustain independence and growth might be considered.

In addition, although UNIFIL is designed as an integrated force, in practice this does not seem to be fully the case. This too is partially due to the interim nature of the Force; but it is also due to the real separations that exist within the Force. The discontinuities within UNIFIL impact strongly on local perceptions concerning the credibility of the Force. They are also exploited by local factions for sectarian purposes. Moreover such discontinuities limit the ability of the Force to operate in the co-ordinated military manner. Certain promising proposals – such as an increased reliance on technology together with a mobile reserve force – have already been suggested. In addition it should be possible to change the nature of the training of a peacekeeping force. Prior to assignment in the field, as well as during it, the various national units should be given more opportunities to train together. The results of such co-training could have a very desirable impact on both the military and social cohesiveness of the force.

NOTES

1. These resources are varied and, in local eyes, highly valuable. They range from civilian jobs with UNIFIL – jobs as interpreters are particularly sought after – to building contracts, to humanitarian assistance, to free dental and medical treatment. Many Mouktars attempt, often successfully, to use these commodities as patronage resources in order to reward clients and hold competitors in check and thereby maintain a political support group. Frequently these resources are simply misused. For instance, one UNIFIL interpreter, who was also a close relative of the local Mouktar, was discovered selling 'permits' which allegedly enabled the bearer to receive preferential treatment from the local UNIFIL dentist.

2. Many of the new leaders now emerging, of which the recently assassinated Douad Douad was representative, are landless, unconnected to the traditional political families and educated.

3. What the GSS actually represents is unclear. The GSS version, which seems to be accepted by UNIFIL, is that the organisation is part of the Israeli intelligence services to which it reports directly and from which its members receive generous monthly salaries. General Security Services translates into Hebrew as *Shin Beth*. GSS leaders have identity cards that appear to be issued by the IDF. However, the IDF in Tel Aviv completely disclaim all responsibility for the GSS and state that *Shin Beth* is not only 100 per cent Israeli, but also 100 per cent Jewish. One SLA officer reported that the GSS is simply an

outgrowth of the intelligence services of the South Lebanese Army over which the SLA has in effect little control.

4. It must be noted that the Israeli occupation has had the same effect, but on a much more massive and potentially devastating scale.

5. It should be noted that income from legal, official employment is also below that required for household survival. A school rector receives approximately $60 per month as does a Lebanese policeman. The monthly salary of a local judge is about $70.

6. In order to put this figure into perspective, it should be noted that the maximum value of the tobacco crop, until recently the south's main money earner, never exceeded $10 million.

7. There are many factors that would suggest that development programmes should be a part of a peacekeeping operation. However, arguably they should be operated not by the peacekeepers themselves but by agencies that possess the required expertise and experience. In the case of Lebanon the need for such programmes in 1978 and 1982, because of the destructions of invasion, and in 1985–86 when the tobacco crop, previously a mainstay of the southern economy, collapsed, was, in my opinion, clearly present. However, it would appear that much of the activity in this realm currently taking place is not only wasteful and inappropriate, but quite possibly counter-productive and detrimental.

8. It should also be noted Western ideas about dirt are not particularly straightforward either. Among other things, dirt is situationally defined. For example, a pair of shoes neatly placed on a closet floor are 'clean'. The same shoes neatly placed next to the lamb roast on the dinner table are 'dirty'.

9.
Country	GDP (million $)	Pop. (millions)	GDP/cap.
France	489 434	54.3	9 013
Fiji	1 124	.6	1 873
Finland	50 662	4.7	10 779
Ghana	6 352	12.2	520
Ireland	17 717	3.4	5 210
Nepal	2 320	15.0	154
Norway	54 719	4.0	13 679

SOURCE: *United Nations Statistical Yearbook*, 1983/84.

10. These figures are based on an exchange rate between the French franc and the Norwegian krone on the one hand and the American dollar of approximately 6.7 on the other.

11. Even at UNIFIL's headquarters at Naqoura a sense of an international solidarity seems tenuous. During their leisure time, few people – except, for some reason, the Irish – go to the international officers' club. Instead, each battalion has built its own leisure centre. There is a Norway House where Norwegians can go to read Norwegian newspapers and enjoy Norwegian breakfasts, with beer, on Sundays. There is a Fiji House where alcohol is forbidden and from which on religious holidays the magnificent choral singing of Fijian soldiers drifts melodiously forth. There is a Finland House, connected, needless to say, to a sauna and so forth. Even in the officers' dining room, a national

territorial system seems to exist with each national unit exercising exclusive claim to particular tables.

12. In the Arab world, blacks are still linked to the image of the slave trade which long pre-dated the European version and in which Arabs were also active. Partly because of local racial attitudes, the presence of black battalions inside UNIFIL is frequently resented. Several civilians with whom I spoke claimed to feel a sense of outrage and insult when stopped and questioned at check points manned by black battalions. Several claimed that they simply refused to stop at such check points. Such attitudes seem to create considerable tensions between the battalions concerned and the local community. Tensions and racial stereotypes are exacerbated when local civilians feel that the military performance of the black battalions is such that the degree of protection expected is not forthcoming.

13. UN Nepalese soldiers are at times mistakenly regarded as Gurkhas. However, Gurkhas come from only one central region of Nepal and as a whole have not been recruited into the Nepalese army. Instead, since the mid-1800s they were recruited by Great Britain and since 1947 into the Indian army where, under British and Indian officers respectively, the Gurkhas gained an excellent military reputation for courage and discipline.

11 The Future of Peacekeeping
Indar Jit Rikhye

POLITICAL ENVIRONMENT

Introduction

A series of dramatic events during 1988 renewed international
interest in peacekeeping and greatly enhanced the prestige of the
United Nations. In June 1988 the introduction of the UN Good
Offices Mission in Afghanistan and Pakistan (UNGOMAP) with
50 UN military observers (UNMOs) to monitor the withdrawal
of Soviet troops from Afghanistan became the first new UN peacekeeping mission in ten years; the last being the UN Interim Force
in Lebanon (UNIFIL) in 1978. Several new peacekeeping missions
have followed: namely, the UN Iran–Iraq Military Observer Group
(UNIIMOG), consisting of 400 UNMOs, to supervise the cease-fire
between the two countries; and a UN Angola Verification Mission
(UNAVEM), consisting of 70 UNMOs, to monitor Cuban and South
African troop withdrawal. In consequence of this agreement the
South Africans have agreed to the transfer of power in Namibia and a
UN Transitional Assistance Group (UNTAG) will be responsible for
helping in elections with a peacekeeping force, including police.
Negotiations to arrange a cease-fire in the Western Sahara are under
way, requiring a UN peacekeeping mission to help with elections.
Similarly a UN peacekeeping force is being considered to halt fighting
in Kampuchea and arrange the withdrawal of Vietnam's troops. The
Nobel Peace Prize for 1988 to UN Peacekeeping operations is a fitting
tribute to the UN, the troop-contributing member states, and the
men and women whose devotion and sacrifice have made peacekeeping possible.

It is evident in the history of the UN that member states may not
always rely upon the UN to help resolve their conflicts, yet they have
time and again turned to peacekeeping to end wars. Peacekeeping
may not always lead to a negotiated settlement of disputes, but it
does succeed in halting or controlling the fighting, which provides
valuable time and opportunity for negotiations to resume. Thus

peacekeeping has evolved into an important and useful tool in present day diplomacy.

Changes in Political Environment

There are conflicts which cannot be resolved unilaterally. The wars in Afghanistan and between Iran and Iraq are examples of this. These two long-term situations were to bring not only the United States, but the Soviet Union, and the rest of the world a new sense of realism: if the UN did not exist, a new international system would be needed to resolve conflicts; therefore it was better to improve the existing organisation than to begin to build a new one.

The summit talks between President Reagan and General Secretary Gorbachev, and the signing of the Intermediate Nuclear Force (INF) Treaty improved the international environment and led to agreements to establish a cease-fire between Iran and Iraq and in other regional conflicts. Within the Soviet Union, Andropov, on succeeding Brezhnev, realised the futility of Soviet military intervention, and initiated steps for the withdrawal of their troops. After Andropov's death, this policy was pursued to conclusion by Gorbachev. This improved climate has afforded new opportunities to cope with conflicts around the world.

The American disillusionment with the UN started with the loss of its virtually automatic majority in the General Assembly some two decades ago, resulting in Third World countries 'block' voting for resolutions opposed by the United States. In his last address to the UN General Assembly,[1] President Reagan, referring to the changes in super power attitudes and hopes of the people of the world said, 'Precisely because of these changes, today the United Nations has the opportunity to live and breathe and work as never before . . . . We are determined that the United Nations should succeed and serve the cause of peace for human kind.'

Just as the American attitudes towards the UN were changing, Gorbachev, in a policy statement on 17 September 1987, brought about a major reversal in the Soviet attitude when he called for an important role for the UN in the resolution of regional conflicts, and peacekeeping, in particular. Sensing the disenchantment of the Soviet people with the intervention in Afghanistan which drained their economy and human resources, the Soviets decided to withdraw their troops from Afghanistan. Thus help from the UN was needed to resolve this conflict.

The Iran–Iraq War caused many anxieties. The Soviet republics, consisting of a variety of ethnic communities, have a lengthy border with Iran and therefore the Ayatollah Khomeni's Islamic fundamentalism and war with Iraq could have brought ill winds to the Soviet people. Also, Kampuchea and Angola, where the Soviets were committed to supporting Vietnam and the Luanda regime respectively, needed multilateral solutions – a service that the UN could best provide. The chasm between the conflicting interests of the super powers began to narrow as co-operation between them became timely.

This improved international political environment has provided many opportunities for multilateral diplomacy and the use of peacekeeping as a useful tool for ending wars. A study of the future of peacekeeping requires an analysis of past history and an indication of immediate future trends. Only then will it be possible to consider probable future conflict situations and the use of peacekeeping in their resolution.

PEACEKEEPING EXPERIENCE

General

Peacekeeping has proved useful, particularly by filling the power vacuum created by the withdrawal of colonial authority. Here peacekeeping facilitated the transfer of power, and when fighting erupted, arranged cessation of hostilities; and failing that, it controlled and limited fighting to allow negotiations to resume. Such operations were also intended to exclude East–West rivalry from the area. Many of these conflicts, for example, the Congo (Zaïre) in 1960–64 and West Irian (1962) were resolved; yet others remain. In situations such as between the Arabs and Israelis, between India and Pakistan, and in Cyprus, peacekeeping succeeded in obtaining precious periods of peace, but because of the failure of the peacemaking process there was renewed fighting.

There were wars due to other causes which required peacekeeping; for example Yemen in 1962. After a coup against the Imam by Nasserite military officers had led to fighting involving Saudi Arabia and Egypt in support of the opposing factions, a United States-negotiated cease-fire required a UN observation force (UNYOM) for its supervision. During the civil war in the Dominican Republic, a UN observer group (UNDOMREP) assisted in the restoration of a cease-fire previously negotiated by the Papal Nuncio.

Current Operations

The current peacekeeping operations include a number of peace-keeping missions which have continued due to the failure of peace-making. In spite of a peace treaty between Egypt and Israel, due to lack of confidence and trust, a non-UN multinational peacekeeping force and observers (MFO) remain in the Sinai; a UN disengagement observer force (UNDOF) is in the Golan Heights between Israel and Syria; a UN peacekeeping force remains in South Lebanon (UNIFIL); and military observers (UNTSO) based in Jerusalem co-operate with other peacekeeping forces and maintain liaison offices in neighbouring Arab capitals. A military observer group (UNMOGIP) remains in Jammu and Kashmir and a UN peace-keeping force (UNFICYP) separates the Turkish-occupied Cyprus from the area controlled by the Greek Republic of Cyprus.

All the other peacekeeping operations were the consequence of decolonisation where economic, ethnic, religious and social or tribal divisions, previously kept in check by colonial powers, erupted on withdrawal of external authority and had to be resolved. The presence of peacekeeping permitted avoidance of war and time to negotiate; it attempted to isolate such conflicts from the East–West rivalry, which would have made solutions even more difficult. The blame for lack of progress in peacemaking has often been attributed to a failure of peacekeeping, which is an unfair judgment, for peacekeeping can only provide a suitable climate for negotiations; it is not a panacea by itself.

Peacekeeping operations are not a guarantee against the resumption of fighting, which may only be achieved with the co-operation of the parties to the conflict. Therefore, if and when peacekeeping operations are prematurely terminated, fighting may resume, for example, the withdrawal of the first UN Emergency Force (UNEF I) from Gaza and the Sinai in 1967. Likewise, if UNIFIL were to be withdrawn before ending the civil war in Lebanon and providing a secure border with Israel, the latter may well expand its security zone inside Lebanon to the line of the Litani River and even beyond, exacerbating the already complex situation in that war-torn country. On the other hand UNIFIL provides some stability in a highly sensitive area and a measure of security for the local inhabitants in its operational area.

Just as in the case of UNIFIL, an early withdrawal of the UN troops in Cyprus would probably lead to renewed fighting; therefore the presence of UNFICYP is crucial, especially now when the communal talks are at a critical stage. Amongst the steps under consideration are the withdrawal of Turkish forces, the disbandment of the National Guard (Greek Cypriot) and the Turkish Cypriot Security Force. The local police forces will remain for security duties and an international force under UN aegis is to assure responsibility for the security of the reunified island state.

UN observers and troops in the Golan Heights are needed by Israel and Syria, since both understand the folly of another war over territory annexed by Israel and claimed by Syria. Similarly UNTSO military observers enhance the performance of UNDOF and UNIFIL and also have responsibilities in the Sinai. They provide a pool of experienced military observers in the area who are readily available to meet new tasks and are an immediate manpower resource to new missions.

A withdrawal of UNMOGIP would probably make little difference in the unresolved Jammu and Kashmir conflict between India and Pakistan. After the Shimla Accord between the two nations, following the 1971 war, a bilateral machinery was established and has operated effectively to resolve border issues. Pakistan continues to report to UNMOGIP alleged violations of the cease-fire line, whereas India ignores it. However, the group remains, since it may only be withdrawn by the agreement of both parties.

There are four new peacekeeping missions: UNGOMAP, UNIIMOG, UNAVEM and UNTAG. UNGOMAP, with 50 UN Military Observers in Afghanistan is a hybrid of a military observer group and the Good Offices of the UN Secretary-General. The mounting of UN peacekeeping operations is difficult enough as they are *ad hoc* in nature, but UNGOMAP encountered even greater problems since this peacekeeping mission was created under the guise of the Good Offices of the Secretary-General.[2] In any event, deploying military observers in a theatre in the absence of a cease-fire was questionable to say the least. If it was mainly intended to observe a Soviet troop withdrawal, the UN mission could have been much smaller, assuming it would equally receive full co-operation of the Soviet military command. The Afghans, the Mujahideen, or for that matter the Pakistanis, had little interest in their presence and even less desire to allow the observers to monitor their actions; nor did they have the capability to provide security to the UN military observers.

The UN military observers in Iran and Iraq are supervising a cease-fire. When the fighting stopped, the rival troops remained *in situ*. In a few places rival troops are only a few metres apart and the task of the observers is made difficult by the absence of an area of separation. So far this group has performed satisfactorily, but it has a difficult task which can only be made easier if negotiation between the two sides progresses.

On 20 December 1988, Angola, Cuba and South Africa agreed on the Brazzaville Protocol for the withdrawal of Cuban troops from Angola and the establishment of UNAVEM for a period of 31 months. The United States-negotiated agreement for the withdrawal of foreign troops from Angola is being supervised by UNAVEM. This mission, expected to proceed smoothly, is due to end with the completion of its task in February 1991.

The UN Security Council had authorised a peacekeeping operation to facilitate transfer of power in Namibia.[3] The initial plan called for the establishment of a UN Transition Assistance Group (UNTAG) consisting of a peacekeeping force to supervise withdrawal of the Republic of South Africa's forces from the territory and the return of Namibians, the South West Africa People's Organization (SWAPO) and Namibian refugees in Angola. With the proliferation of the UN peacekeeping operations, the five permanent members of the Security Council, who share more than half of the peacekeeping costs, in spite of the strong opposition of the frontline, non-aligned states, insisted that the UNTAG budget be almost halved. Although the presence of UNAVEM in Southern Angola, and efforts to end the fighting have eased the situation, the responsibility of UNTAG remains unaltered. Therefore the Secretary-General in his report[4] concerning the implementation of Security Council resolutions 435 and 439 explained that while the number of troops was to be reduced from 7500 to 4650, the police component would be increased from 350 to 500, which would bring the size of the civilian component to 2140. He also requested that additional troops be made available to him on a stand-by basis which could be transported speedily, if required. UNTAG became operational as of 1 April 1989, and will only succeed with the co-operation of South Africa and Namibia.

MANAGEMENT

Political

The management of peacekeeping begins at the Security Council where such missions are authorised. By their inherent nature, Security

Council resolutions are, at best, a compromise. They are often couched in a language which may be interpreted in various ways, resulting in difficulties, especially for commanders and staff in the field who have to translate diplomatic language into precise instructions. In the first instance, it is the UN Secretary-General who is usually called upon to conduct the operation, to translate Security Council resolutions into precise directives to peacekeeping missions, following complex negotiations. The UN staff has gained considerable experience in the last 40 years, yet there are situations where directives are left vague. There may well be explanations why it is so, but when they become issues of life and death for peacekeeping personnel, it becomes paramount that a better way be found. Such issues may concern relations with armed groups not under the control of the host government, and may involve security of the local population, as well as vulnerable points in the economic life and administration of the area of operations, thus necessitating that the peacekeeping troops exercise the right of self defence.

Many of these difficulties stem from a lack of political consensus concerning the conduct of operations among the members of the Security Council, or there may be a lack of political will to implement resolutions. In these situations troop contributors find themselves entrapped, for if they insist on decisive action they may be accused of lacking understanding of complex situations or of taking sides; and when they threaten to pull out, there are appeals to their political wisdom to support peace, for if they were to withdraw their troops, the operation would weaken, thereby threatening a new crisis or even a disaster.

The proper management of peacekeeping operations demands acceptable guidelines. Once arrived at, the task of the Secretary-General and the management of the operations will be greatly facilitated. Such guidelines are also required to prepare and train troops and personnel for the future. A Special Committee for Peacekeeping, the Committee of 33 (now called the Committee of 34, with China added to the list of members) was appointed in 1965 to recommend guidelines for peacekeeping to the General Assembly.

This Committee agreed on all but four essential issues: establishing a sub-organ of the Security Council to manage the operations; the appointment of the commander; the constitution of the forces, including its support units; and the question of termination of the forces. Unable to resolve the remaining differences in the Committee, negotiations were resumed by the four permanent powers, China being excluded at that time. The views of the four permanent members were not far apart, but because there was little political will to resolve their differences, no progress was made. The renewal of peacekeeping to separate the Arabs and Israelis after the October 1973 War, and following the Israeli intervention in South Lebanon in 1978, established that the member states, especially the Permanent Members of the Security Council, could narrow their differences by agreeing to set up UNEF II, UNDOF and UNIFIL. In fact the general guidelines acceptable to member states provided the necessary flexibility to meet the challenges of emerging conflict situations.

The Role of the Secretary-General

The higher conduct of peacekeeping operations has not only suffered from lack of political and financial support by the Security Council and other member states, but its *ad hoc* nature generally requires the UN Secretary-General to be responsible for planning, preparation and conduct of the operations. The earlier type of observer missions, for example, UNTSO and UNMOGIP, were managed by Trygve Lie and his office. He created a Field Service within the General Service of the Secretariat to provide administrative support. Lie had no responsibility for the military operation in Korea, since the UN, in order to avoid Soviet obstruction, had requested the United States to assume responsibility for the conduct of these operations.

Dag Hammarskjöld recognised the limitations brought upon the UN by the Cold War, and the threat of the use of the veto in cases of peace and security issues, and the inability of the UN Secretary-General to rely at that time on his Soviet staff. Therefore, besides his Executive Assistant (an under-secretary), he added two Under-Secretaries for Special Political Affairs for the office of the Secretary-General. He appointed an American, Ralph J. Bunche, a Nobel Peace Laureate, and a Russian, Anatoly Dobrynin, to the new positions. Hammarskjöld's attempt to include Dobrynin in his personal cabinet, with the hope of gaining the support of a senior-level Russian, proved in vain, and Dobrynin reverted to his previous appointment as Under-Secretary for Political and Security Council Affairs, which his country did not wish to lose. However, Hammarskjöld and his successors kept the two positions until the recent reorganisation of the UN Secretariat. The additional Under-Secretaries, together with their staff, henceforth provided the support for Hammarskjöld and his successors for the UN Emergency Force (UNEF) in 1956 and for all subsequent peacekeeping missions.

In time one of the two Under-Secretaries for Special Political Affairs was made responsible for peacekeeping missions, while each of the two was given specific political negotiation responsibilities. The guiding principle for their functions was that the two Under-Secretaries for Special Political Affairs and the Chef de Cabinet (formerly Executive Assistant) worked as a team co-opting any other Secretariat Under-Secretary or senior staff required to support the Secretary-General in the implementation of the wishes of the UN organs.

The inability of the Security Council to deal fully with regional conflicts because of East–West rivalry had gradually led to greater use of the Good Offices of the UN Secretary-General. This required more senior level staff assistance and Kurt Waldheim turned to other Under-Secretaries for support. This practice was continued by Javier Perez de Cuellar. The spread of responsibilities related to political negotiations leading to peacekeeping by higher-level Secretariat officials outside the executive office of the Secretary-General made co-ordination more difficult. The use of UNMOs for UNGOMAP triggered the alarm of the breakdown of the excellent record of higher management of peacekeeping missions. The role of the UNMOs in this mission remains questionable, to say the least, and was ill-managed when started. It was no wonder that it raised hackles in the observer-contributing countries. Realising the situation, Pérez de Cuéllar acted speedily to remedy it.

In a reorganisation of his executive office, the Secretary-General has centralised management of peacekeeping operations in the office of the Under-Secretary for Special Political Affairs for Peacekeeping, and in turn has limited this official's involvement in the political phase of the negotiations, which precedes such operations. This arrangement places peacekeeping operational responsibility with one higher-level official instead of with two Under-Secretaries-General for Special Political Affairs, who had formerly dealt with both the political and operational aspects of peacekeeping.

The new peacekeeping management arrangement provides more centralised political direction for peacemaking by the Secretary-General. The diverse and intensive nature of negotiations to end fighting in different regions requires the Secretary-General to engage a number of personal emissaries who report to him for direction. With expanding needs for peacekeeping, which demand a high degree of specialisation, the Secretary-General has centralised the operational management of peacekeeping. This avoids each peace-keeping operation being managed by different representatives of the Secretary-General, enabling better utilisation of resources and the ability to quickly deal with troop-contributing countries.

There remain two important related matters for consideration. The first concerns administrative and logistics support for peace-keeping. In order to formalise co-ordination between operations managed by an Under-Secretary for Special Political Affairs and the logistic support by Field Service under the Under-Secretary-General for Administration, Pérez de Cuéllar brought field operations to his own office and placed an Assistant Secretary-General in charge. With the two most important aspects of peacekeeping handled within the Executive Office of the Secretary-General, better co-ordination was achieved. Under the recent administrative reform, and consequent reduction in senior Secretariat positions, field operations were reverted to Administration early in 1988.

It is abundantly clear that the administration of peacekeeping is integral to operational management. Just as a commander in the field should and must not be separated from the administrative support of his command, similarly the higher management of peacekeeping requires proper co-ordination. Such an important arrangement can-not be left to individual personal relations, which are important enough, but to a recognised, workable system for co-ordinated action.

The second, and equally important, issue relates to the availability of military expertise to the Secretary-General. Many attempts have been made to provide some military expertise to the UN Secretary-General and his staff, which have yet to prove satisfactory. The political differences between the Permanent Members of the Security Council on key issues relating to the management of peacekeeping operations are central to the question of the use of a military advisory staff for the Secretary-General. Hitherto it has not been possible to activate the Military Staff Committee, consisting of senior military staff of the five Permanent Members, because peacekeeping does not fall into any of the functions described by the UN Charter. A Military Adviser to the Secretary-General is listed in the Executive Office of the Secretary-General; the same person is listed as the Military Adviser in the Office for Special Political Affairs of the Secretary-General. Presumably the Military Adviser has functions at a higher plane with the Secretary-General and deals with the day-to-day operation of peacekeeping missions for the Under-Secretary-General for Special Political Affairs.

The Military Adviser has two assistants of the rank of major or equivalent. With the expansion of the peacekeeping operations, the size of the military staff is unable to meet demands, and outside military expertise, sometimes lacking in high-level UN experience, may be necessary. On occasions the Military Adviser has accompanied the Secretary-General's representative to assist in negotiations that may lead to a peacekeeping operation, leaving only his assistants at Headquarters. There is the danger that outside advisers may have little understanding of the nuances of the Secretary-General's Office, which can only be acquired by experience. When the Military Adviser is away from Headquarters, a suitable military advisory staff officer should be available to ensure that expertise is always available to the Secretary-General and his staff.

Recently the Soviet Union proposed the reactivation of the Military Staff Committee. The United States and the Western Powers responded to the proposal with a certain coolness. Furthermore the troop-contributing countries did not favour the proposal because they want to continue to have a voice in the decision-making process. Besides, some of them have Military Advisers posted to their missions who have little direct contact with the Military Staff Committee. These advisers have access to both the UN Secretariat and the missions, and are determined not to allow only the big powers to decide how their troops are to be used.

The UN Secretariat understands the concerns of troop-contributing countries and is sceptical of direct involvement in peacekeeping by the Military Staff Committee. Amongst the proposals on military advisory functions, the Special Committee on Peacekeeping Operations considered the use of the Military Staff Committee. Suggestions were made that a group of military experts from troop-contributing states and permanent powers be used to provide military advice. However, no clear proposal emerged.

Another limitation is the lack of mutual confidence and understanding between civilians and the military, an affliction of all societies except where military regimes prevail. Diplomacy and general administration demand considerable skills and experience, as does the military profession. While there are common areas of skills and knowledge, each requires specialisation. These skills should be available to the UN Secretary-General.

Logistics

A great deal has been achieved in improving the administrative and logistical support of peacekeeping, but it is only a beginning. Increased support by the great and industrial powers is needed to support operations in the field, since many troop-contributing countries are dependent on other nations for equipment, material supplies and transportation. The UN must eventually establish its own support system to replace an arrangement which was initially created for its Field Service to maintain both small and large military observer missions. Presently each contingent has to rely on its own national resources; the UN purchases available supplies locally, perhaps on a contract basis, and has managed to arrange that some supplies be placed in UN centralised storage. The UN requires resources which it presently lacks. A good logistic system will require a trained staff, sufficient facilities and adequate financing.

Financing

Last, but not least, the limitations of present day peacekeeping experience have been the woeful lack of adequate financing. The failure of member states to pay their dues has resulted in escalating dues to troop-contributing countries. The economies of Nordic countries, Canada and some other member states can withstand failure of the UN to reimburse costs, but it is difficult for countries like Ireland and Nigeria, and unacceptable for small states like Fiji and Ghana. A lack of regular financing also has a devastating effect on planning, administration and logistics. Besides strengthening Security Council resolve to support its own resolutions relating to peacekeeping, the financing of such operations must be put on a solid basis.

A number of approaches to resolving the question of the financing of peacekeeping have been tried: (1) to apportion the cost among all member states, based on the regular scale of assessments; (2) to apportion the costs on the regular scale of assessment, but outside the regular budget; (3) to meet the cost outside the regular budget, apportioning part of the costs on the regular scale of assessments and the remainder on a sliding scale, with the differences being met by voluntary contributions; and (4) all costs being met by voluntary contributions.

However, of all the financial formulas, the most pragmatic is when the costs are largely met, first of all, by the Permanent Members of the Security Council, and secondly by the most developed countries; the remaining costs being shared by the less developed countries in proportion to their regular scale of assessment.

The recent negotiations on the costs of UNTAG are one indication that with increasing demands for peacekeeping, financing arrangements have assumed new prominence. The Secretary-General had asked for $700 million to enable UNTAG to fulfil its missions, with 7500 troops and 2000 civilians, including a police force of 360. However, the Permanent Members of the Security Council decided that since they would provide more than half the share of costs, the UNTAG budget would be limited to $400 million. Negotiations among the permanent and other members and the parties involved required the revision of the mission of the peacekeeping force to make a reduction in number possible. This example makes it more obvious than ever that the financing of peacekeeping must be made a matter of high priority.

THE FUTURE

General

The importance of the presence of UNIFIL to keep peace in South Lebanon and to provide a basis for future negotiations to end the civil war in that country; the need of Israel and Syria to keep UNDOF in the Golan Heights; the useful role of UN military observers of UNTSO in the Middle East; the central role of UNFICYP to keep Cypriot (Greek) troops apart from the Turkish army in Cyprus; and the presence of UNMOGIP in Jammu and Kashmir have been elaborated earlier. It has also been stated that these peacekeeping missions should be made more effective by stronger political support by the Security Council, better co-operation of the parties and increased financing; these steps will facilitate better direction, management and administrative support for the operations.

While the significance of the peacekeeping operations mentioned above to prevent violence is all too obvious, it is still an essential prerequisite for negotiations to continue. Therefore the need to enhance the capability of these operations cannot be overemphasised.

Of the two new peacekeeping operations, the role of the military observers in UNGOMAP was to be greatly reduced once Soviet troops had left Afghanistan on 15 February 1989, but the need for peacekeeping remains. However, in the case of UNIIMOG, difficult negotiations related to the delineation of a cease-fire line have yet to be completed and other negotiations on issues related to Shatt al Arab and territorial waters in the Gulf can be expected to be protracted. The Soviets, among others, have suggested a naval arm for peacekeeping. This suggestion merits consideration.

Among the critical issues related to the maintenance of peace and security in the Gulf is the boundary line in the Shatt al Arab, which limits the territorial waters and freedom on the high seas for the movement of oil tankers vital to the economy of the littoral states, the West, Japan and many developing countries. Therefore UNIIMOG has a vital role in the negotiations between Iran and Iraq being conducted by the UN Secretary-General. Reports on the performance of the observer group have been positive.

An agreement between Morocco on the one hand, and on the other the *Frente Popular para la Liberacion de Saguia el Hamra y de Rio de Oro* (POLISARIO) and Algeria has been concluded with the assistance of the heads of state and governments of the Organization of African Unity (OAU) and the UN Secretary-General.[5] This agreement called for negotiations, presently taking place, between parties to agree to a cease-fire and to introduce a UN peacekeeping force, organising a referendum along the same lines as in Namibia. Consultations by the head of the OAU and the UN Secretary-General are continuing for the implementation of the resolution.

Another peacekeeping operation is under consideration as an essential part of negotiation to end fighting and for withdrawal of Vietnamese troops in Kampuchea. The new operations will greatly increase the present size of UN peacekeeping operations and their cost. In order to meet these demands, the international community will face a number of challenges, for example:

(1)   Manpower needs will require the list of troop-contributing countries to be expanded;
(2)   New contributing countries will require training assistance;
(3)   The costs of peacekeeping will run manifold. Since many states are behind in their peacekeeping dues, a better way of financing must be found;
(4)   The increase in peacekeeping missions will require expanded UN Secretariat ability to manage operations, especially its logistics support and military advisory staff.

NEW ROLES

General

An evaluation of past and present experiences of peacekeeping as well as immediate demands on peacekeeping provide a sufficient basis for forecasting its usefulness in the future. Thus peacekeeping will continue to be needed to end wars and provide an environment for negotiations to resume.

Several suggestions have emerged as possible future peacekeeping roles. Some of these roles listed below and described in this paper are not new:

- peacekeeping during incipiency
- border security
- confidence-building measures
- verification
- peacekeeping during civil wars/law and order assistance
- combating terrorism
- humanitarian aid and security
- drug interdiction
- naval peacekeeping

Peacekeeping During Incipiency

The advantage of peacekeeping during incipiency has been considered but heretofore there has been no occasion to engage such a system because of the inability of the parties and the international community to agree. A changed political climate that may result from improving relations between the super powers may make preventive diplomacy possible, where, in certain situations, peacekeeping could play a part. Security of borders, confidence-building measures including verification are some of the tasks that peacekeeping could undertake before and after a crisis is fully blown.

V. F. Petrovsky, Deputy Head of the USSR delegation to the UN, stated in a speech to the Special Political Committee of the General Assembly on 17 October 1988: 'United Nations peacekeeping operations should not be used to palliate regional problems or to delay substantive decisions but should precede or accompany negotiations on comprehensive settlements'.[6] Petrovsky's suggestions are more or less along the lines of the recommendations made by the UN

Secretary-General in 1982.[7] Border security, verification and confidence-building measures, discussed separately, can all play a useful role during incipiency and deserve further discussion by the Permanent Members of the Security Council and the international community at large.

Border Security

There are very few states that are able to secure their borders against serious external threat. They do, however, attempt to arm themselves relative to a likely threat. When a balance is upset because of unexpected developments, usually by overt defence-spending by a neighbouring state or when it receives external assistance from a big power, then self-reliance is no longer possible. In such situations, a state under threat, real or perceived, is often constrained to obtain external help, which may obligate it to join one or another camp, further threatening regional and international peace and security.

Smaller states are especially vulnerable to a takeover by external assistance to dissidents or straightforward external seizure for ideological, political or economic gain. For example: in Grenada a leftist coup against a legitimate regime brought Cuban assistance, threatening the peace and security of many small states in the Caribbean. Eventually the United States intervened to restore normality. More recently, foreign mercenaries (Tamils from Sri Lanka) helped a former leader in his attempt to take over power in the Maldives. Indian troops had to be called in to deal with the threat.

When states have a growing conflict with a neighbour, as is the case between some of the Central American states, leaving them unable to ensure the security of their borders, they need assistance – which may be sought from a friendly neighbour, another state, or a regional or international arrangement. Such security could prevent the infiltration and movement of unauthorised persons. Border security could be provided by any one or a combination of means available for peacekeeping and could be particularly useful in conflict-avoidance and confidence-building in the future. The question of border security will continue to be crucial in future conflict management, and since most states are unable to take care of their own security, a regional and international system has to be provided.

The border security responsibilities are no different from the supervision of a cease-fire line, since many such lines were drawn in the first instance along international boundaries, with some adjustments. For example, the General Armistice Agreement of 1949, between Israel and neighbouring Arab states established the Armistice Demarcation Lines along the international boundaries agreed to between British Mandatory Palestine and neighbouring Arab states with some changes along the border with Syria and the northern sector in the Sinai. Thus border security and maintenance of cease-fire lines require similar deployment of military observers and/or troops. The main difference between national troops of a state and peacekeeping is in the method of dealing with intrusions and violations. In fact a peacekeeping mission can help create an environment of reduced tension and restore normalcy.

Confidence-Building Measures

Confidence-building measures (CBMs) are a much talked-about topic relating to the maintenance of international peace and security. A UN study has described the need for CBMs to eliminate the sources of tension by peaceful means and thereby contribute to the strengthening of peace and security in the world.[8] The concept of CBMs was first developed in the 1950s within the framework of United States and Soviet Union relationships following the Cold War. Some 20 years later, due to the Helsinki process, it came to be regarded as a European contribution to international balance. A number of CBMs were agreed to in the final document of the Conference on Security and Co-operation in Europe (CSCE) and other related proposals were made at the follow-up conferences at Belgrade and Madrid. CBMs were again negotiated at the Conference on Disarmament in Europe (CDE) in Stockholm (1984).

Recognising the European focus of the CBMs, Chancellor Helmut Schmidt of the Federal Republic of Germany (FRG), in an address to the UN Special Session on Disarmament (SSOD) (1978), said that CBMs could 'serve in all parts of the world to improve the political preconditions for disarmament and arms control'.[9] Subsequently, on the initiative of the FRG, a comprehensive report by the UN on CBMs was prepared by a group of fourteen countries.[10]

This study did not set out specific CBMs for the Third World, but did clarify and develop the concept of confidence-building in the global context to provide guidelines for governments intending to introduce CBMs for the maintenance of international peace and security. The International Peace Academy (IPA) has taken a number of steps to promote discussion of concrete steps, based on the

European experience, that could be useful in dealing with Third World concerns. The IPA's work in Central America has made better progress than other regions.[11]

Hitherto indications are that CBMs can at least be as useful in the Third World as they are expected to be in Europe. There are a number of lessons from the European experience which relate to the definition of 'confidence' and 'measures'. There must be a clear distinction between 'confidence' (as in self-confidence) and 'confidence' (as in trust). Also the term 'measures' means 'steps'. However, there is confusion in talking of measures because one view concentrates on 'military measures', while the other emphasises 'economic, social and other fields'. The Third World generally takes the broader definition of the term 'measures'.

Suspicion of an opposing party leads to an irrational response based on fear and a feeling of vulnerability, which could escalate the conflict. As a crisis develops, suspicion of threats to security could be avoided by preventing or reducing anxiety, doubt and mistrust of the motives of the enemy. Often in a crisis an objective situation is perceived subjectively, or according to how an action is understood from the point of reference of the opponent. Since a conflict tends to distort the perceptions of the parties involved, a third party is essential to clarify the situation and to appeal to the sense of trust and reason of both parties. A third party, such as the UN, can provide a channel of communication and supervision between the two sides via observers, or if necessary, a peacekeeping force. Meetings between parties, visits to the opposite side, including visits to military installations, observation of military manoeuvres and their early notification will all contribute towards creating confidence and easing tensions by diminishing the possibility of miscalculation and misunderstanding.

Verification

The term *verification* became part of the UN's agenda when on 16 December 1985 the General Assembly adopted by consensus Resolution 40/152(O) entitled, 'Verification in all its Aspects'. Initially the term verification was used for disarmament agreements; however, it now has a much wider usage, encompassing other security-related matters. Arms control and limitations agreements between the two super powers are usually verified by the two parties. Mr Eduard A. Shevardnadze, the Soviet Minister for Foreign Affairs, in his address to the General Assembly on 27 September 1988 proposed that the UN could be involved in such arrangements in the future.[12] Similarly the UN could also be called upon to verify regional arrangements.

Given the present day international political climate, the possibility of further negotiations on arms control and reductions by the super powers and the two military blocs is probable. Since the task of verification has similarities to peacekeeping, the UN would indeed be a suitable organisation to render this service. However, there are some issues that will have to be duly considered in undertaking such a responsibility. First, verification cannot be usefully considered without a specific agreement. Second, verification may be used deliberately as a pretext to impede or avoid progress in the negotiations of agreements. Third, perfect viability is elusive and should not stand in the way of concluding agreements.

The definition of the term verification is: to confirm, substantiate, check or test accuracy of exactness, to authenticate; to specify. Verification can be an important CBM, since a third party who checks on the accuracy of the actions of both parties will give an unbiased account, and as each party realises that the 'perceived' threat to their security may not be as great as supposed, this will tend to moderate the conflict. Thus the importance of verification to international security matters cannot be exaggerated. There are a variety of verification tasks in peacekeeping, that is, cease-fires, armistice, and truce observation; and verification of de-militarised and limited weapons zones. In addition there may be tasks related to movement of troops and agreements on military hardware. These tasks may be performed by military observers, as is often the case, but the use of technology has enhanced this capability.

Modern technology has greatly improved surveillance and improved communications. Early warning, accuracy of information and rapid communications will facilitate CBMs and thereby the peacekeeping tasks. For example, the United States' Sinai Support Mission, using modern surveillance techniques and communications, provided limited CBMs and met some Egyptian political needs, as well as helping to reinforce UNEF II operations. High-level fixed wing and satellite surveillance have sharpened imagery. More use of these modern technologies will only enhance peacekeeping capability.

Peacekeeping missions, as a rule, are interposed between two sides, and by their mere presence are in the way of any attempt at aggression by either side. The peacekeepers inform both sides that the agreements are being complied with, and in the case of violations, intervene to restore normality. This monitoring of cease-fire or armistice lines is done by military personnel (civilian technicians may also be used in some situations), and their capability can be greatly enhanced by modern surveillance technology. The IPA has begun a study of the experience of the United States' Sinai Support Mission in the Sinai and has followed the developments of new surveillance technology for peacekeeping.[13]

Peacekeeping during Civil Wars/Law and Order Assistance

There are many conflicts where maintenance of law and order is beyond the resources of the state. How should insurgency and civil war be dealt with in situations like Mozambique, Angola, Central America and elsewhere? Surely there are limits to what external assistance can provide; but the fact remains that such assistance is needed and peacekeeping is an answer.

Many an internal conflict has expanded beyond its country's borders, becoming an inter-state, and sometimes a regional crisis. Divided ethnic groups readily find refuge with the sympathetic populace of neighbouring states, and sometimes recruit them to help fight their adversaries across the borders. For example, the insurgency in Mozambique, which resulted in the blockage of the Beira Corridor, as well as the hostile actions of RENAMO[14] across Mozambique's borders into neighbouring states, led to widening of the conflict. Another example was the civil war in Uganda, which resulted in an influx of refugees into Tanzania and border incidents which culminated in the dispatch of Tanzanian troops to Uganda. Recently the insurgency in Sri Lanka necessitated the island state calling the Indian army for help. In such situations external forces are often persuaded to support one side, further complicating the conflict, for example, India's attempt to stop the tide of refugees from East Pakistan and provide assistance to the dissident forces in East Pakistan led to a war between India and Pakistan in 1971. There is evidence that solutions to some, if not all, of these situations could have been provided by an international or a regional system, for there is less risk of such intervention being perceived as one-sided since responsibility does not rest on only one state. On the other hand the muliplicity of the operation and its control may be the loss of efficacy. However, on balance, this risk is justifiable.

In situations where peacekeeping operations are established, what should the peacekeeping operation do when local administration breaks down and armed groups take the law into their own hands? It is suggested that the peacekeeping troops either assist the remaining local authority or get out. When it takes no action, except in self-defence as the last resort, it is likely to take unnecessary casualties and get no respect from the local population. As in many current conflicts, there are likely to be similar problems which should be faced.

Besides its primary task of separating forces of rival states, the United Nations has gained considerable experience in coping with intra-state wars. In the Congo the UN dealt with the mutiny of the Congolese army, which afterward split into four groups, supporting separate regimes. The UN operation dealt with tribal and factional wars and with foreign mercenaries, and assisted in the restoration of law and order. Although many African states have avoided UN peacekeeping because it failed to protect the head of the government who had initially invited it, and because the super power influence upon the UN operation, which was contrary to the interests of the previous leadership in power, the fact remains that the UN completed its task and left behind a country which was unified and in peace. The countries which contributed troops to the Congo still shy away from such a role. However, in spite of this, the states have continued to provide troops in Cyprus and to the UN forces in Lebanon, where civil war is also rampant.

The United Nations Charter is written around the sovereignty of states and the non-interference by the international organisation in the internal affairs of its members. Yet there is no denying that some internal conflicts become international, and then threaten international peace and security, permitting the UN to respond. Thus there is a very obvious need to consider the many facets of these conflicts and what peacekeeping can do to help in their resolution.

Combating Terrorism

The world community has already made a tentative effort to respond to the threat of international terrorism. The resolution of the United Nations General Assembly,[15] in condemning international terrorism, appealed to all states to join the existing international conventions relating to terrorism, to take necessary domestic means for the elimination of the problem, to co-operate with other states to combat terrorism and to take appropriate measures as necessary by the International Civil Aviation Organization. It further recommended international action to strengthen law enforcement measures and related co-operation between states. This paper addresses itself only to terrorism as a political tool. The perceptions of such terrorism are different in accordance to political beliefs. Some terrorists of yesterday are respected political leaders today and so-called 'criminal' terrorists of today acting to further their political beliefs are potential leaders of tomorrow. Thus political terrorism has to be dealt with at its roots, yet indiscriminate killing and taking innocent victims hostage for political gains is unacceptable behaviour. While most nations have arrived at some manageable basis for dealing with acts of hijacking and terrorism, similar political activities by extremist groups present challenges which still need to be fully met.

There are several politically-motivated terrorist organisations around the world, some of which are integral to liberation movements, whereas others are totally committed to violence. The Palestine Liberation Organization (PLO), for instance, includes elements who wage war across the borders into Israel (called terrorism by those who are not sympathetic to the PLO) and military targets abroad, especially those that belong to states that are friendly to Israel; then there are groups that commit acts of violence against innocent civilians of countries that support Israel. Most Arab states have at one time or another harboured different PLO groups. Iraq, Libya and Syria are known to have permitted bases to known terrorist groups.

The United States chose to act unilaterally against Libya because it would have been impossible to obtain an agreement for international action of this kind; and probably because military and political risks were greater had they decided to act against Syria, which harbours some of the most important active terrorist groups in the world. Terrorist acts are usually committed against democracies. The media of the free world gives them great attention and this results in influencing the public to take an interest in the cause of the protagonists because democracies are vulnerable to human rights concerns. The PLO only gained world-wide attention after the airliner hijackings in the early 1970s. This has not spared the Soviets, or other persons of authoritarian regimes, except that terrorists' activities are seldom reported. The fact remains that acts of terrorism receive considerable publicity in the free world, compared to countries with strict information controls. Thus democracies are more susceptible to influence by the strategy of terror.

The record of terrorism used during the anti-colonial struggle as an instrument for change was credible enough to encourage its future use. Although in other situations it may not have proved all that effective in producing immediate results, there is no denying that terrorists gain publicity, as well as increase the cost for those who oppose their cause and attract international attention. In spite of the recent offensive of some states against terrorism, conditions are ripe for further escalation, with the ominous possibility of the use of chemical weapons and some form of nuclear device. An informal agreement by the United States and the Soviet Union in 1985 allows sharing of information about any nation preparing to use such weapons. This needs to be implemented in letter and spirit. However, terrorism is likely to remain at a relatively lower level in the scale of expected violence between opposing groups, and possibly between states which choose war.

There are existing intelligence agencies dealing with terrorist activities. However, an arrangement for pooling information on politically-known and potential terrorists has to be established. The possible creation of an international agency, perhaps attached to or as a subsidiary to Interpol, merits consideration. This agency should collect relevant data and make information available to legitimate security services to combat terrorism.

The security of airports is a domestic responsibility and security during flight is the responsibility of the airlines. While there have been instances of breaches of airport security, a majority of acts have occurred in flight. Thereafter hijacked aircraft are forced to land at a given destination or to refuel to continue flight. This is where counter-action is possible.

The Israeli commando raid on Entebbe to free their hijacked citizens and the West German commando raid on Mogadishu were the only two known dramatic rescue missions. Some others were less successful. The attempt by Egyptian commandos to rescue their hijacked Egypt Air flight at Malta ended in tragedy. The inability of Cypriot authorities to relieve a hijacked Gulf Air aircraft at Larnaca, which then flew on to Algiers, also ended in serious straits. A way must be found to improve relief and the international community should consider an élite international peacekeeping unit, highly skilled in hostage relief and rescue, to undertake this responsibility.

Humanitarian Aid and Security

The need for security of humanitarian assistance activities has become increasingly obvious after witnessing the sufferings of refugees in Africa and elsewhere. In the Sudan and in the Horn of Africa aid was denied for political reasons. In Mozambique anti-government insurgency waged by RENAMO has made determined efforts to abort efforts of governments and non-governmental aid agencies in providing relief. Kampuchean refugee camps inside Thailand are attacked to deny relief and to loot supplies for use by raiding troops. This litany of forcible prevention of aid to refugees is unending.

Although the 1949 Geneva Convention ensuring legal protection for refugees was ratified by 140 nations, the blockage of aid comes from governments themselves, by liberation movements, or a combination of the two. Though it is difficult to understand the morality of such actions, the strategic value is easily apparent. Starvation of populations is aimed at reducing resistance and has been effectively employed throughout history. The failure of governments to provide timely relief eventually creates a new crisis. The secession of East Pakistan and the fall of its leader of the freedom struggle, Mujibul Rahman, and Haile Selassie in Ethiopia, are typical examples of people not forgetting gross neglect.

There are several UN agencies involved in refugee relief, but none have built-in security arrangements, since this is what governments are expected to provide. The International Committee of the Red Cross (ICRC) and other private humanitarian organisations were empowered to assist and protect civilian populations under the Geneva Accord, but they lack the means to provide physical protection, aside from the question of enforcement capability. The Swedes, on the basis of the Congo experience, have a technical battalion on stand-by which has only a self-defence capability. In spite of these difficulties, some private relief organisations have attempted limited aid operations over the objectives of the governments with some success. These attempts do not really point towards any long-term solutions.

A role for peacekeeping in security assistance to humanitarian aid poses problems, many of them no different from those encountered in normal operations. There must be respect for national sovereignty and non-interference in internal affairs of the state. Peacekeeping operations in the Congo, Cyprus and now in South Lebanon indicate that in limited ways these essential UN Charter concerns can be handled. The UN forces are normally concerned with government-controlled forces. Yet the operations mentioned above have provided valuable experience in dealing with factions not under government control and national liberation movements which usually have little respect for international law.

The civil war in Mozambique affected the indigenous people because of the blocking of the Beira railway system which prevented the use of the port of Beira by the neighbouring countries, Malawi, Tanzania and Zimbabwe. In the absence of any available regional or international arrangement, these three countries entered into a security operation with Mozambique, resulting in a joint military force of some 12 000, to secure the Beira Corridor; and the railway system and the port have been reopened. The international community, wary of stepping across the lines of sovereignty and non-interference in the internal affairs of a state, has remained on the sidelines. These operations by the adjoining African states are an enormous undertaking for which they deserve support.

Drug Interdiction

The question of the use of military forces for drug interdiction is being debated in many countries, notably the United States. Already there is an ever-increasing realisation of the need for education and the prevention of the use of drugs. In any case, the enormous task of drug interdiction is perpetual, a task which is akin to the prevention of smuggling, in which considerable experience exists. It is the enormity of the task and the critical risk to health and life which demands the availability of all resources to prevent the illegal entry of drugs.

The United States and a number of other countries have employed elements[16] of their defence and security forces for surveillance and attacks on selected targets in the supply line. Also co-operative efforts exist in some regions, such as in the China–Burma–Thailand triangle and the South Asian Association for Regional Co-operation (SARC). Many of these tasks overlap with anti-smuggling measures which are undertaken or reinforced by the armed forces. Satellite imagery, high-level aircraft photography, aerial surveillance, coastal and land patrolling are all being employed. Thus there are several tasks that are in common with peacekeeping functions, whereas search-and-destroy missions of drug-producing fields, factories, and storage are police or enforcement actions and therefore beyond the limits of peacekeeping norms. It would be logical then to separate the surveillance functions from search-and-destroy missions. A multi-lateral surveillance system for drug interdiction could be developed on the basis of present experience. On the other hand, search-and-destroy missions should primarily rely on national efforts, a task that will be greatly facilitated by the former.

Across land frontiers, joint patrolling and surveillance have been employed and could be greatly improved by a para-military force; and in critical situations, ground troops supported by air, as well as naval patrols in territorial waters, could be effectively used. In the United States, it is the Coast Guard which carries out these functions; whereas in other countries it is generally the responsibility of the navy, with coastal-type vessels. It is possible for such ground and maritime craft to be supported by high-level aerial surveillance.

Naval Peacekeeping

The need for naval peacekeeping arose after the Iran and Iraq war had spread to the Persian Gulf, which resulted in an increased number of attacks on tankers and oil installations. In a resolution[17] on 20 July 1987, the UN Security Council demanded that 'as a first step towards a negotiated settlement, Iran and Iraq observe an immediate cease-fire, discontinue all military actions on land, at sea and in the air, and withdraw all forces to the international borders without delay'. This resolution also requested the UN Secretary-General to supervise the cease-fire, a task that included peacekeeping at sea for the first time in the history of the UN.

Earlier during the war, responding to Kuwait's request to the Permanent Members of the Council for protection of shipping, the Soviets had immediately responded by supplying a few tankers, with their own registry, and an escort of small naval vessels with mine-sweeping capability. The United States had replaced the British naval units based in Bahrain in the early 1970s, and were already well-placed to respond. President Reagan chose to flag Kuwaiti oil tankers and provided a reinforced fleet of about 30 ships for escort and protection of shipping in the Gulf. Other western powers sent more ships with the primary intent of protecting their own commercial shipping. Although the western fleet did not operate as such, there was some co-operation between their navies on an informal basis, presenting a formidable challenge to any hostile action. This came mostly from Iraq, whose aircraft relentlessly attacked Iranian oil targets and tankers, regardless of their registry. Of course Iran also succeeded in causing damage to tankers transporting oil from the Arab Gulf states.

After the Security Council called for a cease-fire and the UN began considering a peacekeeping arrangement, the Soviets proposed a naval peacekeeping arm to replace the naval units operating in the Gulf. The Soviet Union was obviously concerned with a major western naval presence in the Gulf, within easy air-striking distance of their territory. However, they were genuinely concerned, as were many others, that the presence of so many diverse naval units might result in an incident which could cause serious consequences. The Reagan Administration rejected this suggestion because they said the UN had no past experience for this task, nor was it suitably equipped for it. It is worth remembering that the UN had little experience in managing a peacekeeping land force with air transport and ships when it first launched such an operation to end fighting in the Suez Canal in 1956. The fact was that the United States has major political and strategic interests in the Gulf and the region, and it also badly needed to improve its image at home after Irangate.

The UN did have some experience in handling naval craft in support of the UN mediation efforts by Count Folke Bernadotte in 1948; and in West Irian in 1962, a country with thousands of miles of coastline accessible only by air and sea. More recently, Iran's naval ships were promised by the Shah to patrol the Straits of Tiran, on the flanks of UNEF II, but this did not materialise after his overthrow. Now a three-ship Italian naval unit, part of the MFO in the Sinai, patrols the Straits of Tiran to ensure the freedom of shipping between the Red Sea and the Gulf of Aqaba.

There are a number of tasks that could be performed by a naval arm of UNIIMOG. These include the marking and monitoring of a cease-fire line in the Shatt al Arab and the continuation of the line to the high seas to the limits of the territorial waters. The Shatt will require clearing and the UN would be the best to supervise it. Such needs raise crucial questions relating to the Law of the Sea. Since the Soviet suggestion for a UN naval peacekeeping force in the Persian Gulf was mooted, some members of the American delegation to the UN have argued that the whole question of the freedom of the high seas was so crucial that it was not open to debate. There are indeed complex issues involved in a peacekeeping arrangement on the high seas, yet a solution that would end the conflict in the Gulf, and bring peace to the region, should be encouraged.

There are three possible tasks for peacekeeping on the oceans: the Antarctic Treaty prescribes a non-military order without prejudicing military freedom of the high seas south of the sixty-degree latitude;

the Partial Test Ban Treaty and the Sea Bed Arms Control Treaty both contain some prohibitions relating to nuclear weapons; and the Treaty of Tlateoleo (1967) limits weapons beneath the bed of the territorial borders of its signatories.

The second task for naval peacekeeping would be the prospect of peacekeeping as manifested by the UN; and the third relates to the maintenance of international peace and security. Therefore there is an urgent need to address related issues immediately in order to facilitate the implementation of the cease-fire between Iran and Iraq, which is an essential prerequisite for negotiations to find a peaceful solution to the conflict in the Gulf.

CONCLUSIONS

The possibility of establishing a more rigorous framework for the prevention and settlement of international disputes rests upon the common will of the UN member states and respect for national sovereignty and integrity as well as upon respect for international authority and compliance with its decisions. Since the eventual success of peacekeeping depends on the ability to promote peace-making, a greater effort by the UN is required in this respect. As peacekeeping is the start of the process of peacemaking, its success is essential for what will follow. Therefore, the members of the Security Council must show greater will to support their resolutions, for there will be little progress if there are no teeth for implementing the Council's decisions.

Peacekeeping can play a useful role in conflict avoidance. Confidence-building measures and verification can contribute significantly to prevent escalation of conflicts, just as they do to prevent recurrence of fighting. Progress in technology has greatly enhanced communications and verification. However, peacekeepers need a better understanding of the available technology and how best to harness it to strengthen their operations.

The role of the Secretary-General has often emerged as more acceptable than that of other UN organs. Thus his role must be strengthened and the capability of his office enhanced by providing him with suitable political and military staff to perform his duties.

The present political climate is ripe for reopening a dialogue on peacekeeping matters, first between the super powers, then among the Permanent Members of the Security Council, and eventually among the troop-contributing states. On the basis of the experience of peacekeeping operations since the October 1973 Arab–Israeli war, it has become clear that, given the need and the will of the member states, the few remaining differences could easily be resolved.

There is also a need to enlarge the number of troop-contributing countries. In this respect stand-by arrangements as designed by the Nordic countries and Canada among others provide a useful example. Many of the contributing countries will require assistance in their training and preparation. The pioneering work of the International Peace Academy, a non-governmental organisation (NGO), will continue to be vital in the development of training models and research. Yet the UN will have to assume responsibility for guidance and assistance to troop-contributing countries.

The financial and logistics support of peacekeeping cannot be ignored. Since financing in this case is essentially a political question, it has to be dealt with at an early stage of the resumed negotiations on peacekeeping. Once peacekeeping is placed on a sound financial basis, its logistics will be facilitated.

The demands of maintaining international peace and security require that peacekeeping be more readily available for a variety of tasks beyond traditional roles. Many wars are caused by liberation movements and insurgency which soon spill over the borders. An international co-operative effort is required to deal with international terrorism. This age has seen more suffering by man-made disasters than by those which nature inflicts on mankind. A way must be found to remove the insecurity of relief operations. Arms control and limitations agreements require verification.

After 40 years, peacekeeping is better understood and appreciated. The UN Charter signed at the end of World War II had envisaged prevention of another similar war by enforcement action if necessary. The Great Alliance hardly survived a decade after the war and the global geopolitical scene has changed beyond imagination. Time has shown that the solutions of the past are no longer applicable to the present. Although many states have resorted to the use of force to serve their ends, there is reluctance to use force collectively to achieve peace. This has given peacekeeping the recognition that it has been receiving. The award of the Nobel Peace Prize to UN peacekeeping is a worthy recognition of its important role in the peaceful resolution of conflicts.

NOTES AND REFERENCES

1. UN Document A/43/PV.4, 26 September 1988, p. 22.
2. Security Council Resolution 662 (1988) and S/19834. Also, see *Geneva Accords: Agreement on the Settlement of the Situation Relating to Afghanistan* (UN/DPI/935–40420–July 1988–20M) para. 7.
3. UN Security Council Resolution S/RES/435, 30 September 1978.
4. UN Document S/20412, 23 January 1989.
5. UN General Assembly Resolution 41/16, 31 October 1986.
6. UN Document A/SPC/43/SR.5, 17 October 1988.
7. UN General Assembly Document A/37/1, 7 September 1982.
8. UN Document A/36/474, para. 4.
9. *Bulletin of the Federal Republic of Germany*, no. 55 (30 May 1978) p. 534.
10. IPA Disarmament Study Group, 'Building Confidence in Europe', *Bulletin of Peace Proposals*, no. 2 (1980) p. 226.
11. Jack Child (ed.), *Conflict in Central America: Approaches to Peace and Security* (New York: St Martin's Press; London: C. Hurst and Company, 1986), published for the International Peace Academy.
12. UN Document A/43/PV.6, 27 September 1988.
13. Hugh Hanning (ed.), *Peacekeeping and Technology: Concepts for the Future* (New York: International Peace Academy, 1983). Also, Hugh Hanning (ed.), *Weapons of Peace* (IPA publication, 1980, out of Print).
14. The Mozambican National Resistance (sometimes called the MNR), an armed insurgency group formed by Rhodesia to wage war against the Frelimo-government and to gather intelligence on *freedom-fighters* seeking to bring down the regime in Salisbury. It collapsed in 1980.
15. UN Document A/RES/40/61, 9 December 1985.
16. *The New York Times*, 7 January 1989, reported that, 'Select National Guard forces, including helicopter units and military police detachments, will be used increasingly this year in anti-drug activities.'
17. UN Document S/RES/598, 20 July 1987.

Appendix

THE INTERNATIONAL PEACE ACADEMY

The International Peace Academy works in partnership with the United Nations, regional organisations and governments world-wide in peacekeeping and related techniques in conflict resolution. In twenty years of off-the-record workshops, training seminars and consultation, the Academy has built an influential, global network of over 4000 diplomats, peacekeeping officers and policy-makers from 150 nations. It is a non-governmental, independent organisation which brings together all parties to conflicts to explore peaceful and lasting solutions. The Academy has no counterpart anywhere in the world today that puts into practice the skills of peacekeeping and peacemaking.

NORWEGIAN INSTITUTE OF INTERNATIONAL AFFAIRS

The Norwegian Institute of International Affairs (NIIA) was established in the autumn of 1958 by an Act of Parliament and began its work the year after. The objectives of NIIA are to contribute towards increased understanding of international problems and issues, to disseminate information on international relations, and to promote studies on the problems of international co-operation and the causes of international conflicts. The Institute's field of activities includes research, analysis and information on international questions. The Institute is independent and politically neutral and professionally free in its performance of activities.